Maury County, Tennessee

Marriages
1807-1837

- Vol #1 -

(2 Volumes in 1)

Southern Historical Press, Inc.
1981

Please direct all correspondence and orders to:

SOUTHERN HISTORICAL PRESS, Inc.
PO BOX 1267
375 West Broad Street
Greenville, SC   29601
southernhistoricalpress@gmail.com

ISBN #0-89308-885-4

Forward

Copied from Original Marriage Bonds in the basement of
Maury County Court House by Mrs. Evelyn B. Shackleford,
Mrs. Marise P. Lightfoot, Mrs. Virginia W. Alexander
and Mrs. Rose H. Priest

NAME	DATE	BONDSMAN
Abernathy, Harley D. to Sally Abernathy	Oct. 22, 1810	John McTire
Adair, Isaac to Polly Granger	July 24, 1811	Wm. McGhee
Adair, Jacob to Tempy Wilkenson	Apr. 24, 1815	Wm. Reece
Adams, William to Rebecca Craig	Sept. 11, 1811	Geo. Agnew
Adkins, David to Mary Duckworth	Apr. 26, 1814	John Duckworth
Agnew, John C. to Mary Carathers	July 22, 1835	Carol Morris
Akin, Peter to Elizabeth Locke	June, 1828	W. M. Biffle
Akin Pleasant J. to Betsy Rodgers	Feb. 14, 1827	Robert Rodgers
Akin, Samuel W. to Eliza. C. Alexander	Oct. 2, 1822	James Patton
Alderson, Jeremiah to Sally B. McGimpsy	Feb. 22, 1827	Thos. P. Johnson
Alderson, John B. to Amanda Shelton	Sept. 18, 1828	Saml. Phillips
Alexander, James to Metilda Kirkpatrick	Feb. 3, 1808	David Alexander
Alexander, James M. to Margarite Copeland	Aug. 19, 1822	Alexander Johnston
Alexander, Jonah to Elizabeth King	Mar. 4, 1811	Samuel King
Allen, Abraham to Elizabeth Kendrick	May 14, 1814	John Elliott
Allen, Benjamin to Sally Voorhies	Aug. 10, 1811	John Voorhies
Allen, Charles to Elizabeth Gill	June 6, 1808	Nathaniel Gholson
Allen, James to Elizabeth Reynolds	Mar. 26, 1812	Jesse Tomlinson
Allen, Josiah L. to Patsy Smith	Oct. 25, 1819	John C. MacKean
Allison, Bazile B. to Catherine Longley	Jan. 23, 1823	A. O. Harris
Allison, Hugh to Fanny Howell	July 23, 1823	Robert Johnston
Allred, William to Sally Warren	Mar. 5, 1814	James Burns
Anderson, John to Charity McPeters	Aug. 26, 1808	Thomas Robertson
Anderson, John to Nancy Branch	Feb. 9, 1822	Wm. Anderson
Anderson, Samuel Y. to Peggy McCurdy	Aug. 14, 1811	Andrew Boyd
Anderson, William J. to Eliza Wallan	May 1, 1828	Robert Childress
		Dana Looney
Andrews, Joseph A. to Nancy D. Richardson	Jan.10, 1827	T. W. King
Andrews, Micheal L. to Sally Dearon	May 1, 1832	D. F. Andrews
Appleby, Benjamine to Jemima King	Feb. 22, 1836	Alex. McLure
Armstrong, Josiah to Margaret Holland	Dec. 13, 1836	John Spencer
Arnold, David to Polly M. Powell	Dec. 14, 1814	William Nix
Arnold, George to Jane Nixon	Nov. 23, 1835	G. P. Webb
Arnold, Robert to Polly Gordon	Dec. 6, 1810	Moses Arnold
Ashton, James to Mary Stewart	Aug. 15, 1827	Robert Madding
Ayers, John to Ann Rever	Sept. 12, 1832	Park L. Higgins
Ayres, James to Tabitha Williams	Feb. 8, 1817	Arthur Ayres
Backum, James to Ruth Robiason	Oct. 5, 1835	James Williams
Bailey, Benjamin to Eleanor Osborn	June 28, 1832	James Neely
Bailey, Brittan to Sarah Lee	Dec. 1, 1827	Daniel C. Brown
Baird, John to Rebecca Stone	June 16, 1823	Wm. H. Cooper
Baker, Stephen to Polly Cooper	18	Henry Williams
Baldridge, James to Lyddia Pickins	Sept. 11, 1809	John Craig
Baldridge, John to Matilda R. Hoge	Sept. 10, 1832	E. M. Dickson
Baily, Anderson to Martha Young	Dec. 17, 1836	Wm. Pope
Ball, Daniel to Patsy Williams	Jan. 30, 1828	John Renfro
Ball, Ensley to Polly Sprinkles	Dec. 31, 1829	Moses Gordon
Banks, George to Sally Hill	Nov. 26, 1832	George Ross
Barham, William W. to Hannah Mayfield	Jan. 22, 1829	John H. Stokey
Barker, James to Nancy Mills	June 4, 1829	James Presgrove
Barlew, Wiley to Dorcus Tankisly	Nov. 25, 1816	James Bingham
Barns, William to Martha Garret	Sept. 2, 1832	Tho. Timmons
Barr, John W. To Agnes McCord	May 22, 1811	William McCord
Bartlett, Cyrus H. to Becky Radford	Aug. 13, 1828	James James ?
Bartlett, Thomas to Nancy Brooks	Apr. 30, 1811	Andrew Forgey
Bass, William to Catherine Scott	Mar. 2, 1829	Henry Hawkins
Bailey, Anderdson P. to Martha Young	Dec. 17, 1836	Wm. Pope

NAME	DATE	BONDSMAN
Batts, Thomas F. to Sally Shaddin	Feb. 14, 1823	Jesse Rogers
Baucom, Josiah S. to Priscilla Tuttle	Feb. 17, 1826	Avery K. Baucom
Beard, Martin to Lydia Cox	Feb. 24, 1814	William Craig
Beasley, Edward to Nancy Crosswill	Sept. 18, 1823	John Ferrell
Beasley, John W. to Rachel Wantland	July 3, 1827	Eli Fields
Beechum, Jesse to Susannah Bridges	Sept. 18, 1822	Zadoc Winn
Bell, John to Polly Alexander	Sept. 17, 1814	Thomas Bell
Bell, John to Sally Vincent	Jan. 24, 1822	Jesse Vincent
Bell, Sterling to Polly Spencer	Oct. 10, 1808	Thomas Bell
Benderman, John A. To Sara L. Matthews	Feb. 21, 1832	E. M. Matthews
Benderman, William D. to Delany Culberth	Apr. 10, 1833	Robert McCissick
Bennett, Moses to Sara Woolard	Feb. 2, 1835	Eli Cheek
Benton, Robert to Isabella Edmonds	Dec. 21, 1832	Jn. Edmonds
Bevil, William to Rebecca Duggen	Jan. 25, 1822	David C. Burris
Biffle, John to Polly Chambers	May 17, 1814	Samuel Aiken
Bigbia, Joseph to Eliza Madox	June 15, 1832	John Guill
Bingham, James N. to Rebecca Smith	Sept. 16, 1828	J. B. Hamilton
Bigham, Robert to Sara McKee	July 22, 1836	Beverly Dodson
Bills, Isaac N. to Catherine M. Rutledge	Nov. 23, 1826	Jonathan D. Bills
Bird, Liberty to Catherine McCallester	Aug. 15, 1832	William Costen
Bishop, Edmond to Anna Russell	Oct. 18, 1810	Benjamin Lewis
Bishop, Regen to Rebecca Howell	Mar. 1, 1811	John Moorehead
Bizzell, William to Sara Scott	Jan. 21, 1835	Elias Fogleman
Black, James C. to Catherine Fitzgerald	Sept. 23, 1828	James Beatey
Black, John to Margaret A. Baldridge	Dec. 16, 1823	William Black
Black, William to Mary Vaughn	Dec. 2, 1823	Amize Black
Blackburn, Robert E. to Adeline Kelsey	June 28, 1832	S. Jaggers
Blackburn, Silvanus W. to Catherine Brewer	Dec. 15, 1827	Wm. M. Vaughn
Blackman, Stephen to Matilda Campbell	Sept. 7, 1826	Barton Jenkins
Blackwell, James to Grizy A. Fielder	May 1, 1833	Jess Fitzgerald
Blanton, John to Ann J. Buyers	Mar. 23, 1819	J. Guest
Bledsoe, Young to Henrietta Wilkes	Dec. 10, 1823	Hugh Forgey
Boaz, Robert to Ailey Pulling	July 10, 1829	James Richardson
Bogard, John J. to Nancy Hickman	Jan. 11, 1822	James Tidwell
Boles, Charles to Amy Southerland	Oct. 18, 1822	Alston Southerland
Bone, Young to Amy McDaniel	Dec. 10, 1836	Holliday McGuire
Booker, Isham to Malinda Harvey	May 11, 1829	James Harden
Boyd, Robert to Mary Farris	Sept. 21, 1829	Tho. D. Cathey
Braden, Patrick to Sara Johnson	Apr. 2, 1832	John Whitaker
Bradley, David S. to Elizabeth Kirk	Apr. 1, 1822	John W. Smith
Branch, T. M. to Nancy McKee	Mar. 30, 1835	James Bowman
Brandford, Alexander to Rebecca Brown	Aug. 18, 1836	Anderson Pogue
Brasfield, Wilie to Emmaline Shaw	Feb. 19, 1822	James Jones
Breshears, Brazeal to Sally Head	Mar. 24, 1811	W. W. Thompson
Bridges, Oliver to Sara J. B. Farrer	Nov. 21, 1836	Claiburne Harris
Bridleman, John to Lucy Landers	Mar. 24, 1814	William Voorhees
Brooks, Aaron to Lydia Currey	Mar. 19, 1828	Isaac Currey
Brooks, Anderson to Rachel Hart	Mar. 29, 1822	Alfred Brooks
Brooks, Hezikiah to Betsy Porter	May 11, 1814	Calaway Hardin
Brooks, James to Jane Bailey	Oct. 27, 1829	Thornton Chamrer
Brooks, James to Easther Hopkins	Nov. 24, 1810	Samuel Crawford
Brown, Butler to Mary A. Baily	May 28, 1836	Alex. Beckum
Brown, Daniel C. to Susan S. Yancy	Sept. 24, 1822	D. H. Sanders
Brown, Jesse to Mary L. Nance	Dec. 21, 1829	Jas. H. Nance
Brown, James to Mary Howard	Feb. 10, 1835	Wm. Braden
Brown, Jethro to Sara Cutbirth	July 29, 1811	John M. Taylor
Brown, John to Elizabeth Brown	Jan. 21, 1823	McClintick Brown

NAME	DATE	BONDSMAN
Brown, John M. to Elvira Potts	Nov. 5, 1835	Wm. Cockran
Brown, Willey to Mary Smith	Aug. 26, 1828	John Stratton
Sol. by Robert Henderson, J.P.		
Brown, William to Jane Smith	Oct. 30, 1819	A. Brown
Brown, William R. to Sarah P. Lewellin	Mar. 20, 1827	P. Nelson
Brown, William S. to Sophia McClanhan	July 14, 1829	Wm. G. Yancy
Brownlo, Andrew to Miriah McFarland	Nov. 17, 1827	John Rhea
Bryant, Richard to Nancy Fergurson	Jan. 19, 1827	D. B. Crawford
Bryant, Willis to Charity Hutchison	Aug. 25, 1815	James Ivey
Buckner, Anthony H. to Isabella Mitchell	Feb. 26, 1827	Zebina Conkey
Bullock, Allen to Lucinda Pruhit	Aug. 24, 1827	William Akin
Bunch, Solomon Bunch to Ann Brown	May 13, 1823	John Jenkins
Burkett, Price to Jane Jones	Mar. 28, 1833	Benj. Burkett
Burkit, Daniel to Massey Honneycut	June 1, 1809	James Love
Burnett, John F. to Milly Thompson	June 29, 1823	Thos. P. Thomson
Burpo, Jacob to Peggy Alvis	Apr. 17, 1827	Alexander Burpo
Burris, Jacob R. to Nancy Raines	June 29, 1832	H. A. McMacken
Butcher, Eli to Lavinia Arnold	18__	David Harris
Butler, Elias to Ann Bullock	Dec. 30, 1823	William Allen
Butler, John to Betsy Hays	Apr. 26, 1811	Jacob Daimwood
Butler, John to Mary Newcomb	Sept. 12, 1836	Nelson Newcomb
Butler, John to Eliz. Henson	July 30, 1832	B. D. Butler
Bynum, Eliz. to Matilda Henderson	Aug. 23, 1819	Luke Bynum
Byrnes, John M. to Mary Nevils	Jan. 9, 1833	R. B. Foster
Byrum, Young to Jane Hood	Jan. 30, 1827	Franklin Clark
Caldwell, Amos to Sally Dodson	Aug. 14, 1809	Allen C. Yates
Caldwell, Benjamin H. to Miriah Kirby	Feb. 10, 1835	John Caldwell
Caldwell, George to Juley Capell	Mar. 13, 1810	Amos Caldwell
Caldwell, John to Patsy C. Rutledge	June 5 ___	James Rutledge
Caldwell, William H. to Margaret Weber	Feb. 8, 1835	Benjamin Caldwell
Caldwill, H. (A) ? to Nancy E. Doak	Jan. 8, 1829	T. Doak
Campbell, Charles to Alsey Phillips	Feb. 11, 1829	Jas. A. Deaton
Campbell, David to Lucy Cooper	June 23, 1809	John M. Armstrong
Campbell, Hiram to Sally Gordon	June 15, 1814	James Gordon
Campbell, John P. to Louisa Chairs	Aug. 24, 1827	Marshall T. Polk
Campbell, John P. to Lewanza W. Smith	Sept. 25, 1827	Joseph L. Baker
Campbell, John to Martha A. Bingham	Mar. 29, 1829	Thos. Kittles
Capps, Allisa to Frances Brown	Nov. 23, 1827	Wm. R. Miller
Carithers, Robert to Elizabeth Blair	No Date-1814 records	Saml. Crawford
Carl, John to Sally Cone	Aug. 7, 1828	James Woodward
Carney, James (No Bride)	Sept. 29, 1826	Joseph Hart
Carter, Benjamin to Elizabeth K. Lindsay	June 13, 1822	Guston Kearney
Carter, Kintchen to Kessiah Johnston	Feb. 6, 1822	Charles Harrington
Carathiers, Hugh A. To Ellen Hampton	Jan. 31, 1832	Samuel Reding
Caskey, Robert to Jane Hill	July 3, 1823	Saml. G. Cunningham
Cathel, Joseph M. to Rachel Jones	Dec. 10, 1825	Saml. Rogers
Cathey, Griffith to Rebecca Finley	Mar. 2, 1825	Noah Sessioms
Cathey, Hugh to Margaret Hope	Mar. 19, 1833	William Hope
Cathey, James to Agnes Walker	Sept. 5, 1835	Nimrod Graham
Cathey, Josiah to Polly Cooke	Dec. 21, 1827	Francis L. Cooke
Caudle, Isham to Sarah Arnold	Apr. 27, 1822	William Arnold
Cayce, George to Margaret McEarly	Mar. 22, 1836	Riley Casey
Chaffin, Edward H. to Ruth Whiteside	Sept. 23, 1835	T. Groves
Chaffin, Hillary G. to Susanna Kirby	Aug. 20, 1836	Thomas Dugger
Chathem, John to Nancy Mills	June 1, 1822	Samuel Lastley
Childress, James to Susan Caskey	May 15, 1832	Adrian Childress

NAME	DATE	BONDSMAN
Childress, William to Elizabeth Davis	Mar. 7, 1832	John Caskey
Chitty, Benjamin to Nancy Ware	July 12, 1814	George Cockburn
Choate, John S. to Lucinda Stallings	Oct. 15, 1829	Benedict Stallings
Chumley, Young to Nancy Akin	Aug. 11, 1826	William Voorhies
Churchwell, Elias to Arramandy Brewer	July 14, 1823	John Blackburn
Churchwell, Robert to Mary Johnson	Feb. 9, 1825	A. Calhon
Churchwell, William to Peggy Ayres	Dec. 26, 1807	Joseph Ayres
Clairdys, Benjamin to Nancy J. Kilpatrick	Dec. 28, 182_	George G. Farrar
Clanton, Anderson to Eleanor Hail	Sept. 10, 1828	John Bachelor ?
Clark, William to Lucy Osborn	July 17, 1828	James Forbes
Clayton, John to Nancy Bridges	June 16, 1814	Bagely Clayton
Clemens, Hargis to Sara Roane	Feb. 18, 1836	John Chandler
Cockman, Ammon to Frances B. Cockman	Jan. 1, 1828	Geo. B. Jopling
Cockran, John T. to Sara Milican	Dec. 19, 1832	William Cockran
Cockran, David to Elizabeth Phiffer	Mar. 22, 1836	Sample Orr
Coffey, William G. To Elizabeth Bondham	Feb. 14, 1822	Robert Caskey
Coggins, John to Nancy Smith	Nov. 4, 1835	James Emerson
Coggins, Robert to Synthya Hall	Feb. 26, 1835	Elijah Rustin
Cohea, Richard (No Bride)	No Date	John M. Lankford
Cohorn, William to Saberry Robertson	July 10, 1822	Micajah Blackwell
Cole, Edward to Polly Hodges	Mar. 24, 1823	William Cole
Cole, Isaac to Polly Franks	June 17, 1828	William Melton
Cole, Pilmoore to Catherine Land	May 18, 1833	McBride Godwin
Cole, William to Peggy McWilliams	Mar. 9, 1811	Hugh McWilliams
Collier, Cole to Sophia Cooper	Apr. 3, 1829	Thos. Hargis
Collins, John to Mary A. Cole	Dec. 5, 1836	Jordon Johnston
Collins, Thomas W. to Jincy Edwards	Jan. 1, 1822	John Robinson
Combs, Layborn to Polly Scott	Nov. 8, 1826	John Adcock
Comstock, Ephriam H.F. to Nancy Goodman	Oct. 14, 1823	Robert Bates
Connally, Eli W. to Mary C. Stanford	18__	Waston Hoge
Cooper, Mathew to Elizabeth J. Frierson	July 7, 1835	Edmond Frierson
Cooper, William to Lydia Hubbard	18__	Jonathan D. Bills
Cooper, William to Sara Craftin	Aug. 7, 1825	Saml. McDowell
Copeland, James C. to Sarah Webb	Aug, 7, 1826	Meredith Webb
Cottle, William to Margaret Kelley	Sept. 6, 1811	Robert Johnston
Courts, Charles to Clary Hudspeth	Oct. 14, 1808	Henry Branch
Covey, Archibald to Margaret A. Matthews	Apr. 12, 1836	William Branch
Covey, Riley to Polly Tharp	Dec. 14, 1836	T. A. Blair
Covey, Thomas to Lucinda Morrison	Jan. 15, 1836	Eli Reddin
Cowan, William to Sally Wallace	Dec. 18, 1809	Elias Frierson
Cowden, William to Elizabeth Scott	Feb. 8, 1810	James Scott
Craddock, George (No Bride)	Nov. 27, 1826	Hardin Williams
Crafton, William D. to Elizabeth Curtis	Aug. 29, 1822	Stephen Akin
Craig, David to Mary Isom	Oct. 4, 1828	A. Johnson
Craig, John to Betsey Monry (Money?)	Oct. 12, 1809	John Raggan
Craig, John to Nancy Gordon	Feb. 6, 1835	John Gordon
Crawford, Alexander to Esther Alexander	Dec. 20, 1808	Wilson Henderson?
Crawford, James to Barithenia Owens (Burns)	Aug. 22, 1815	Archibald Moorely
Crawley, Samuel to Margaret Hay	Setp. 20 ?	George Hay
Crenshaw, John to Malinda Kindle	Jan. 21, 1828	B. R. Harris
Crisp, John H. to Mary Jones	182_?	James C. Hill
Cromwell, George to Catherine Pickard	June 15, 1829	Isaac Pickard
Crosby, Robert to Eliza P. Coleman	Nov. 4, 1823	Josiah Alderson
Cross, Joseph O. to Elisa Harlin	Oct. 2, 18277	B. R. Harris
Crassin, Elijah to Rebecca Baker	Feb. 10, 1827	John Secrist
Culverson, Andrew to Polly Fitzgerald	Apr. 7, 1828	Thos. Fitzgerald
Culvertson, Aaron to Mary Wharten	Jan. 27, 1826	Andrew Culvertson

NAME	DATE	BONDSMAN
Cummings, John to Mahala Hood	Nov. 3, 1823	Daniel A. McCoy
Cunningham, James to Peggy Rodgers	Aug. 21, 1822	Thomas Currey
Cunningham, Matthew to Lilah Griffin	Aug. 6, 1822	Will H. Johnson
Currey, James E. to Mary Williams	May 15, 1829	Isaac J. Currey
Curry, James to Fedilia Parks	Dec. 15, 1835	James Branch
Cutburth, David to Jane Reed	Oct. 7, 1814	William Reed
Cutlough, Saml. D. to Harriet C. Wallis	Jan. 1, 1829	Thos. J. Porter
Dagley, John to Sarah Boyd	Nov. 29, 1808	Jacob Lindsey
Damron, Simon to Polly Ferril	Oct. 7, 1826	Samuel McKee
Daniel, John M. to Phebe King	Oct. 13, 1829	Silas Harlan
Dark, Anderson to Margarette Basham	July 28, 1829	Nathaniel Moore
Davidson, James to Elizabeth Swin?	Mar. 18, 1827	John Davidson
Davidson, John E. to Mary N. Holmes	May 30, 1810	Samuel J. Rogers
Davidson, John to Hester Wilson	Aug. 29, 1828	John O'Brian
Davis, Benjamin to Molly Blackwell	Apr. 20, 1822	John Cohorn
Davis, John to Dicy Tombs	June 10, 1809	Reuben Parks
Davis, John to Rachel Bennett	Feb. 23, 1828	Kendrick Arnold
Davis, Joseph to Hannah Lamb	July 12, 1828	Demsy Watson
Davis, William to Nancy Griffin	Dec. 24, 1826	Lorenzo Dowell
Davis, William H. to Catherine Brasier	Oct. 5, 1822	Isiah Garrison
Davis, Willis to Nancy Kendrick	Apr. 2, 1814	Moses Sprinkles
Dearing, Berry to Nancy Davis	Oct. 4, 1814	Aaron Reynolds
Denby, Robert to Mary H. Denby	July 23, 1823	Zacheriah Stiles
Denton, Williamson to Mary Collier	Jan. 10, 1836	Albert Collier
Derryberry, H. W. to Margaret Swaim	Dec. 30, 1832	J. W. Swaim
Dickey, Adam to Martha E. Booker	May 10, 1836	Ed. Shegogg
Dickey, Benoni to Margaret G. Frierson	June 23, 1809	William Frierson
Dickson, D. M. to Martha W. Buckner	Dec. 10, 1832	William Buckner
Dickson, James to Elizabeth McCalla	Feb. 12, 1823	Samuel Edmundson
Dickson, Robert C. to Sarah C. Edmondson	Oct. 30, 1823	Saml. Edmondson
Dicky, George M. to Ann Stone	Dec. 26, 1808	Tilman Spencer
Dillard, Henry B. to Lucy O. Driggs	Dec. 28, 1826	Ridin H. Simons
Dillingham, Berryman to Eliz. Dyer	Nov. 10, 1836	S. F. Dyer
Dobbin, James to Eliza Webster	Feb. 23, 1814	John T. Moore
Dodson, Elisha to Ann Dodson	May 19, 1808	Greenham Dodson
Dodson, Fortunatus to Sophia Falas (Phalas)	Mar. 20, 1827	D. Dodson
Dodson, Hightower to Sara Hanks	June 25, 1832	Elijah Hanks
Dodson, Jerome to Margaret Tate	Aug. 4, 1836	John H. Caldwell
Dodson, Samuel to Betsey McDonnill	Nov. 26, 1808	Alexander Black
Dodson, William to Kizy Hill	Aug. 20, 1814	Thomas Hanks
Dogget, Soloman to Polly N. Morgan	Oct. 19, 1829	James Caburt
Dogget, Solomon to Eliza J. Rodgers	Oct. 15, 1836	Hugh Rodgers
Doggett, Thomas to Anna Lunnon	Apr. 9, 1828	Miller Doggett
Dooley, Esom B. to Patsy Caldwell	Mar. 2, 1814	David Bell
Dooley, Paris F. to Cinthia E. Davidson	Aug. 12, 1822	Edward H. Chaffin
Dorser, Cornelius to Polly Livisay	July 9, 1828	William Livesay
Dorsey, Robert to Jane Segraves	Nov. 12, 1823	Arthur Lockhart
Dortch, William to Sarah Rust	Nov. 1, 1826	William Roundtree
Dotson, Greenham to Marcy Brooks	Jan. 9, 1808	Samuel Brooks
Dotson, Jordon to Polly Etton	Sept. 21, 1809	Elisha Dotson
Dotson, Willis to Matilda Rainey	Feb. 12, 1822	D.H.E. Saunders
Dotton, Lacy W. to Virginia Stratton	Jan. 3, 1836	Jessie Leftwich
Dounaldson, Francis to Nancy Germain	May 13, 1814	John Cloud
Dowdy, Alfred to Nancy Berryman	Aug. 4, 1829	Wm. Maxwell, Wm. Dowdy, Tho. Elliott
Dowell, Lorenzo to Ann Booker	Sept. 6, 1826	Jos. N. Puckett

NAME	DATE	BONDSMAN
Downey, David to Judah Few	July 18, 1826	John Few
Duncan, Jerimiah to Elizabeth Underwood	Mar. 11, 1835	Endymon Baker
Duncan, Joseph to Minny Phillips	(No date-in 1822box)	Wm. Duncan
Duncan, L. H. to Emily L. Webster	July 3, 1828	David Looney
Duncan, Matthew L. to Sarah Spence	Nov. 29, 1829	L. S. Duncan
Duncan, Tyrrell to Lydia Smith	Jan. 1, 1828	William Duncan
Dungan, Nathan to Lily Hamilton	Jan. 9, 1826	Richard Overby
Dunlap, Samuel to Saṕah Stephenson	Sept. 30, 1817	James Stephenson
Dunn, Samuel A. to Rinney Goodman	Sept. 9, 1823	Talliferro Goodman
Dunnagan, John C. to Mary A. Buchanon	June 30, 1836	Arthur Potter
Durham, James to Prudence Perdue	Jan. 31, 1835	Issac Pickard
Dyer, Felix to Elizabeth Smith	Dec. 10, 1832	Joseph Harrison
Dyer, William to Hannah Brasier	Oct. 5, 1822	Adam Andrews
Dysart, Milton to Margaret Ewing	Nov. 25, 1835	Cary Dysart
Eagle, Phillip to Betty Long	Mar. 9, 1819	John Hardison
Early, John to Sarah Kilby (Killy?)	Dec. 19, 1808	John Kilby (Killy?)
East, Thos. M. to Sariah J. Alderson	Sept. 4, 1829	J. H. Walker
Edgin, Jacob B. to Martha Heilton	Aug. 14, 1837	John Edgin
Edmondson, Joseph to Jane Ann Wilkes	Feb. 27, 1829	Wm. S. Wilkes
Edmondson, Saml. D. to Margarette Edmondson	Oct. 2, 1829	A. C. Mitchell
Edmonson, John to Mary H. Baker	Mar. 13, 1832	Allen Brown
Edwards, Hazel W. to Polly Neeley	Nov. 7, 1829	L. Dowell
Edwards, William to Sarah Williams	Feb. 28, 1811	Adonyah Edwards
Edwards, William to Polly Oakly	Apr. 21, 1828	Washington Oakley
Edwards, William H. to Mary Almond	Jan. 31, 1822	John W. Nelson
Elliott, John R. to Matilda Stone	June 1, 1829	W. H. Baldridge
Elliott, Thomas to Mary Murrell	Aug. 4, 1829	Alfred & Wm. Dowdey
Elliott, Thomas to Susan Griffith	Dec. 25, 1835	Anderson Williams
Ellis, Francis to Rebecca Edmond	Feb. 13, 1822	Robert Edmond
Ellis, James to Nancy Wrenn	Aug. 13, 1810	Micajah Brooks
Eloiss, Edmond to Pheby Farriss	Dec. 28, 1808	John Stephenson
Emerson, Mathew to Margaret Phillips	Oct. 9, 1835	John Phillips
Erwin, David to Polly Beard	Nov. 2, 1809	Joseph Young
Erwin, James to Jane Kennedy	July 7, 1810	John Erwin
Erwin, John P. to Susan M. Darnell	18__	Wm. Cathey
Erwin, Wm. H. to Catherine Strayhorn	Dec. 10, 1826	Nathan B. Erwin
Estis, Henderson to Marthy White	Dec. 23, 1835	A. C. Dickey
Evans, James R. to Milly J. Miller	Sept. 10, 1823	John Jackson
Ewing, Andrew to Sarah M. Hudspeth	Mar. 27, 1829	Tho. Tompkins
Ewing, ? to Polly Glasscock	18__	____ Bills?
Ewing, James to (No Bride)	Feb. 15, 1827	Noah R. Randall
Fanin, John H. to Sarah Woodall	Mar. 26, 1829	David Humphreys
Faris, John to Eliz. McKannon	Apr. 30, 1822	Archibald McKannon
Faris, John P. to Elizabeth Lusk	July 22, 1822	Hugh Douglass
Fariss, James to Peggy Whiteside	Aug. 14, 1809	Robert Whiteside
Farlow, Samuel to Mary Avery	Jan. 30, 1827	Elijah R. Hart
Farras, Peter to Polly Vincent	18__	Henry Wollard
Farrer, Wiley E. to Rachel Reynolds	Sept. 18, 1826	John Johnson
Farrer, Wm. B. to Martha Blackmon	June 16, 1835	John Williams
Farris, Abraham (No Bride)	18__	William Fox
Farris, Issac to Milinda Walker	Nov. 13, 1835	Wm. Cockran
Ferrill, Isaac to Nancy Davis	Feb. 16, 1828	David Looney
Finch, Keeble to Katherine Thurmond	June 2, 1836	Richard Finch
Finch, Richard to Malinda Griffin	July 22, 1835	Bolin Finch
Fisher, Jacob to Nancy Helm	June 25, 1823	Joel Yarborough

NAME	DATE	BONDSMAN
Fitzgerald, Darril to Ann Witherinton	Dec. 10, 1832	Samuel Church
Fitzgerald, Jackson to Sally Moore	June 1, 1814.	Mastin Fitzgerald
Fitzgerald, James to Polly Ladd	Aug. 23, 1819	Nathaniel Fitzgerald
Fitzgerald, John to Nancy Hanks	Oct. 2, 1809	Thomas Hanks
Fitzgerald, John to Julia A. Adkisson	Nov. 7, 1835	George Shelton
Fleeman, Julius to Elizabeth Cisco	Oct. 14, 1815	George Gullett
Fleming, William O. to Winnefred Richardson	June 24, 1829	Robt. A. Reed
Fletcher, Wesley to Elizabeth Abshaw	Jan. 23, 1828	Bazel Williams
Flin, Isham to Patsy Mayfield	Mar. 5, 1822	A. B. Mayfield
Fly, Jeremiah N. to N ancy Oakley	Mar. 10, 1823	Henry Caps (Cass?)
Fly, John to Lydia Newton	June 18, 1811	James Birmingham
Fly, William to Mary Mitchell	Nov. 10, 1809	John Mitchell
Flynt, Abijah to Polly Gideon	Sept. 20, 1808	Sam Wood
Foglemon, David to Mary Bostick	Oct. 25, 1832	Andrew Hudson
Follis, John to Mary E. Sorrey	Dec. 9, 1835	Wash. Oakley
Follis, William to Nancy Mayes	Oct. 18, 1810	George Hay
Forbes, Ruben to Lavina Rogers	Feb. 18, 1832	Wm. P. Weems
Forgason, John M.C. to Jenny Johnson	Feb. 1, 1822	Joseph Knox
Fox, Joseph to Nancy Hannah Church	Feb. 27, 1811	Thomas Church
Freeland, Robert D. to Ann Maria Headon	Oct. 21, 1823	Thos. S. Headon
Freeman, Silas to Frances Nickols	Mar. 10, 1827	Benjamin Rose
Frierson, Joshia B. to Ann E. Brown	Feb. 7, 1832	R. B. Mayes
Fry, Joseph to Mary Amis	18__	David Looney
Furlow, Thomas to Miriah Eagle	Jan. 21, 1836	Henry Eagle
Fuzzell, James to Angeline Cruise	May 8, 1833	Alex. Fuzzell
Fuzzell, John to Dissie Ragsdale	Mar. 20, 1830	Pleasant Rankin
Galloway, Enoch to Eliz. Trimble	July 1, 1836	Thomas Taylor
Galloway, T. to Jane Neely	July 18, 1836	Charles Harris
Galyean, Joshua to Eliza Ann Hill	July 5, 1828	Dicemus Harrison
Gannaway, Edmund to Sarah Tomlinson	Feb. 4, 1826	Gregory Gannoway
Garner, James R. to Patsy Curry	June 11, 1822	George Chambers
Garrett, George to Lucy Chaffin	Oct. 10, 1822	William Garrett
Garrett, William to Elenor Lewallen	Aug. 5, 1822	Samuel Dougherty
Garrigan, John to Polly Cash	Jan. 1811	William Garrigan
Garrigus, Benjamin to Jane Simpson	Feb. 10, 1823	Jesse Garrigus
Gattin, William V. H. to Elizabeth Henderson	Jan. 30, 1823	John Knox
Gee, Joseph to Polly Jones	Sept. 17, 1822	John C. Hamilton
Gholson, Nathaniel to Patsey Gill	May 25, 1808	Charles Allen
Gholson, William to Sarah Thomas	Nov. 12, 1810	Pleasant Nelson
Gibson, J. W. to Hannah Dickie	Apr. 22, 1832	Issac Goff
Gilbreath, Mathew to Elizabeth Redding	Jun. 22, 1835	Eli Redding
Giles, James H. to Mary Roberts	Feb. 28, 1831	
Gill, James to Mary Jenkins	Mar. 9, 1822	John Gill
Gill, James M. to Susannah Toney	July 12, 1828	Wm. S. Moore
Gill, Robert R. to Sara M. Johnson	Apr. 25, 1832	
Gillispie, James D. to Sarah R. Cheatham	Jan. 26, 1829	William Gillespie
Gillespie, John to Jane Boyd	Jan. 15, 1822	John H. Bills
Gillespie, John to Permelia Cheatham	Aug. 28, 1827	James Gillespie
Gillespie, John M. to Namoni Gillespie	Dec. 1, 1832	Jacob Utzman
Gilliam, Allen to Elizabeth Coleburn	June 13, 1836	Wm. T. Gilliam
Gilliam, John to Martha Gilliam	Feb. 1, 1822	William Gilliam
Gilmer, Jerimiah to Nancy Patterson	May 9, 1835	Wm. Gilmer
Ginger, Lewis to Elizabeth Miller	Oct. 2, 1823	James Bradshaw
Gladd, Lewis to Polly Boyd	Apr. 29, 1822	Robert Glass
Glover, Howell L. to Permelia Taylor	Jan. 15, 1827	Archibald Scott
Glover, Joshua to Peggy Milligan	July 13, 1822	Will Bradshaw
Glover, Phinibos T. to Susannah Simpson	Mar. 30, 1819	John Simpson

NAME	DATE	BONDSMAN
Glymph, Henry to Sara Jones	Dec. 30, 1823	William Glymph
Goad, Andrew to Malinda Deson	Dec. 30, 1827	John R. Rainey
Goad, Robert to Polly Mahoe	Oct. 13, 1809	Caleb Henley
Goad, Robert to Susannah Hood	Nov. 12, 182_	Sandford Dove
Goforth, Hiram to Priscy Halcomb	Mar. 29, 1815	Samuel Job
Goforth, William to Irena Johnson	Sept. 11, 1835	Daniel Booker
Good, Andrew to Rebecca M. Hill	Mar. 18, 1822	William Reeves
Good, Robert to Rebecca Griffith	Dec. 5, 1832	Seaborn Miller?
Goodloe, W. H. to Emily C. Williams	Sept. 8, 1828	John P. Spindle
Goodman, Joseph to Polly Booth	May 18, 1818	Vincent Booth
Goodman, Robinson to Polly Sutherland	July 9, 1829	William Goodman
Goodrich, John to Eliza Adkisson	Oct. 7, 1835	S. R. Nickels
Goodridge, Benj. U. to Amanda M. Miller	Jan. 28, 1829	Wm. Hannah
Goodwin, Jacob to Susan Dickey	Oct. 17, 1827	Minor Wilkes
Goodwin, James C. to Rebecca Evans	Nov. 2, 1826	Abraham Petty
Gordon, James to Nancy Tomlinson	Nov. 26, 1816	Bird M. Turner
Gordon, John to Elizabeth Tomblin	Dec. 11, 1809	Joseph Stockard
Gordon, Powhattan to C.M. Coleman	June 21, 1828	T. J. Porter
Gosset, Elijah to Betsey Edwards	Dec. 28, 1809	James Byers
Gowan, Andrew to Lucy Elliott	Aug. 2, 1811	John McElvans?
Gracy, Joseph to Elizabeth Bradshaw	Oct. 6, 1835	Wm. Crafford
Graham, Peter to Martha Bowdin	Aug. 6, 1828	J. J. Alderson
Grant, James to Mary Timmons	Oct. 14, 1828	Green B. Grant
Graves, Thomas to Polly Weaver	Dec. 15, 1828	Jos. C. Record
Gray, Charles to Polly Stanfield	Feb. 13, 1810	John Whiteside
Gray, Jesse to Sarah Evans	Jan. 12, 1829	Wm. Edmondson
Green, Abel to Hanna Tillman	Dec. 26, 1832	Thomas Weaver
Green, James to Elizabeth Hinson	Mar. 7, 1832	John Hinson
Green, Mortimer to Pazzidda Wadkins	Apr. 7, 1835	Andrew Patterson
Green, Nathaniel to Elizabeth Mosely	July 8, 1822	Robert B. Newsom
Green, William to Margaret Tomason	Jan. 6, 1836	Aaron McManus
Greene, William to Candice Record	June 18, 1835	William Duncan
Greenfield, George T. to Keren Sanford	Nov. 2, 1826	James Holland
Gregory, John B. to Eliza Patton	Dec. 27, 1827	Green Huckaba
Grey, Skipwith to Virginia Kery	Oct. 5, 1836	William Littlefield
Griffith, Benjamin to Frances Murphy	Dec. 20, 1836	Anthony Goldson
Grigsby, William R. to Katherine Baily	Feb. 13, 1836	William Richardson
Grimes, Alexander to Sally Hart	June 1, 1814	James Grimes
Grimes, James to Rebecca Dean	Aug. 20, 1814	John Thompson
Grimes, John to Elizabeth Price	Dec. 14, 1835	William Grimes
Grimes, Lloyd to Nancy Kerr	June 21, 1814	James Grimes
Grimes, Richard to Mary Akin	May 14, 1836	William Koonce
Grimes, William to Rachel Kerr	Mar. 25, 1822	Elijah King
Groves, John to Rosanna Collins	May 9, 1835	Corda Denton
Grubbs, John to Henrietta Brown	Feb. 5, 1822	Jesse Burchum
Guest, Joshua to Polly Cherry	July 11, 1814	Pleasant Nelson
Gullet, James to Patience Knight	Feb. 1, 1810	William McNeil
Gullett, Thompson to Priscilla Deanes	May 9, 1822	James P. Deanes
Gunter, Joseph John to Elizabeth Williams	Aug. 2, 1822	Archibald Gunter
Hackney, James to Betsy Brown	Nov. 22, 1832	John Arnold
Hadly, Ambrose to Lousia McLeod	Feb. 7, 1823	Murdock McLeod
Hail, William to Nancy Bass	Dec. 16, 1832	M. Bass
Halcomb, Jason to Martha Johnson	Mar. 7, 1835	Wm. Goforth
Hale, Robert to Rachel Johnston	Aug. 22, 1822	Samuel Lastly
Haley, Seabron to Martha Butler	Jan. 5, 1832	John Hines
Hall, Darling to Margaret Egnew	Apr. 29, 1809	Robert Anderson
Hall, David to Hannah Phillips	Jan. 17, 1810	Joseph Hall

NAME	DATE	BONDSMAN
Hall, Henry, Jr, to Sally Stokes	Apr. 14, 1810	Henry Hall, Sr.
Hall, Isaac C. to Prudence Gillespie	Apr. 2, 1828	Jacob Utzman
Hall, John to Prudence McFarlin	Apr. 23, 1810	James McFarland
Hall, (Noll?) John to Anny Wimloe	Feb. 21, 1814	Henry Hall
Hall, Joseph A. to Malvina Wright	Apr. 22, 1828	R. A. Parker
Hall, John M. to Margarette Faires	July 10, 1829	James Faires
Hall, Joseph to Anna Caroline Walters	Oct. 16, 1826	Lemuel Walters
Hall, Mansell to Delphia Porter	Jan. 4, 1810	John Lee
Hamblett, William to Sarah Collins	Mar. 12, 1823	B. W. Hardin
Hamilton, James to Peggy Irvin	Jan. 20, 1814	Joseph Brown
Hamond, John S. to Ruth Brooks	Jan. 27, 1823	Hugh B. Porter
Hancock, John W. to Louisa Lane	May 11, 1829	T. W. Hancock
Hancock, Stephen M. to Emeline Lane	June 27, 1832	Samuel B. Reves
Hanes, Joseph to Jane Baker	Sept. 4, 1810	John Baker
Hanks, Elijah to Polly Woolveton	June 4, 1811	John Woolveton
Hanks, Moses to Mary Montgomery	May 21, 1808	John Mitchell
Hanna, Andrew to Naomi Bryson	Nov. 13, 1835	E. M. Matthews
Harbison, Thomas to Jane Alderson	Jan. 30, 1828	Elijah Adkins
Hardin, Burger to Kenyan Hardin	Mar. 9, 1811	Francis Wisdom
Hardin, William to Elizabeth Herrington	Jan. 5, 1826	William Tom
Hardison, Ezra to Serinia Derrybetry	Jan. 16, 1835	Robert Hardison
Hardison, Humphrey to Hariel Woolard	Mar. 6, 1826	Charles Hardison
Hardison, Ira to Penelope Hardison	18__	William Hardison
Hardison, John to Polly Strain	Sept. 4, 1827	Thomas Church
Hardison, Joseph to Apha Woolard	Feb. 13, 182_	Simon Daniel
Hardison, Joshua to Martha Long	Oct. 13, 1814	David Long
Harlan, Elijah to Eliz. Tinsley	Aug. 23, 1811	Thomas Sims
Harmon, George to Elizabeth Ring	July 5, 1833	Sessom Rainwater
Harper, Joshua to Polly Oakley	Jan. 20, 1836	Geo. Potts
Harrington, Abel to Betsy Blackburn	Feb. 2, 1829	Shubble Blackburn
Harris, Giles to Caroline M. Daniel	Dec. 21, 1826	William Perry
Harris, James to Elizabeth Standield	Jan. 14, 1811	John Stanfield
Harris, John to Betsey Young	Jan. 2, 1810	Zephemiah Johnson
Harris, John to Nancy McAslin	Feb. 20, 1827	Andrew McAslin
Harris, Samuel to Jane B. Smith	Jan. 29, 1829	Wm. S. Burney
Harris, Sephas to Mary Gooch	Dec. 21, 1835	John Woodward
Hart, Joseph to Frances M. Alderson	Feb. 21, 1822	Taswell Anderson
Harvey, Joel(Hickman Co.) Polly Harvey	Sept. 1, 1810	John Aldridge
Haskins, Daniel to Eliz A. Elam	Aug. 26, 1827	Thomas Gregory
Hawkins, Benjamin to Adeline Morris	Nov. 26, 1835	Noah Morris
Hayes, James to Betsey Kilcrease	Jan. 15, 1811	Jacob Damon
Hayes, Willie G. to Martha Kitrell	July 21, 1829	L. A. Kitrell
Haynes, David to Patience House	Oct. 26, 1835	William House
Haynes, James to Mary D. Puckett	Dec. 14, 1833	Oliver Bridges
Haynes, Levi to Rebecca Orr	Dec. 16, 1832	James L. Haynes
Hays, Wm. & Powell, Mark to Caroline Moppins (couldn't tell which was groom)	May 22, 1819	
Headlee, Joseph to Martha C. Steele	Feb. 25, 1823	Caleb Headley
Helm, Malichi to Elizabeth Porter	May 8, 1814	Linea Helm
Helm, William to Cynthia Stuart	Feb. 12, 1827	John Fisher
Helton, Jessie to Catherine Agent	Mar. 19, 1835	Noah Hawkins
Hemphill, Robert to Evelina Cooper	Feb. 25, 1833	John Cooper
Henderson, Ezekial to Easter Hanna	Feb. 14, 1826	James Matthews
Hensley, John to Easter Johnston	Jan. 19, 1829	Wm. Sharp
Herald, Noah to Lydia Reynolds	Sept. 16, 1826	Thomas Reynolds
Herron, Alanson (No Bride)	Feb. 17, 1827	Thomas Bord
Henry, Hesekiah to Nancy Bennett	Aug. 7, 1823	Malcomb Gilchrist

NAME	DATE	BONDSMAN
Hicks, Gilbert to Elizabeth Allen	Apr. 2, 1832	William Akin
Hicks, John to Elizabeth Bandfield	Apr. 18, 1814	Abner Heraldson
Hicks, John H. to Perdytha Loronce	Nov. 27, 1826	David Craig
Hicks, Temple to Sally Bullock	May 24, 1814	William Carr
Hicks, Thomas to Mary A. White	Jan. 25, 1829	John L. Riger
Higgins, Charles to Vicey Hudson	Oct. 15, 1811	Zodock Hyatt
Higgins, Michael to Mary Childress	Dec. 14, 1827	Simpson Neeley
Hight, Richard B. to Sally Bobbitt	May 5, 1823	Sion H. Hight
Hill, Bennet to Caroline Frazier	July 2, 1829	James A. Tidwell
Hill, John R. to Eliz. H. Kennedy	Oct. 7, 1829	A. A. Dickerson
Hill, Joseph to Rosannah McFarland	Mar. 26, 1810	James McFarland
		John Hall
Hill, William H. to Sarah Brown	Sept. 18, 1810	Jesse Brown
Hilliard, Anderson to W. H. Mangrum	Oct. 9, 1832	Andrew Hudson
Hobbs, Jordan to Patsy Nicholson	Sept. 18, 1822	Charles Weems
Hodges, Forsythe to Drusilla Liggett	Jan. 19, 1829	J. W. Wortham
Hogan, William to Anny Atkison	May 13, 1813	Cyrus Alexander
Holcomb, John R. to Patience Dowell	Feb. 24, 1829	William Timmons
Holding, Samuel to Elvira H. Gullet	Feb. 13, 1827	T. J. Porter
Holland, Amos to Sophia Steward	Oct. 30, 1836	John Dillehay
Holland, Newton to Rosena Brittleman	Feb. 4, 1836	Robert Elder
Holmes, John to Martha A. Evans	Oct. 16, 1832	John Oliphant
Holmes, Robert to Nancy Forgey	Oct. 27, 1832	David Mitchell
Holt, Darril D. to Elizabeth Bowden	Nov. 27, 1835	Josiah Smith
Holt, Isaac to Martha C. Wilson	Aug. 14, 1826	T. J. Porter
Holt, Milton B. to Mariah Smith	Nov. 3, 1826	John Hale
Hood, William to Catherine Owins	Aug. 21, 1823	Jordan Adkison
Howell, Jethro to Elizabeth White	Mar. 27, 1822	Buford Turner
Howell, Major to Mary Meese	Jan. 2, 1827	John Howell
Hudson, Solomon to Martha Pickins	Mar. 8, 1836	Jas. Carothers
Hudson, Young to Eliza Pickens	Feb. 8, 1836	Lytle Dooley
Hudspeth, Counsil to Parnita Edmundson	Jan. 21, 1810	James Birmingham
Hudspeth, Joel to Elizabeth Smith	May 20, 1822	William Hudspeth
Hudspeth, William to Matilda Powell	Feb. 9, 1826	William Shelton
Huey, Green to Susan Bobo	Feb. 15, 1832	Robert M. White
Huey, James to Jane Bradly	Feb. 29, 1832	Thorton Chandler
Huey, William to Susan Bradly	Nov. 5, 1835	Wash. Miller
Huff, Martin to Hannah Baker	Apr. 21, 1823	Thomas Hanks?
Huggins, Anderson to Rebecca Tuttle	Oct. 1, 1832	Wm. T. Knowis
Hughey, John to Candess Dotson	Feb. 8, 1808	John McKnight
Hunter, Elisha to Elizabeth Record	June 19, 1809	Isaac Brooks
Hunter, William to Elinor Stockard	Sept. 28, 1810	Richard Stockard
Irwin, George to Mary A. Pettiswood	Jan. 6, 1836	Stark B. Wood
Isom, Dudley to Elizabeth P. Kennedy	June 17, 1822	A. T. Isom
Jackson, Gilom to Mary Kitrell	Dec. 2, 1832	Robert Wright
Jackson, Thomas G. to Elizabeth Calvert	Jan. 17, 1829	Berry F. Morgton?
Jeaton, James A. to Elizabeth Wilkes	Apr. 21, 1829	Rich. Wilkes
Jennings, Benj. to Nancy Williams	July 24, 1832	Geo. F. Benton
Jenkins, Michael to Margaret Williams	Mar. 14, 182_	Mortimer Black
Jennings, William to Margarette Williams	Feb. 6, 1827	Thomas Vincent
Johns, Daniel to Mary H. Jossey	Oct. 26, 1836	Augustus Sowell
Johnson, Berry to Nancy Neeley	Aug. 11, 1832	Watson Cassele
Johnson, Cassel to Cinthia Cheatom	Sept. 4, 1832	Watson Cassil
Johnson, Daniel to Celia Cole	Jan. 30, 1828	Absalom Adkins
Johnson, James to Mazie Mays	Jan. 4, 1836	Elias P. Mays
Johnson, Gideon to Celia Travis (Frasier?)	July 16, 1811	Francis McBrae

NAME	DATE	BONDSMAN
Johnson, Hugh N. to Mary Fitzgerald	Dec. 12, 1835	J. H. Fitzgerald
Johnson, John to Isabella Kerr	Feb. 21, 1814	Nathaniel Johnson
Johnson, Joseph to Patsey S. Caldwell	Feb. 12, 1810	Micajah Davis
Johnson, Mordica to Winney Storey	Jan. 25, 1823	James Bradshaw
Johnson, Nathan to Susan Davis	Sept. 2, 1836	William Goforth
Johnson, Neill to Peggy Dean	Aug. 22, 1811	Wm. Dean & Angus Johnson
Johnson, Robert to Mary Murrell	Apr. 29, 1822	Coleman Chaffin
Johnson, Simon to Massey Swim	Apr. 9, 1832	James Halcomb
Johnson, William to Mary Altz.	Aug. 31, 1822	James Johnson
Johnson, William J. to Sally Wade	Dec. 15, 1814	John T. Moore
Johnston, Alexander to Lottie Mitchell	May 3, 1829	J. J. Craig
Johnston, James to Ann Johnston	May 9, 1822	John Johnston
Johnston, Joshua W. to Swan Henderson	Oct. 16, 1828	J. F. McWhister?
Johnston, M. C. to Sara Gordon	July 7, 1835	Thomas Caperton
Jones, Edward D. to Kitty Willis	May 10, 1819	John S. Longley
Jones, Elisha to Charlotte Shelton	Feb. 11, 1835	Wm. M. Branch
Jones, James to Nancy M. Jones	Dec. 4, 1814	William T. Lewis
Jones, James to Martha Jackson	Mar. 23, 1829	Bradford Darall?
Jones, Joshua to Jane Covey	Jan. 21, 1835	James Bowman
Jones, Joseph to Frankey Taylor	July 2, 1808	Gibson Stewart
Jones, Robert to Mary Moore	Jan. 19, 1832	N. F. Smith
Jones, Stephen to Susan Keeble	July 20, 1835	Charlie Old
Justice, Zachariah to Lucy Wolverton	Oct. 24, 1827	Reuben Hill
Justice, William to Mary Dotson	Mar. 7, 1827	Vestal Mash
Kates, William to Sarah Randall	Apr. 10, 1822	James Randall
Keeble, John G. to Martha Cheatham	Jan. 16, 1835	William Hardin
Keele, David to Mary Sweet	July 5, 1832	A. H. Williams
Keith, Thomas G. to Elizabeth Boon	Aug. 30, 1819	John Galbraith
Kelly, James to Elizabeth Barbour	Apr. 6, 1836	Willie D. Kelly
Kelly, (Coly?) Patrick to Betsy Gwinn	Mar. 2, 1814	Samuel Davis
Kelly, Willie to Eliza Barbaur	Feb. 6, 1836	James Kelly
Kellum, Jordon to Mary I. Ervine	May 20, 1829	Jonas E. Thomas
Kelsay, Thomas to Hester J. Sealey	Feb. 14, 1828	J. T. Faris
Kenddy, Eli to Margaret L. Finly	Aug. 16, 1814	Francis McBride
Kennedy, Eli to Elizabeth Curry	Jan. 23, 1823	J. R. Shelton
Kennedy, Francis H. to Caroline P. Davis	Oct. 8, 1829	J. A. W. Jackson
Kennedy, John to Elizabeth Baldridge	Aug. 23, 1822	James Baldridge
Kennedy, Thomas B. to Nancy Tomlinson	Feb. 28, 1827	David D. Deanes
Kennedy, Thomas to Priscilla Quintard	Aug. 19, 1828	Fenwell Bunland
Kerr, Andrew to Eliz. Norris	Oct. 31, 1832	Washington Webb
Key, Thomas to Nancy Cherry	July 4, 1829	Samuel Keef?
Kilburn, Adam to Mildred Watkins	Jan. 2, 1826	B. C. Wallis
Kilian, Adam to Polly Spencer	July 6, 1814	James Lynch
Killingsworth, James to Nancy Cooke	Sept. 23, 1822	William Cooke
Kilpatrick, Andrew to Louisa Bell	Sept. 11, 1828	Thos. G. Caldwell
Kilpatrick, Eleazer to Nancy Cathell	June 4, 1811	Josiah Cathell
Kincade, Isaac to Nancy Hood	July 12, 1828	Isaac Dark
King, Alexander to Elizabeth Shields	Aug. 4, 1819	Henry Coffey
King, Samuel to Isabella Shields	Jan. 24, 1811	James Shields
Kirby, Ethelbert to Nancy Polk	Sept. 8, ___	
Kirby, Hardy to Elizabeth Latta	Dec. 11, 1827	Samuel B. Reavis
Kirk, Natus to Priscilla Knight	Mar. 11, 1809	William Daniel
Kitchens, John B. to Nancy Kennedy	Nov. 13, 1832	W. M. Kennedy
Klyce, John to Sara Ridley	Oct. 8, 1832	R. B. Mays
Knox, Joseph to Levoisa Paxton	Sept. 21, 1822	Samuel J. Rogers

NAME	DATE	BONDSMAN
Koonce, James to Polly Hart	May 30, 1808	Bartholemew Stephens
Koonce, John to Martha Howard	Feb. 11, 1829	J. D. Aldisson
Kurtz, (Curtis) Martin to Marg. Sutherland	July 17, 1829	? Master
Kyle, Pryor to Jinny Cooper	July 14, 1809	David Campbell
Lamb, Barden to Polly Johnson	Mar. 2, 1827	Dempsy Watson
Lamb, John to Ann Thomas	Mar. 19, 1836	John Black
Lancaster, Eli to Alley Williams	May 7, 1811	Thomas Lancaster
Lanes, William to Emla Campbell	18__	William Moore
Langford, Jesse to Winnefred T. Sanders	Feb. 12, 1823	Jas. L. Turner
Langham, Andrew to Sara Roper	Sept. 30, 1836	Benj. Pulliam
Langston, Noah to Eliz. Mayhoe	July 18, 1832	Wm. Sweat
Lankford, Benjamin to Sarah Ellison	Sept. 18, 1837	John Blackburn
Lankford, John to Betsy Grurdin	June 21, 1814	Henry Brooks
Lane,J.(Larue?), to Clara Hardin	May 13, 1811	Joseph Larue
Lasslay, Samuel to Charity Johnson	Mar. 11, 1822	Andrew Derryberry
Lawrence, John to Nelly Haynes	Apr. 10, 1813	Jacob Lowrence
Lea, Lilburn to Elizabeth Richmon	Feb. 14, 1823	Bradford Bynum
Leach, David to Nancy Gilchrist	Feb. 4, 1817	John D. Fleming
Leaper, John to Nancy Compton	Aug. 1, 1810	Samuel Leaper
Ledbetter, Ziriah to Rebecca Barnes	Sept. 1832	Shadrick Wren
Lee, Mathew to Delilah Loid	Jan. 11, 1832	John L. Lee
Lee, William T. to Elizabeth Almon	Dec. 15, 1827	Samuel C. Love
Leeper, Hugh to Sally Davis	July 18, 1822	John Alderson
Leigh, Thomas J. to Harriett Donaldson	Jan. 13, 1823	Alfred M. Donaldson
Lemaster, Joseph to Elizabeth Miller	Mar. 7, 1822	Alexander McKay
Lewis, Rich. to Mariah Craig	Mar. 2, 1829	Wm. Walker
Lindsay, John to Sally Kelly	Aug. 6, 1822	Thomas Kelly
Lindsey, Isaac to Polly Taylor	June 29, 1808	Burgess Hardin
Lindsey, Sterling to Lucy Johnston	Feb. 9, 1826	Hardin Williams
Lion, William to Elizabeth Norwell	May 3, 1814	John McKissick
Lions, Richard to Sela Ghasgill	Oct. 13, 1823	John Liversay
Little, John to Nancy Perkins	Jan. 9, 1832	David Partee
Liveray, John to Peggy Lyon	Aug. 24, 1814	Jesse Liveray
Liversay, William to Martha Dorsey	Mar. 25, 1826?	Thomas Liversay
Livesy, Lorenzo to Dililah Mayes	Mar. 10, 1823	John Livesy
Lock, William to Elizabeth Smith	Nov. 15, 1823	Francis Hamilton
Lockart, Moses to Patsey Myers	June 29, 1811	William Smith
Locke, James to Lucinda Tankesley	June 19, 1811	John Tankesley
Lockhart, Arthur to Sarah Seagraves	Feb. 25, 1822	James Randall
Lockridge, Robert to Eliza Buchanan	July 25, 1827	Thomas J. Lentz
Logan, Robert to Polly Edwards	Feb. 5, 1811	Joseph Kincaid
Loney, C. P. to Orra Dorch	Apr. 21, 1829	David R. Dorch
Loney, James to Lucretia Williams	Sept. 2, 1822	Nimrod Porter
Long, Anderson to Ann Pearson	Dec. 5, 1832	John Thomas
Long, George to Jennett Sansom	Dec. 21, 1835	George Perry
Long, John to Susannah Dewall	Nov. 17, 1832	Josiah Long
Long, Joseph to Sarah Hardison	May 31, 1822	Jesse Leftwich
Long, Ware to Nancy Huggins	July 21, 1828	Andrew Agnew
Looney, R. G. to Eliza Carathers	Jan. 18, 1832	P. W. Porter
Louallen, Clayborn to Nancy Hill	May 29, 1833	Butler Noles
Louallen, William to Anny Gifford	May 9, 1832	John Arnold
Loven, William to Betsy Holloday	Apr. 16, 1822	Jeremiah Holloday
Lovin, Presley to Susannah Peoples	Feb. 18, 1817	Reuben Peoples
Lumpkin, John to Eliz. Dooley	Dec. 3, 1835	Micheal Lancaster
Lusk, James to Eleanor R. Lusk	Sept. 3, 1827	James Hodge

NAME	DATE	BONDSMAN
Madding, Rawley to Sally Bridgeman	Apr. 14, 1828	Francis
Madison, James to Elizabeth Fields	Sept. 12, 1832	William Pickard
Maguire, Holliday to Eliza Cayce	May 12, 1836	Thomas Cayce
Mangrum, Edward to Esther Allen	Jan. 21, 1832	John Baugus
Manning, Douglas to Mary M. Duffee	Apr. 26, 1828	John S. Erwin
Marine, Moses to Prudence Ferrell	May 30, 1836	James Chaffen
Marsh, Shelby to Dorinda Jones	Sept. 4, 1837	John Daniel
Martin, G. W. to N.W. J. Hiller	Aug. 12, 1828	D. C. Topp
Martin, James R. to Polly McCrackin	Jan. 6, 1823	Elijah R. Hart
Martin, William to Nelly Davis	July 5, 1809	William Dearing
Martin, Zachrach to Eliz. Hudson	Apr. 9, 1832	James Garral
Mash, Vestal to Elizabeth Justice	Aug. 29, 1822	Charles Merryman
Mason, William to Ruth Headlee	Dec. 18, 1827	Caleb Headlee, J.P.
Matthews, Henry to Matilda Doston	Mar. 4, 1826	Andrew Doston
Matthews, Robert F. to Sally E. Bills	Oct. 24, 1822	Thomas E. Ridley
Maxey, Merit to Eliza M. Shell	Aug. 23, 1823	Thomas Ellett
May, Peter to Margaret Blithe	Jan. 16, 1817	Malice Pamenter
Mayberry, Frederick to Betsey Turnbean	Aug. 3, 1810	Elijah Mayfield
Mayberry, Micheal to Mary Williams	July 7, 1835	Stephen Oakley
Mayes, Elias P. to Mary D. Gardner	June 4, 1836	Joseph Johnson
Mayes, Isaac to Ruthy Edwards	Sept. 20, 1810	Adam Bell
Mayes, John to Ann D. Sharlock	Jan. 23, 1827	M. D. Cooper
Mayfield, Eliajah to Rachel Mayberry	May 28, 1810	David Mayberry
Mays, David to Dicey White	Feb. 23, 1829	James Turner
Mays, Davis to Rhody Edmondson	Mar. 30, 1822	David Mays
Mays, Isaac to Susan Garner	Apr. 6, 1828	William Garner
McAndles, John to Margaret Hannah	June 26, 1822	James W. Matthews
McBride, Francis to Margaret Perry	Mar. 16, 1814	John Whittaker
McBride, Jesse to Ann Thomason	182	Thomas W. Vincent
McBride, Samuel to Polly Voorhies	Apr. 1, 1815	Henry Peyton
McCabe, Charles to Nancy Rogers	Dec. 1, 1832	Willie Hite
McCafferty, Edward to Sally Ninon	Sept. 23, 1808	John Stanfield
McCallester, William to Polly Webb	May 30, 1810	Meredith Webb
McCallister, William to Leahanna Herrod	Aug. 28, 1810	Issac Grooms
McCarty, Andrew to Ruthy Rees	Aug. 11, 1808	James Rees, Jr.
McCasland, Andrew to Mitilda Kennemore	May 23, 1835	? King
McCastin, Branson to Susannah Weaver	June 19, 1828	William Lyter?
McClain, James to Elizabeth Rickets	Mar. 23, 1835	James Pugh
McCollum, Samuel to Sally Gray	Sept. 2, 1808	Lemuel White
McCormick, John to Betsy Butler	Aug. 9, 1822	George Driskell
McCowan, Joshua W. to Marthy Shepard	Apr. 23, 1828	Samuel D. McAlister
McCoy, Samuel to Martha McColley	June 4, 1808	Jesse C. McCoy
McCrackin, Ephriam to Mary Mitchell	July 19, 1811	James Mitchell
McCracken, John to Margaret McMeen	Apr. 2, 1833	Henry Hadly
McCrady, Ephriam to Sarah M. Wingfild	Feb. 11, 1826	James Kennedy
McCrady, William to Rebecca Moore	Nov. 29, 1835	Person Yates
McCullum, Davis to Polly McQuatlean?	Oct. 17, 1827	John W. Record
McDaniel, John to Betsey Tinsley	Aug. 1, 1811	Spencer Tinsley?
McDaniel, Mumford to Elizabeth Neely	Nov. 5, 1827	Issac Neely
McDaniel, Mumford to Hixey Hight	Jan. 7, 1836	William McFaddin
McFall, Thomas to Betsey Fergerson	Oct. 30, 1810	Daniel Fergerson
McFarlin, James to Polly Hall	Apr. 23, 1810	John Hall
McGee, Wiley to Nancy Jones	Feb. 13, 1833	George Jones
McGimsey, Thomas to Dance Partee (alis Sherman)	Jan. 14, 1822	B. W. Hardin
McIlvane, John to Kerem Mackates	May 7, 1822	Abraham Roland
McIntosh, Hector to Nancy Wiggs	Mar. 12, 1832	J. H. Fitzgerald
McKain, Joshua M.E. to Eliz. Roberson	Jan. 23, 1832	James Rodgers

NAME	DATE	BONDSMAN
McKean, John C. to Margaret Kearing	Sept. 29, 1819	John B. Groves
McKee, Samuel to Sarah Polk	Feb. 22, 1826	David Looney
McKee, William to Jane Ray	Nov. 23, 1826	William Roundtree
McKennon, John to Eliza A. Herrington	Feb. 12, 1828	Geo. G. McKennon
McKey, James to Eliz. Rhodes	Dec. 10, 1832	S. Y. Blackburn
McMackin, Hugh A. to Emily Pillow	Sept. 21, 1822	Andrew Johnston
McManus, William to Polly Powell	Aug. 24, 1827	William Phillips
McMillian, John to Elizabeth Jones	June 23, 1835	C. G. Ewing
McNeely, Joseph E. to Elizabeth Sanford	May 22, 1828	Wm. Childers
Meade, Phillip to Elizabeth Donaldson	18__	Joel Goad
Meek, Samuel to Esther Hawkins	Oct. 24, 1822	Campbell Stricklin
Metcaff, Jackson to Eliza Hill	Apr. 29, 1833	Johnson Maning
Metcalf, Thomas to Elizabeth Bridges	182_	Cyrus Bridges
Mills, Samuel to Margaret Lythe	Mar. 20, 1835	Rob Craig
Miller, Daniel B. to Susanna Brown	Jan. 21, 1810	William Lorne
Miller, John to Nancy Turner	Sept. 16, 1829	T. W. Smith
Miller, John to Easter Mangrum	Sept. 30, 1836	John Kilcrease
Miller, John T. to Miss Hannah Williams	Oct. 9, 1826	Mark Powell
Miller, Joseph H. to Maria W. Campbell	Feb. 22, 1811	Jesse Brown, B.F.Lewis
Miller, Joseph H. to Mary Roundtree	Oct. 21, 1822	John Jameson
Miller, Richard to Mary Alexander	Jan. 17, 1823	Eli Alexander
Miller, Stephen to Patsy Kenedy	Feb. 16, 1811	James Erwin
Miller, Thomas to Nancy Moore	Apr. 5, 1832	Allen Brown
Miller, Vincent to Mildred Miller	July 14, 1828	Frank A. Polk
Millican, Thomas to Cynthia Gifford	May 3, 1829	Henry J. Freeman
Mills, Branchton to Celia Ellemore	Apr. 3, 1828	William Melton
Mills, James to Elizabeth McAfee	Oct. 9, 1832	Sample Mills
Mills, Jonathon to Katherine Huey	July 29, 1823	John Baugus
Mills, Sanders to Drucia Cannon	Aug. 30, 1814	Wiley Richardson
Mitchell, Anderson to Emily Witherspoon	Apr. 20, 1833	Edmond Williams
Mitchell, Andrew to Betsy Wren	Oct. 27, 1814	David Mitchell
Mitchell, David to Minerva Cathey	Sept. 4, 1832	Anderson Mitchell
Mitchell, John to Martha Murhead	Sept. 17, 1814	Robert Olliphant
Mitchell, Lesserberry to Avery Hill	Nov. 24, 1823	Wyatt Hill
Mitchell, Thomas to Betsey Evans	Dec. 18, 1810	Jessé Evans
Montgomery, Jacob to Rachel Guardner	May 20, 1811	Benj. H. Lewis
Montgomery, James to Susanna Craig	June 19, 1809	John Craig
Montgomery, Robert to Cynthia Toney	Feb. 13, 1817	Beverly Phillips
Moore, Denson to Margarette Cook	Apr. 4, 1823	Joel R. Smith
Moore, James to Abbigale Grimes	Dec. 6, 1811	Joel Wilson
Moore, James C. to Diamah E. Frierson	Aug. 24, 1829	Robert Ransom
Moore, Lewis to Lethe Braek?	June 21, 1828	Alsey Braek
Moore, Nathaniel to Elisa Smith	May 3, 1829	Pistill Patton?
Moore, Shadrick to Sally Johnson	Sept. 27, 1823	Vawn C. Scott
Moore, Walker to Jane Davis	Mar. 13, 1829	J. L. Campbell
Moore, William F. to Mahala Nichols	Mar. 12, 1832	Wm. J__?
Morris, Elijah to Elizabeth Wadkins	Apr. 27, 1835	Robert Morris
Morris, James to Annis Clark	Feb. 25, 1823	Robert Porter
Morris, Jessie to Louisa J. Goodman	Jan. 24, 1833	J. C. Choate
Morris, James to Elizabeth Hutchinson	Nov. 8, 1823	James Hutchinson
Morrow, John to Elizabeth Randal	July 18, 1823	James Randal
Morton, Joseph T. to Lucinda Hancock	(No Date)	S. M. Harwell
Mosely, Bryant to Hannah West	Oct. 22, 1822	Evin Lewis
Mozley, Archibald to Hixy Hight	July 9, 1836	John Harris
Murfree, Nathaniel G. to Charlotte Perry	July 29, 1822	Simpson Perry
Murphey, David to Nancy Brown	Apr. 3, 1822	Biriah Hawkins
Murphey, William to Nancy Hudspeth	May 17, 1814	Maxamillian Redding
Murrell, Jeffrey S. to Mary Staggs	Aug. 14, 1828	L. Walton

NAME	DATE	BOARDMAN
Neal, William to Sara Shaddon	Jan. 27, 1835	Bryant Paydon
Neal, Matthew to Lydia Owens	Nov. 16, 1818	Joseph Porter
Neeley, Andrew to Comfort Hunter	Feb. 15, 1829	R. H. Simmons
Neeley, Charles to Louisa Polk	Jan. 19, 1808	Thomas McNeil
Neeley, John to Mary Davis	Aug. 24, 1822	Hugh Whiteside
Neeley, Thomas to Synthia Reed	Feb. 20, 1817	James Campbell
Nelson, William to Naomi Jagurs	June 1, 1814	Pleasant Nelson
Nicholson, Nathaniel to Katherine Kilcrease Jan. 21, 1835 Jn. Simmons		
Nix, William to Betsy Spratt	Nov. 11, 1814	Robert Arnold
Nolen, Matthew to Nancy Duke	Mar. 1, 1827	James Pugh
Noles, Allen to Elisa Bateman	June 30, 182_	Paris F. Dooley
Norris, James G. to May Dougherty	May 18, 1835	
North, Isom to Martha Baker	Aug. 13, 1835	James Napier
Nunn, Thomas to Sara Gill	May 14, 1835	Mark Jackson
Oadham, John to Lydia Vincent	Dec. 20, 1836	George Vincent
Oakes, Layburn to Tiny Ferrell	Dec. 8, 1823	David Geriger
Odum, Littleberry to Polly Cochran	Sept. 20, 1822	John Odum
O'Neel, James to Rebecca Hamblet	(No date-1816 box)	Wesley Witherspoon
Orr, James to Elizabeth Lawrance	July 29, 1809	Jacob Lawrance
Orr, Joshua to Nancy Kindrick	Mar. 11, 1809	Jones Kendrick, Jr.
Osborn, Phillip to Martha Gregory	Mar. 19, 1833	Thomas Gregory
Osbourne, Thomas to Margaret Maise (Mays)	182_	John Akin
Overton, Jesse to Susanna Alexander	Feb. 26, 1810	Eleezer Alexander
Owen, John to Martha Strange	Nov. 29, 1827	(Permission of Mother,
Martha Jane Strange, father being dead for dau. to Marry John Owen)		
Owen, John to Martha Jane Stewart	Dec. 14, 1827	P. N. Porter
Owens, Andrew to Jenny McCrackin	Dec. 7, 1816	Joseph McCrackin
Pace, Thomas to Catherine Donahoo	(In 1816 Box)	Henry Webster
Pain, Richard to Jane Holland	May 22, 1828	John Knox
Parchment, John to Patsy Follis (Hollis)	July 20, 1809	Abraham Follis
Patterson, Solomon to Barsheba Elton	Aug. 27, 1811	Joab Patterson
Patterson, William to Ann Irvine	Jan. 30, 1833	Flemming Rankes
Patton, Archibald to Jane C.M. Longley	Dec. 21, 1827	Samuel Rivis
Peck, Isiah to Lydia O'Neal	Aug. 27, 1810	Jonathon O'Neal
Perkins, Hardin to Sophia S. Holland	June 27, 1814	Peter Cheatham
Perritt, Larkin to Sarah Shickly	Dec. 27, 1829	Jordon Hobbs
Perry, Daniel to Vesta Crawford	Aug. 29, 1828	Shadrack Tillmon
Perry, Green B. to Ann Hart	Oct. 27, 1823	James W. Jennings
Perry, William to Nancy McCord	Aug. 17, 1828	Samuel Caruthers
		Josiah Perry
Petty, George to Fanny Williams	Dec. 9, 1823	Gideon G. Williams
Petty, Hardy to Susan Wrenn	Feb. 21, 1831	Peter Wrenn
Petty, Hardy to Sara Mays	July 24, 1832	William Skelly
Petty, Richard to Susan Williams	Sept. 21, 1828	George W. Petty
Phillips, Lemuel to Eliza P. Goff	June 5, 1833	Andrew Hudson
Phillips, Samuel to Rebecca O. Cross	May 15, 1828	Thomas J. Porter
Pibler, (Pebles?) Wm. to Betsey Ivey	Aug. 12, 1811	James Ivey
Pickard, Alexander to Polly Mitchell	Sept. 12, 1814	David Mitchell
Pickard, Alexander to Elizabeth Craig	Sept. 16, 1826	Alex. A. Pickard
Pickard, Henry J. to Maria Johnson	Jan. 14, 1836	Berry Mangrum
Pickard, Isaac W. to Sarah Ephland	Feb. 4, 1829	J. Williams
Pickens, David to Susan Byers	Apr. 16, 1810	Alexander Gillespie
Pickens, (Perkins?) James to Tabithia Jack	July 23, 1810	Robert Hooten
Pigg, Alfred to Nancy Paine	Dec. 13, 1836	John Simpson
Pigg, Anderson to Isabella McManas	Sept. 15, 1828	Levi London
Pilkinton, John N. to Mary A. Campbell	Jan. 14, 1835	John Campbell
Pillow, John to Margaret Adkins	May 3, 1818	George Patton

NAME	DATE	BONDSMAN
Pimento, Maliki to Jane Ramsey	Nov. 14, 1808	George Dior (Dier?)
Pinkard, William to Matilda Warfield	June 4, 1832	M. F. Pinkard
Pipking Phillip to Polly White	Sept. 17, 1827	Chesley Rainey
Pipkins, Gillford to Sally Mozely	182_	John Pettillo
POLK Pogue, Joseph to Hannah Lamaster	Dec. 31, 1810	John Lamaster
Polk, Ezekial to Sophia Leonard	Nov. 24, 1810	Horatio De Priest
Polk, John to Polly McBridge	July 28, 1814	William Polk
Pollard, Joseph H. to Mary A. Richards	Feb. 27, 1832	M. Richards
Porter, Elias to Ann Shaw	Sept. 1, 1835	Richard Looney
Porter, Parry to Jane Looney	Feb. 9, 1832	J. Porter
Porter, Robert to Mary Ann Roake	Sept. 17, 1810	Wm. R. Nunn
Powell, Daniel to Rebecca Cawtrey	Nov. 13, 1826	Larkin Dearen
Powell, Eli to Synthia Turbyfield	Nov. 27, 1836	Willie Johnson
Powell, Fanning to Katherine Powell	May 8, 1832	Edmond Guin
Powell, Isom to Sally Knox	July 13, 1814	Alexander Kelly
Powell, John to Polly Harden	Apr. 27, 1814	Peter Powell
Powell, John A. to Susan Arnold	Sept. 8, 1814	Sion S. Record
Powell, Lewis to Mary Hinson	Aug. 9, 1832	T. Hinson
Powell, Nathaniel to Barbary Fogleman	182_	J. A. Gillespie
Powell, Thomas to Mary McKain	Dec. 3, 1829	Joshua McKain
Prewitt, Mark to Sarah D. Wilks	Jan. 12, 1828	Claiborne Harris
Prichit, John to Martha Robinson	Jan. 5, 1828	James Taylor
Puckett, Pleasant to Katherine Vaughn	Nov. 16, 1835	Wilson Denton
Puckett, William to Mary Griffin	Aug. 23, 1826	Wiley Griffin
Pullen, William to Sally Bailey	Jan. 15, 1810	Bird Hurt
Pullin, Joseph to Catherine Dugger	Jan. 8, 1828	Robert Boaz
Pusell, (Fussell) Joshia to Eliza. Fitzgerald	Jan. 31, 1832	W. Coston
Radford, Samuel to Cynthia Kilpatrick	Nov. 14, 1809	Ebonezah Kilpatrick
Ramsey, John to Elizabeth Kennedy	Sept. 25, 1822	James Kennedy
Rankin, David to Rebecca Jobe	Oct. 20, 1810	Jesse Job
Rankin, Pleasant (No Bride)	Dec. 6, 1826	John Renfrae
Ray, James to Nancy Osteen	Oct. 12, 1836	Andrew Akin
Ray, William W. to Arsenath Blackburn	June 4, 1836	John Blackburn
Rea, Nathan to France Moody	Aug. 13, 1823	Benjamin Spencer
Read, W. T. to Catherine Wantling	Apr. 21, 1829	Samuel Frierson
Reasonover, Early to Levina Grant	Jan. 6, 1835	James Moore
Reddin, Isaac to Elizabeth Bobo	Dec. 22, 1829	Samuel Reding
Reece, James to Rebecca Simpson	Nov. 11, 1809	William Stephenson
Reeves, Thomas to Sally Murphy	? 24, 1827	W. J. Bridges
Reemiy, Allen to Jane Campbell	May 18, 1835	Reddin Simmons
Renfro, Lewis to Nancy Huckeberry	Dec. 27, 1820	Moses Renfro
Renfrow, John to Rachel Rankins	May 30, 1822	Shelton Renfrow
Renfrow, Shelton to Peggy Goforth	July 8, 1822	William Renfrow
Reynolds, Aaron to Masse (Maye?) Davis	Dec. 24, 1810	Thomas Mitchell
Reynolds, James to Cynthia A. Williams	Sept. 21, 1829	James Allen
Rhea, Elijah to Jane Bacum	March 2, 1835	Alexander Ray
Rhedding, Abijah to Mahala Mitchell	Jan. 5, 1809	Thomas Mitchell
Rhyne, John to Elizabeth Mitchell	May 29, 1835	Robert Thompson
Richards, Thomas to Lucinda Chumley	Sept. 19, 1827	Rich. Baugass
Richardson, Wiley to Nancy P. Crofton	Dec. 18, 1816	John W. Nelson
Rieves, Elijah to Polly Stallings	July 14, 1819	George Hamilton
Rivet, James to Louisa Hight	July 26, 1832	Geo. D. Harmon
Ring, Lewis to Jinny Hogg	Mar. 24, 1823	Edward Harris
Roach, Abner to Sally Koonce	Dec. 31, 1827	John H. Koonce
Roach, William to Patsey Aiken	Sept. 21, 1810	William Aiken
Roads, Jessie to Martha Helm	Dec. 31, 1832	William Carr

NAME	DATE	BONDSMAN
Robason, Henry to Zilly Whitly	July 20, 1829	Daniel Nellums
		I. E. Thomas
Robertson, Benjamin to Martha Goodloe	Sept. 30, 1823	Allen Brown
		Hillary Langtry
Robertson, John to Betsey Robertson	Apr. 24, 1810	John Dickson
Robertson, Michael to Betsey Robertson	Nov. 7, 1809	Bluford Turner
Robertson, Starkey to Elizabeth Crawford	Oct. 4, 1823	William Crawford
Robinson, Jacob to Mary C. Bobitt	July 16, 1829	Thomas Oakley
Robinson, James to Martha Forsythe	Oct. 19, 1835	Stephen Harrison
Rodery, Washington to Emily J. Overton	Oct. 21, 1829	Thomas McMeens
Rodes, Tyree to Cynthia Holland	Apr. 5, 1811	Benjamin Lewis
Rodgers, Robert to Aratillia Hall	Nov. 20, 1832	Pearson Yates
Rodgers, Thomas to Jane S. Wilks	Dec. 21, 1829	Thomas Wilks
Rodgers, William to Nancy Calwell	Jan. 23, 1817	James Mills
Rogers, Jesse to Lucy Akin	May 17, 1827	Pleasant Akin
Rook, Jacob to Elizabeth Asque	Nov. 24, 1810	William Asque
Ross, Hugh to Betsey Brooks	Oct. 4, 1809	Isaac Brooks
Ross, James to Nancy Pritchett	July 13, 1814	James Pritchett
Ross, William to Rebecca Armstrong	Mar. 27, 1828	Thos. Ross
Roundtree, David to Victory McKee	Feb. 15, 1827	William Roundtree
Rummage, James to Sarah Barker	Sept. 6, 1819	Brittan J. Baucom
Rush (Rusk?), Andrew to Leah Dale	Aug. 31, 1814	Reddick Robertson
Rust, Samuel to Sarah C. Wilson	Dec. 28, 1826	William Dortch
Ruston, Elijah to Betsy Coggins	Jan. 14, 1829	Lawrence McMinus
Rutledge, James to Nancy Armstrong	Jan. 16, 1811	James Purcell
Rutledge, Samuel to Bethia Carter	Dec. 26, 1823	E. B. Dooley
Rutledge, William to Sarah Sims	Dec. 10, 1809	Joel Rutledge
Rutledge, William to Margaret C. Reid	Dec. 21, 1814	Pleasant Nelson
Ryne, Andrew to Eliza Hays	May 5, 1836	John Burns
Sanders, John to Cynthia Pillow	Oct. 30, 1832	Thomas Craighead
Sanders, L. D. to Sally Spivy	July 14, 1829	James G. Campbell
Sanders, Moses to Amanda Fausett	Jan. 5, 1826	William Fausett
Sandford, Robert J. to Elizabeth Yancy	May 22, 1823	James L. Turner
Sansom, Dorrell to Mary E. Brown	Oct. 15, 1822	M. Caruthers
Sawyer, Costin to Sally Roach	May 8, 1811	William Roach
Sawyers, Payton R. to Nancy Brisley	Apr. 24, 1832	A. G. Sawyers
Scott, Elias to Peggy Laird	Feb. 27, 1822	Andrew Laird
Scott, James to Peggy Wallan	Jan. 19, 1811	Ezekial Wallan
Scott, James to Sarah Williams	Jan. 8, 1826	Thomas Wolverton
Scruggs, Jesse T. to Susanna Thornton	June 4, 1823	Job H. Thomas
Sealey, Enoch to Hester Estes	Feb. 22, 1828	Thrashly A. Estes
Sewell, James to Ann Alexander	Mar. 21, 1832	Andrew Hill
Sewell, Joseph to Elizabeth Stone	Feb. 11, 1809	Samuel Long
Shackelford, Richard to Eliza Buchanan	July 24, 1827	Walter S. Jenkins
Shaddin, John to Mary Rogers	Aug. 13, 1814	Martin Beard
Shannon, Jefferson to Rachel Randal	Jan. 23, 1823	Stokely Vittets
Shannon, Owen to Peggy Sloan	Nov. 22, 1808	William Adams
Sharp, George to Elizabeth Hensley	July 8, 1836	Robert Tarrant
Sharp, John to Nancy Hensly	Apr. 11, 1828	John Hensly
Shaw, James to Betsy Shaw	Mar. 12, 1822	James Jennings
Shell, William to Jane Campbell	Apr. 13, 1814	George McNutt
Shelton, Elijah to Elizabeth Shelton	Aug. 20, 1822	Joel Shelton
Shelton, Gideon to Elizabeth Woolverton	Sept. 26, 1826	John Fitzgerald
Shelton, Stephen to (No Bride)	No Date	Zephemah Johnson
Sherald, Itty to Polly Parr	June 28, 1809	William Simpson
Sherman, Parson to Elizabeth Dood	Sept. 29, 1835	H. J. Hoge

NAME	DATE	BONDSMAN
Shores, James C. to Elizabeth Scott	Oct. 31, 1832	William Gordon
Simmons, John to Nancy Patterson	Oct. 26, 1835	David Hays
Simmons, Readin H. to Eliz. P. Briggs	Aug. 27, 1828	Barton M. Jenkins
Simmons, Thomas to Barbery Grinder	Feb. 23, 1836	John Odham
Simons, Flemmon to Polly Kilchrist	Mar. 31, 1810	James Hutchison
Simpson, Abel to Polly Gordon	Dec. 18, 1814	John H. Brown
Simpson, William to Elizabeth Stephenson	July 29, 1809	Pleasant Jones
Sims, Minor to Melinda Cooke	Apr. 1, 1833	James Robertson
Sims, Nicholas to Amanda Zollicoffer	Oct. 23, 1832	James Briscoe
Shelton, Edmond to Elizabeth Beshary	Jan. 30, 1833	
Shelton, John to Elizabeth Wadill?	Dec. 5, 1821	Andrew Caradine
Slauter, Francis to Lourania Evans	Jan. 17, 1822	William K. Hill
Smith, Daniel to Mary L. Cathey	Oct. 19, 1835	William Nichols
Smith, Lawrence to Mary Overstreet	Nov. 8, 1836	William Crawford
Smith, John W. to Nancy Tooms	Feb. 12, 1823	Garner Tooms
Smith, Moses to Pamelia Eakin	Nov. 17, 1808	Simon Johnson
Smith, Moses to Fanny Mayberry	Apr. 17, 1813	Moses Lockhard
Smith, Robert O. to Mary Payton	Dec. 31, 1832	J. W. Barr
Smith, Samuel to Mary Shaw	Aug. 6, 1827	Wm. H. Goodloe
Smoot, John M. to Betsy Holland	Jan. 27, 1827	Gray P. Webb
Southern, Willis to Emily Bobitt	Sept. 21, 1836	Alex. McDaniel
Sowell, Ryon to Anny Letsinger	Jan. 10, 1823	Augustus Brown
Sparkman, Seth to Rebecca Latta	July 8, 1822	Thomas Latta
Spencer, James to Jane Green	Dec. 23, 1835	Alex_____?
Spivey, William to Sally Wilkes	Mar. 8, 1828	Richard Wilkes
Sprinkle, Micajah to Susan Kendrick	Nov. 28, 1808	Jesse Kendrick
Spruell, Pleasant to Jane Barket	182_	Thomas L. Dillard
Staggs, Fleming to Sally Locke	Jan. 31, 1810	Mathis Speers
Stallings, Benedict to Sarah Choate	Dec. 16, 1829	Joseph Choate
Stanfield, Thomas to Rachel Burns	Aug. 21, 1810	George Burns
Stanfield, William to Sally Bolin	May 24, 1814	Joel Dabs
Stanfield, William to Jane Mason	Feb. 16, 1832	John Butler
Steel, Aaron to Nancy Davis	Mar. 6, 1819	Lile McKesson
Steel, James A. Tof Frankie Harris	Dec. 30, 1823	John H. Money
Steel, Micheal to Mary A. Pursel	Jan. 23, 1833	James Haynes
Stephens, James to Sara A. Majors	(No Date)	Samuel English
Stephens, John to Polly Hines	Dec. 20, 1808	Charles Stephens
Stephens, John H. to Susan Williams	Dec. 16, 1832	John Callahan
Stephenson, Chesley to Martha B. Penn	Nov. 22, 1836	John Bynum
Stephenson, James to Mary Fleming	May 26, 1808	David Frierson
Stephenson, John to Elizabeth Hill	182_	Holliday Maquire
Stephenson, William to Mariah Johnson	Oct. 28, 1810	Theron E. Balch
Stewart, James to Miriah Turner	May 26, 1835	Richard Gilmore
Stockard, Joseph to Elizabeth Croford	Jan. 13, 1810	David Craig
Stone, Eli to Mary Jones	May 10, 1828	Fountain G. Stone
Stone, Hudley to Mary Jenkins	Feb. 4, 1811	Walter S. Jenkins
Stone, John to Betsy Isbile	Aug. 8, 1814	Beverly Phillips
Stone, Robert to Maacah Gentry	May 4, 1832	? Gentry
Stone, Thomas to Nancy Dogan	Mar. 12, 1814	Samuel Craig
Story, Parrish to Polly McManus	Oct. 4, 1823	Martin Kendrick
Strahan, John to Hannah Patton	Nov. 9, 1814	John T. Moore
Stratton, Henry to Mary Rogers	May 7, 1836	Samuel H. Watson
Strayhorn, John to Mary Stevens	Dec. 18, 1832	William Akin
Stuart, John to Mary L. Henderson	Sept. 25, 1828	Moses Crafford
Sutherland, A. to Rachel Huckeby	Oct. 7, 1826	John Butler
Sweet, James to Mary Wiggs	Jan. 1, 1832	A. M. Williams

NAME	DATE	BONDSMAN
Tade, Joseph to Jane Stephenson	Feb. 26, 1810	John Chambers
Tally, Daniel to Judah Forbes	July 4, 1828	Tartton Renfro?
Tate, Owen to Martha J. Shaddin	Sept. 24, 1835	David Dobbins
Taylor, William to Ann Adams	Nov. 30, 1808	Thomas Rheardon
Taylor, William to Sally Rearden	Oct. 23, 1809	Joseph Jones
Theobold, William to Minerva Daniel	Nov. 1, 1836	Isaac Bills
Terry, David to Betsey Love	Jan. 26, 1811	Joel Love
Thomas, David to Nancy Hurton	Oct. 31, 1808	James Hurton
Thomas, Elisah to Alley Gurley	Sept. 21, 1809	Jeremiah Gurley
Thomas, James to Rebecca Black	Feb. 15, 1836	John Black
Thompson, Aaron to Margaret Mills	Feb. 9, 1827	John D. Neal (Head)
Thompson, Ebenezer to Barbara Gray	Apr. 14, 1810	George Burns
Thompson, F. D. to Elizabeth Morgan	May 4, 1810	James T. Sandford
Thompson, J. M. to Ruth Davidson	Dec. 10, 1832	Hiram Faim
Thompson, Leonard to Silva Graves	Sept. 11, 1827	William Duncan
Thompson, Silas to Sara A. Lockhart	July 28, 1835	Henry Wade
Thompson, William to Sally Wiley	Feb. 19, 1820	Andrew Wiley
Thurman, Fleming to Rebecca Librey	July 19, 1814	Thomas Taylor
Thurmond, William to Nancy Sandord	Apr. 5, 1836	John Baily
Tidwell, Francis to Betsy Forbes	Dec. 30, 1826	Darling Tidwell
Tidwell, Thomas to Polly Boyd	Feb. 1, 1820	W. B. Porter
Tinin (Linin?) Jesse, to Little Bets	Aug. 9, 1814	John Thompson
Tombs, Anthony to Caroline Young	July 16, 1835	Sam Redding
Tombs, William to Betsy Duff	May 28, 1808	Benjamin Rawlings
Tomlinson, Hugh to Sarah Nuan?	Dec. 26, 1827	Joshua Kilpatrick
Tomlinson, Hugh to Elizabeth McKracken	Dec. 24, 1829	Wm. S. Moore
Tomlinson, James to Martha Gannaway	Aug. 5, 1822	Henry B. Cannon
Toney, Mark A. to Martha Taylor	Apr. 26, 1823	William Miller
Trotter, John to Polly Fields	May 11, 1822	John Sanders
Tull, Josiah to Margarette Butler	Jan. 3, 1829	Ephriam Stanfield
Turnbough, Hugh to Polly Powell	Aug. 6, 1814	Lewis Powell
Turnbow, Chesley to Sabry Rose	Oct. 4, 1827	Sampson Cutbirth
Turnbow, James to Phililia Coffey	Aug. 2, 1811	Chesley Coffey
Turner, Alexander to Elizabeth Thomas	Oct. 1, 1822	Andrew Nelson
Turner, Arthur to Nancy Nix	July 21, 1832	John Ephland
Turner, Elijah to Nancy Lester	May 21, 1828	Thomas P. Start
Turner, Littleberry to Sarah Smith	Dec. 13, 1826	Elias Minican
Turner, Thomas to Ann Nichols	Dec. 25, 1810	Joshia Nichols
Underwood, David to Nancy Bradley	Jan. 8, 1835	Tilman Mills
Underwood, Edmund to Mary Whetherly	Apr. 14, 1832	Tillman Mills
Underwood, John to Permilia Henry	Mar. 2, 1829	Temple Mills
Veach, Silas to Rachel McConnell	June 4, 1822	Archibald McKennon
Vincint, Moses to Rebecca Waldrop	Feb. 10, 1810	William Vincint
Vincent, Watkins to Elizabeth Odum	Aug. 6, 1819	David Vincent
Voorhees, Peter J. to Polly Roberts	Mar. 4, 1811	Benj. Lewis, Isaac Hardin
Wadkins, George to Clarenda Abry	Dec. 17, 1827	James L. Crawford
Wadkins, John to Judy Wadkins	Apr. 13, 1835	John Hudson
Wadkins, William to Matilda Mason	Feb. 10, 1832	T. L. Henson
Waldrop, Michael to Rebecca Brown	Jan. 8, 1810	Absalom Brown
Waldrum, Henry B. to Lidonia Carlisle	Sept. 9, 1828	William Waldrum
Walker, Green H. to Nancy Potts	Dec. 6, 1829	W. H. Campbell
Walker, John H. to Judith Ames	Dec. 16, 1836	John Terrell
Walker, Joseph A. to Adeline Nelson	Jan. 4, 1832	F. Bostick
Wantlan, Samuel to Anney Alderson	Feb. 17, 1828	John W. Beasley

NAME	DATE	BONDSMAN
Ward, Hezekiah to Elizabeth Ridley	May 2, 1822	James K. Polk
(License Also - May 2, 1822		
Warden, Samuel to Louisa Harris	Sept. 22, 1832	David Kincaid
Watkins, Thomas A. to Eliz. Rilly	Feb. 26, 1830	Lemuel Walters
Watson, James to Phebe Lamb	Mar. 1, 1829	Drew Lamb
Watson, John to Peggy Pickins	Feb. 27, 1809	John Pickins
Watson, Thomas to Ibby Egnew	Aug. 25, 1808	William Thompson
Weatherly, Danl. to Elizabeth Saunders	July 23, 1827	Wm. Melton
Webb, John to Tina Davis	Oct. 28, 1828	James Rhea
Webster, George to Betsy Hubbard	May 17, 1819	Joshua Guest
Webster, Levi to Arina Metcalf	Dec. 2, 1827	Geo. Metcalf
Wells, James J. to Frankie Furgerson	Jan 14, 1811	Henry Davis
Wells, William to Rachel Rankin	182_	Francis Slauter
West, B. M. to Elizabeth Jones	Feb. 6, 1828	Henry Freeman
Wheatley, Francis to Charity L. Brown	Nov. 6, 1823	William Dickson
Wheatley, Thomas to Milly Johnson	Mar. 23, 1815	Wiley Johnson
Wheeton, Newsom to Polly Berry	June 6, 1828	Joseph Berry
Whitaker, John to Betsy Love	Dec. 22, 1807	William Whitaker
White, Israel to Martha Hill	Feb. 10, 1827	Hannan White
White, John L. to Mary C. Jordan	July 31, 1828	James Lansdown
White, Josiah to Pheby Jackson	Aug. 1, 1811	Isaac Stanfill
White, Reuben to Emmarando B. Waldrup	Nov. 4, 1816	William Waldrup
White, Sherwood to Susan Kendrick	Mar. 27, 1813	Magnuss Davis
White, William to Polly Sewell	Sept. 24, 1835	Alexander Graves
Whiteside, Adam to Elizabeth Sprewell	Mar. 2, 1816	John Burns
Whiteside, John to Betsey Young	Dec. 25, 1810	Jacob Young
Whitesides, Robert to Rhoda Faires	Dec. 26, 1809	Samuel Whitesides
Whitson, James to Betsy Long	May 6, 1811	James Walker
Wicker, Abel to Mary O. Glasby	Jan. 5, 1828	John Stratton
Wier, Robert to Narcissa C. Pepin?	July 19, 1827	Thos. J. Porter
Wiggs, Nedham B. to Elizabeth Radford	Feb. 29, 1836	Shadrick Green
Wiley, Alexander to Sally Faris	May 22, 1822	Andrew Hill
Wiley, Andrew M. to Polly Whiteside	Mar. 2, 1822	Abraham Whiteside
Wiley, David to Martha Dickey	Nov. 18, 1816	Matthew Wiley
Wiley, John C. to Jane Davis	Feb. 6, 1833	John M. Caskey
Wilkes, Minor to Patsy Courtny	Aug. 6, 1819	Thomas Wilkes
Wilkins, Samuel J. to Rebecca Paul	Oct. 20, 1823	James C. Alderson
Wilkins, Samuel J. to Nancy Jones	Oct. 15, 1829	G. W. Egnew
Wilkenson, Stephen to Lucinda Evans	Feb. 7, 1836	John Butler
Wilks, David to Elizabeth Spivy	Apr. 14, 1832	William Spivy
Williams, Alexander to Elizabeth Jones	June 11, 1814	Joseph Hodge
Williams, Edmond to Elizabeth K. Dowell	June 26, 1823	J. N. Porter
Williams, John to Sarah Hall	Aug. 15, 1811	William Hall
Williams, John to Harriet M. Yancy	Mar. 14, 1814	William Yancey
(attached note of permission shows Wm. Yancy as her father)		
Williams, John to Candis Spickard	Dec. 2, 1823	Mark Grimes
Williams, Joseph to Martha Pigg	June 12, 1828	John R. Groves
Williams, Peter to Mary G. Beasley	(In box 1826-27)	John H. Hill
Williams, Samuel to Vicey Hutchinson	May 7, 1811	Thomas Lancaster
Williams, William to Nancy Smith	Sept. 12, 1809	John Williams
Wills (Wells?) Bryant to Nancy Bramblet	July 14, 1814	William Bramblet
Wills, David to Elizabeth Fitzpatrick	Sept. 9, 1836	John L. Redding
Wills, Thomas to Mary Davis	Feb. 16, 1829	Samuel Davis
Wilson, David to Anna Hanes	Aug. 7, 1810	Joseph Hanes
Wilson, George C. to Eliza Knox	Oct. 10, 1832	C. W. Trainum
Winn, Phillip W. to Joanna W.M. Houser	July 6, 1835	Geo. Webster
Winn, Zadoc to Elizabeth Breckum	Sept. 19, 1822	Jesse Breckum

NAME	DATE	BONDSMAN
Wire, Josiah to Susan Fuzzell	July 16, 1829	R. H. Flippen
Witherspoon, John to Sara Perry	Jan. 4, 1836	Nathan Perry
Witherspoon, Wesley to Sarah Whitson	Dec. 18, 1816	William Whitson
Wolf, John to Betsy Simmons	Aug. 22, 1814	Peter Wolf
Wolverton, William to Jane Jenkins	Nov. 27, 1826	John Woolverton
Wood, Curtis to Peggy Sewell	June 20, 1808	Jonah Goforth
Woodall, Wash. to Jane Hodge	Mar. 5, 1832	John Dowd
Woodard, George to Eliza McKissick	Jan. 8, 1823	Mitthais Garrigas
Woods, Allen N. to Martha Ewing	Jan. 21, 1832	David Ewing
Woodward, Thomas to Peggy Kilpatrick	Aug. 1, 1829 ?	William Kilpatrick
Woollard, Churchill to Mary Darden	Feb. 17, 1826	James B. Woollard
Wooldridge, Alfred to Paralee N. Stevens	Jun. 9, 1836	Labon Walters
Wortham, Wm. G. D. to Ann W. Mack	Oct. 31, 1832	William Wortham
Wright, Robert to Permelia A. Wright	May 27, 1837	Dariell Jackson
Wyatt, Francis to Sally Wright	Feb. 20, 1809	Samuel Sebastian
Yancey, William J. to Ann Lusk	Oct. 30, 1829	A. K. Erwin
Yandell, James to Jean Leach	May 15, 1809	David Leach
Yates, John to Malinda McLeon	Jan. 20, 1836	J. Adkisson
Young, Josiah to Eliza Foster	Jan. 10, 1835	John W. Lemaster
Younger, James to Margaret Hinson	Feb. 18, 1835	Tilman Hinson

IN DE INDEX

Name	No.
Chumley, Lucinda	16
Church, Nancy H.	77
Cisco, Elizabeth	7
Clark, Annis	14
Cockman, Frances	4
Cochran, Polly	15
Coffey, Phililia	19
Coggins, Betsy	17
Cole, Celia	10
Cole, Mary	4
Coleburn, Eliz.	7
Coleman, C. M.	8
Coleman, Eliza	4
Collier, Mary	5
Collins, Rosanna	8
Collins, Sarah	9
Compton, Nancy	12
Cone, Sally	3
Cooke, Milinda	18
Cook, Margarette	14
Cooke, Nancy	11
Cooke, Polly	3
Cooper, Evelina	9
Cooper, Jinny	12
Cooper, Lucy	3
Cooper, Polly	1
Cooper, Sophia	4
Copeland, Margarite	1
Courtny, Patsy	20
Covey, Jane	11
Cox, Lydia	2
Craftin, Sara	4
Craig, Eliz.	15
Craig, Mariah	12
Craig, Rebecca	1
Craig, Susanna	14
Crawford, Eliz.	17
Crawford, Vesta	15
Croford, Eliz.	18
Crofton, Nancy	16
Cross, Rebecca	15
Crosswill, Nancy	2
Cruise, Angeline	7
Curry, Eliz.	11
Curry, Lydia	2
Curry, Patsy	7
Curtis, Elizabeth	4
Cutberth, Delany	2
Cutbirth, Sarah	2
Dale, Leah	17
Daniel, Caroline	9
Daniel, Minerva	19
Darden, Mary	21
Darnell, Susan	6
Davidson, Cinthia	5
Davidson, Ruth	19
Davis, Caroline	11
Davis, Eliza	4

Name	No.
Davis, Jane	20, 14
Davis, Mary	15, 20
Davis, Masse	16
Davis, Nancy	6, 5,18
Davis, Nelly	13
Davis, Sally	12
Davis, Susan	11
Davis, Tina	20
Dean, Peggy	11
Dean, Rebecca	8
Deanes, Priscilla	8
Dearon, Sally	1
Denby, Mary	5
Derryberry, Ser.	9
Deson, Malinda	8
Dewall, Susannah	12
Dickey, Martha	20
Dickey, Susan	8
Dickie, Hannah	7
Doak, Nancy	3
Dodson, Ann	5
Dodson, Sally	3
Dogan, Nancy	18
Donaldson, Eliz.	14
Donaldson, Harriett	12
Donahoo, Cath.	15
Dood, Eliz.	17
Dooley, Eliz.	12
Dorch, Orra	12
Dorsey, Martha	12
Doston, Matilda	13
Dotson, Candess	10
Dotson, Mary	11
Dougherty, May	15
Dowell, Eliz.	20
Dowell, Patience	10
Duckworth, Mary	1
Duff, Betsy	19
Duffee, Mary	13
Dugger, Cath.	16
Dugger, Rebecca	2
Duke, Nancy	15
Dyer, Eliz.	5
Eagle, Miriah	7
Eakin, Pamelia	18
Edmond, Rebecca	6
Edmonds, Isabella	2
Edmondson, Marg.	6
Edmondson, Rhody	13
Edmondson, Sarah	5
Edmundson, Parnita	10
Edwards, Betsey	8
Edwards, Jincy	4
Edwards, Polly	12
Edwards, Ruthy	13
Egnew, Ibby	20
Egnew, Margaret	8
Elam, Eliz.	9

Name	No.
Ellemore, Celia	14
Elliott, Lucy	8
Ellison, Sarah	12
Elton, Barsheba	15
Ephland, Sarah	15
Ervine, Mary	11
Estes, Hester	17
Etton, Polly	5
Evans, Betsey	14
Evans, Lourania	18
Evans, Lucinda	20
Evans, Martha	10
Evans, Rebecca	8
Evans, Sarah	8
Ewing, Margaret	6
Ewing, Martha	21
Faires, Margarette	9
Faires, Rhoda	20
Falas, Sophia	5
Faris, Sally	20
Farrer, Sara	2
Farris, Mary	2
Farriss, Pheby	6
Fausett, Amanda	17
Fergerson, Betsey	13
Fergurson, Nancy	3
Ferrell, Prudence	13
Ferrell, Tiny	15
Ferril, Polly	5
Few, Judah	6
Fielder, Grizy	2
Fields, Eliz.	13
Fields, Polly	19
Finly, Margaret	11
Finley, Rebecca	3
Fitzgerald, Cath.	2
Fitzgerald, Eliz.	16
Fitzgerald, Mary	11
Fitzgerald, Polly	4
Fitzpatrick, Eliz.	20
Fleming, Mary	18
Fogleman, Barbary	16
Follis, Patsy	15
Forbes, Betsy	19
Forbes, Judah	19
Forgey, Nancy	10
Forsythe, Martha	17
Foster, Eliza	21
Franks, Polly	4
Frazier, Caroline	10
Frierson, Diamah	14
Frierson, Eliz.	4
Frierson, Margaret	5
Furgerson, Frankie	20
Fuzzell, Susan	21
Gannaway, Martha	19
Gardner, Mary	13

Name		Name		Name	
Garner, Susan	13	Hanes, Anna	20	Hodge, Jane	21
Garret, Martha	1	Hanks, Nancy	7	Hodges, Polly	4
Gentry, Maacah	18	Hanks, Sara	5	Hoge, Matilda	1
Germain, Nancy	5	Hanna, Easter	9	Hogg, Jinny	16
Ghasgill, Sela	12	Hannah, Margaret	13	Holland, Betsy	18
Gideon, Polly	7	Harden, Polly	16	Holland, Cynthia	17
Gifford, Anny	12	Hardin, Clara	12	Holland, Jane	15
Gifford, Cynthia	14	Hardin, Kenyan	9	Holland, Marg.	1
Gilchrist, Nancy	12	Hardison, Penelope	9	Holland, Sophia	15
Gill, Elizabeth	1	Hardison, Sarah	12	Holloday, Betsy	12
Gill, Patsey	7	Harlin, Elisa	4	Holmes, Mary	5
Gill, Sara	15	Harris, Frankie	18	Honneycut, Massey	3
Gillispie, Namoni	7	Harris, Louisa	20	Hopkins, Easther	2
Gillespie, Prudence	9	Hart, Ann	15	Hood, Jane	3
Gilliam, Martha	7	Hart, Polly	12	Hood, Mahala	5
Glasby, Mary	20	Hart, Rachel	2	Hood, Nancy	11
Glasscock, Polly	6	Hart, Sally	8	Hood, Susannah	8
Goff, Eliza	15	Harvey, Malinda	2	Hope, Marg.	3
Goforth, Peggy	16	Harvey, Polly	9	House, Patience	9
Gooch, Mary	9	Hawkins, Esther	14	Houser, Joanna	20
Goodloe, Martha	17	Hay, Margaret	4	Howard, Martha	12
Goodman, Louisa	14	Hays, Eliza	17	Howard, Mary	2
Goodman, Nancy	4	Hays, Betsy	3	Howell, Fanny	1
Goodman, Rinney	6	Haynes, Nelly	12	Howell, Rebecca	2
Gordon, Nancy	4	Head, Sally	2	Hubbard, Betsy	20
Gordon, Polly	18,1	Headlee, Ruth	13	Hubbard, Lydia	4
Gordon, Sally	3	Headon, Ann M.	7	Huckeberry, Nancy	16
Gordon, Sara	11	Helm, Martha	16	Huckeby, Rachel	18
Grant, Levina	16	Helm, Nancy	6	Hudson, Eliz.	13
Granger, Polly	1	Henderson, Eliz.	7	Hudson, Vicey	10
Graves, Silva	19	Henderson, Mary	18	Hudspeth, Clary	4
Gray, Barbara	19	Henderson, Matilda	3	Hudspeth, Nancy	14
Gray, Sally	13	Henderson, Swan	11	Hudspeth, Sarah	6
Green, Jane	18	Henry, Permelia	19	Huey, Katherine	14
Gregory, Martha	15	Hensley, Eliz.	17	Huggins, Nancy	12
Griffin, Lilah	5	Hensly, Nancy	17	Hunter, Comfort	15
Griffin, Malinda	6	Henson, Eliz.	3	Hurton, Nancy	19
Griffin, Mary	16	Herrington, Eliz.	9	Hutchison, Charity	3
Griffin, Nancy	5	Herrington, Eliza	14	Hutchinson, Eliz.	14
Griffith, Rebecca	8	Herrod, Leahanna	13	Hutchinson, Vicey	20
Griffith, Susan	6	Hickman, Nancy	2		
Grimes, Abbigale	14	Hight, Hixy	13, 14	Irvin, Peggy	9
Grinder, Barbery	18	Hight, Louisa	16	Irvine, Ann	15
Grurdin, Betsy	12	Hill, Avery	14	Isbile, Betsy	18
Guardner, Rachel	14	Hill, Eliza	14	Isom, Mary	4
Gullet, Elvira	10	Hill, Eliz.	18	Ivey, Betsey	15
Gurley, Alley	19	Hill, Eliza	7		
Gwinn, Betsy	11	Hill, Jane	3	Jack, Tabithia	15
		Hill, Kizy	5	Jackson, Martha	11
Hail, Eleanor	4	Hill, Martha	20	Jackson, Pheby	20
Halcomb, Priscy	8	Hill, Nancy	12	Jagurs, Naomi	15
Hall, Aratillia	17	Hill, Rebecca	8	Jenkins, Jane	21
Hall, Polly	13	Hill, Sally	1	Jenkins, Mary	7
Hall, Sarah	20	Hiller, N. W.	13	Jenkins, Mary	18
Hall, Synthya	4	Hieton, Martha	6	Jobe, Rebecca	16
Hamblet, Rebecca	15	Hines, Polly	18	Johnson, Charity	12
Hamilton, Lily	6	Hinson, Eliz.	8	Johnson, Irena	8
Hampton, Eliz.	3	Hinson, Marg.	21	Johnson, Jenny	7
Hancock, Lucinda	14	Hinson, Mary	16	Johnson, Maria	15

Johnson, Martha	8	Knight, Priscilla	11	Mayberry, Fanny	18	25
Johnson, Mary	4	Knox, Eliza	20	Mayberry, Rachel	13	
Johnson, Milly	20	Knox, Sally	16	Mayes, Dililah	12	
Johnson, Polly	12	Koonce, Sally	16	Mayes, Nancy	7	
Johnson, Sally	14	Koeble, Susan	11	Mayfield, Hannah	1	
Johnson, Sara	7,2			Mayfield, Patsy	7	
Johnston, Ann	11	Ladd, Polly	7	Mayhoe, Eliz.	12	
Johnston, Easter	9	Laird, Peggy	17	Mays, Mazie	10	
Johnston, Kessiah	3	Lamaster, Hannah	16	Mays, Sara	15	
Johnston, Lucy	12	Lamb, Hannah	5	McAfee, Eliz.	14	
Johnston, Mariah	18	Lamb, Phebe	20	McAslin, Nancy	9	
Johnston, Rachel	8	Land, Catherine	4	McBridge, Polly	16	
Jones, Dorinda	13	Landers, Lucy	2	McCalla, Eliz.	5	
Jones, Elizabeth	20,14	Lane, Emeline	9	McCallester, Cath.	2	
Jones, Eliz. T.	20	Lane, Louisa	9	McClanahan, Sophia	3	
Jones, Jane	3	Latta, Eliz.	11	McEarly, Marg.	3	
Jones, Mary	18, 4	Latta, Rebecca	18	McColley, Martha	13	
Jones, Nancy	11,20, 13	Lawrance, Eliz.	15	McConnell, Rachel	19	
Jones, Polly	7	Leach, Jean	21	McCord, Agnes	1	
Jones, Rachel	3	Lee, Sarah	4	McCord, Nancy	15	
Jones, Sara	8	Leonard, Sophia	16	McCrackin, Jenny	15	
Jordan, Mary	20	Lester, Nancy	19	McCrackin, Polly	13	
Joss ey, Mary	10	Letsinger, Anny	18	McCurdy, Peggy	1	
Justice, Eliz.	13	Lewallen, Elenor	7	McDaniel, Amy	2	
		Lewellin, Sarah	3	McDonnill, Betsey	5	
Kearing, Marg.	14	Librey, Rebecca	19	McFarland, Mariah	3	
Kelley, Marg.	4	Liggett, Drusilla	10	McRarland, Rosannah	10	
Kelly, Sally	12	Lindsay, Eliz.	3	McFarlin, Prudence	9	
Kelsey, Adeline	2	Livisay, Polly	5	McGimpsy, Sally	1	
Kendrick, Eliz.	1	Locke, Eliz.	1	McKain, Mary	16	
Kendrick, Nancy	5	Locke, Sally	18	McKannon, Eliz.	6	
Kendrick, Susan	20,18	Lockhart, Sara	19	McKee, Nandy	2	
Keneddy, Patsy	14	Loid, Delilah	12	McKee, Sara	2	
Kennedy, Eliz.	16	Long, Betsy	20	McKee, Victory	17	
Kennedy, Jane	6	Long, Betty	6	McKissick, Eliza	21	
Kennedy, Nancy	11	Long, Martha	9	McKracken, Eliz.	19	
Kennemore, Mitilda	13	Longley, Catherine	1	McLeod, Lousia	8	
Kerr, Isabella	11	Longley, Jane	15	McLeon, Malinda	21	
Kerr, Nancy	8	Looney, Jane	16	McManas, Isabella	15	
Kerr, Rachel	8	Loronce, Perdytha	10	McPeters, Charity	1	
Kery, Va.	8	Love, Betsey	20, 19	McQuatlean, Polly	13	
Kilby, Sarah	6	Lunnon, Anna	5	McManus, Polly	18	
Kilchrist, Polly	18	Lusk, Ann	21	McMeen, Marg.	13	
Kilcrease, Betsey	9	Lusk, Eleanor	12	McWilliams, Peggy	4	
Kilcrease, Kath.	15	Lusk, Eliz.	6	Meese, Mary	10	
Kilpatrick, Cynthia	16	Lyon, Peggy	12	Metcalf, Arina	20	
Kilpatrick, Nancy	4	Lythe, Marg.	14	Miller, Amanda	8	
Kilpatrick, Peggy	21			Miller, Eliz.	12,7	
Kindle, Malinda	4	Mack, Ann	21	Miller, Mildred	14	
Kindrick, Nancy	15	Mackates, Kerem	13	Miller, Milly	6	
King, Eliz.	1	Maddox, Eliza	2	Milicain, Sara	4	
King, Jemima	1	Mahoe, Polly	8	Milligan, Peggy	7	
King, Phebe	5	Maise, Margaret	15	Mills, Margaret	19	
Kirby, Miriah	3	Majors, Sara	18	Mills, Nancy	3, 1	
Kirby, Susanna	3	Mangrum, Easter	14	Mitchell, Eliz.	16	
Kirk, Eliz.	2	Mangrum, W. H.	10	Mitchell, Isabella	3	
Kirkpatrick, Metilda	1	Mason, Jane	18	Mitchell, Lottie	11	
Kitrell, Martha	9	Mason, Matilda	19	Mitchell, Mahala	16	
Kitrell, Mary	10	Matthews, Marg.	4	Mitchell, Mary	13,7	
Knight, Patience	8	Matthews, Sara	2	Mitchell, Polly	15	

```
Wilks, Sarah          16
Williams, Alley       12
Williams, Cynthia     16
Williams, Eliz.        8
Williams, Emily        8
Williams, Fanny       15
Williams, Hannah      14
Williams, Lucretia    12
Williams, Margaret    10
Williams, Margarette  10
Williams, Mary       5,13
Williams, Nancy       10
Williams, Patsy        1
Williams, Sarah      17,6
Williams, Susan     18,15
Williams, Tabitha      1
Willis, Kitty         11
Wilson, Hester         5
Wilson, Martha        10
Wilson, Sarah         17
Wimloe, Anny           9
Wingfield, Sarah      13
Witherinton, Ann       7
Witherspoon, Emily    14
Wolverton, Lucy       11
Woodall, Sarah         6
Woolard, Apha          9
Woolard, Hariol        9
Woolard, Sara          2
Woolveton, Polly       9
Woolverton, Eliz.     17
Wren, Betsy           14
Wrenn, Nancy           6
Wrenn, Susan          15
Wright, Malvina        9
Wright, Permelia      21
Wright, Sally         21

Yancy, Eliz.          17
Yancy, Harriet        20
Yancy, Susan           2
Young, Betsey       20, 9
Young, Caroline       19
Young, Martha         21

Zollicoffer, Amanda   18
```

Maury County, Tennessee

Marriages
1838-1852

- Vol #2 -

(2 Volumes in 1)

Southern Historical Press, Inc.
1981

Forward

Maury County was established by an Act of the General Assembly of Tennessee at Knoxville on November 16, 1807, from a part of Williamson County. Maury is the parent county of Giles. Lawrence and Lewis Counties. Our records begin with the formation of the county. Maury County has produced many prominent families. We hope these records will be of help to those doing genealogical research on the families of Maury County.

We meant at first to copy only the marriages licenses in Marriage Book 1 covering the years 1807-1837. When we found that there were many marriage bonds in the basement of the Court House with no license recorded for the bond, we decided to copy those bonds.

We wish to thank Mrs. Marise P. Lightfoot, and Mrs. Evelyn Shackleford for helping us copy the bonds. We wish also to thank Mr. Roy Pogue, County Court Clerk and his staff for being so courteous and helpful to us. Our husbands certainly deserve a word of thanks for being so understanding during this that we have been working on this project.

We omitted some names from the index of licenses but added them at the end. We trust that you will be able to find them.

A   <u>Date Issued</u>

Abernathy, Dr. C. Clayton to Martha J. Stockard   17 Aug. 1851
     Sol. 18 August 1851, G. W. Mitchell, M.G.

Acuff, Abram L. to Louisa Bailey   29 June 1839
     Sol. 30 June 1839, William W. Grimes, M.G.

Acuff, William to Nancy C. Bailey   11 Dec. 1839
     Sol. 12 Dec. 1839, R. Stockard, J. P.

Adcock, Jesse to Martha Pillow   8 Mar. 1851
     Sol. 9 March 1851, Joseph F. Jordan, J. P.

Adcock, Reuben to Sarah Barnes   23 July 1846
     (Did not marry.)

Adcock, Reuben to Sarah Barnes   13 Mar. 1849
     Sol. 14 March 1849, Coleman Goad, J. P.

Adkins, James to Malvina Brochean   27 Feb. 1849
     Sol. 27 Feb. 1849, Henry Harris, J. P.

Adkins, John to Jane Vaughan   24 Oct. 1842
     Sol, 26 Oct. 1842, B. Gresham, J. P.

Adkins, John to Nancy A. Aldred   12 Nov. 1845
     Sol. 12 Nov. 1845, Samuel Wheatley, J. P.

Adkins, Moses to Frances Helton   13 Feb. 1840

Adkisson, John to Mariah Witt   6 May 1851
     Sol. 6 May 1851, J. W. Westmoreland, J. P.

Adkisson, John G. to Eliza V. Craig   20 Mar. 1849
     Sol. 20 March 1849, A. W. Wortham, J. P.

Adkisson, William G. to Susan G. Lawhorn   12 Dec. 1850
     Sol. 12 December 1850, W. S. Langdon, M. G.

Adkisson, William K. to Priscilla L. Crandford   27 Dec. 1851
     Sol. 30 December 1851, Aroma Clark, J. P.

Agnew, Thomas P. to Margaret Thompson   12 March 1838
     Sol. 28 March 1838, R. F. Durham, J. P.

Akin, David A. to Mary J. Sowell   7 Feb. 1848
     Sol. 7 Feb. 1848, Parke Street, J. P.

Akin, James to Mary J. Porter   9 April 1844
     Sol. 10 April 1844, Joseph Sherman, M. G.

Akin, James to Elizabeth B. Porter   8 May 1850
     Sol. 8 May 1850, William Mack, M. G.

Akin, James H. to Susannah Maddox   6 Oct. 1851
     Sol. 6 October 1851, Aroma Clark, J. P.

Akin, Lewis S. to Elizabeth C. Smith   9 May 1838
     Sol. May 10, 1838, G. W. Mitchell, M. G.

Akin, Nathaniel B. to Elizabeth A. Blakely   18 Aug. 1852

Akin, Samuel V. to Argent H. Hart   6 Jan. 1838
     Sol. 18 Jan. 1838, John H. Koonce, J.P.

Alderson, Bathus C. to Sarah J. Vanhook   2 Mar. 1840
     Sol. 5 March 1840, G. W. Mitchell, M. G.

Alderson, James F. to L. D. Oliphant   14 Aug. 1849

Alderson, James F. to Sarah C. Alderson   27 Sept. 1851
     Sol. 27 Sept. 1851, William W. Coleman, J. P.

Alderson, Josiah to Milly Fitgerald   25 Nov. 1842
     Sol. 26 November 1842, G. Hanks, J. P.

Alderson, Robert, Sr. to Elizabeth Dodson   18 Feb. 1840
     Sol. 18 Feb. 1840, William Harris, M. G.

Alderson, Samuel S. to Margaret J. Alexander   17 Jan. 1838
     Sol. 18 Jan. 1838, James P. Adkins, J. P.

Alderson, Samuel S. to Josephine Hunter   6 Feb. 1849

Alderson, William to Winny Dodson   23 Dec. 1840

Alderson, William to Nancy Wilks   20 Oct. 1842
     Sol. 20 Oct. 1842, E. Hanks, M. G.

Alderson, William B. to Louisa J. Burnham   28 Mar. 1850
     Sol. 31 March 1850, A. T. Gray, J. P.

Aldridge, Edmund H. to Matilda L. Tanner   26 June 1852
     Sol. 27 June 1852, Edward R. Puckett, J. P.

Aldridge, Isaac H. to Lucy A. T. (no surname)   12 July 1851
     Sol. 16 July 1851, J. W. Westmoreland, J. P.

Alexander, John N. to Maria E. Howard   9 Oct. 1850
     Sol. 9 Oct. 1850, James Brownlow, M. G.

Alexander, Randal to Feseby Odam   27 Dec. 1850
     Sol. 27 Dec. 1850, F. A. Burke, J. P.

Alexander, S. R. to Ellen J. O'Nell   14 May 1852
     Sol. 16 May 1852, W. H. Baldridge, M. G.

Alexander, William A. to Margaret Y. Baldridge   5 Jan. 1848
     Sol. 5 Jan. 1848, J. T. Moss, M. G.

Alexander, William R. to Lydia C. Foster   2 Dec. 1850
     Sol. 5 Dec. 1850

Allen, Addison to Sarah D. Freeland   28 Nov. 1849
     Sol. 1 Dec. 1849, F. A. Burke, J. P.

Allen, Benjamin to Damanus Tidwell   14 Jan. 1850
     Sol. 17 Jan. 1850, R. Baker, J. P.

Allen, Berryman to Zane M. Ham   22 Apr. 1840

Allen, Harris O. to Julia Cocke   11 Nov. 1841
     Sol. 11 Nov. 1841, William Davis, M. G.

Allen, James to Nancy Mitchell   13 Mar. 1849
     Sol. 17 March 1849, Coleman Goad, J. P.

Allen, John M. to Eliza Bradley   11 June 1840

Allen, Joseph H. to Letha A. Choat   29 Nov. 1849
     Sol. 30 Nov. 1849, Joseph Foster, J. P.

Allen, Robert B. to Elizabeth J. Hanks   19 Aug. 1845
     Sol. 20 August 1845, M. B. Molloy, Minister

Alley, Hamblin to Martha Fitzgerald   6 Feb. 1841
     Sol. 7 Feb. 1841, R. A. Glenn, J. P.

Allred, Aaron to Nancy Jane Haley   3 Aug. 1841
     Sol. 12 Aug. 1841, James Smith, J. P.

Alsobrooks, Kindred N. to Mary Beckum   7 Feb. 1840
     Sol. 13 Feb. 1840, John Hunter, M. G.

Ament, John M. to Mary E. Brooks   23 Feb. 1847
     Sol. 25 Feb. 1847, M. B. Molloy, M. G.

Amis, John D. to Margaret H. Daniel   8 June 1852
     Sol. 10 June 1852, Jeremiah Stephens, M. G.

Amis, William to Nancy F. Wilson   28 Sept. 1843
     Sol. 12 October 1843, Samuel Wheatley, J. P.

Anderson, Garland to Maria A. Crowder   20 Dec. 1838
     Sol. 20 December 1838, Parke Street, J. P.

Anderson, James M. to Margaret C. Nelson   8 Nov. 1852
     Sol. 9 Nov. 1852, W. J. Kirkpatrick, M. G.

Anderson, Lafayette to Wealthy A. Howell   31 Dec. 1838
     Sol. 1 January 1838, T. E. Kirkpatrick, M. G.

Anderson, William B. to Nancy A. Turner   11 Oct. 1847
     Sol. 11 October 1847

Anderson, William F. to Jennete M. Thompson   24 Apr. 1845
     Sol. 24 April 1845, Joseph Brown, M. G.

Andrews, B. B. to Sarah H. Crawford   29 Sept. 1846
     Sol. 1 October 1846, R. L. Andrews

Andrews, James M. to Permelia J. Derryberry   27 Apr. 1852
     Sol. 27 April 1852, Asa Hardison

Andrews, John M. to Hannah E. Watson   22 June 1842
     Sol. 23 June 1842, Benony Gresham, J. P.

Andrews, Littleberry B. to Martha J. Thurmond   20 July 1850
      Sol. 21 July 1850, Joseph Foster, J. P.

Andrews, William B. to Permelia R. Andrews   14 Aug. 1838
      Sol. 14 Aug. 1838, William Watkins, J. P.

Andrews, W. B. to Mary Hanks   2 Jan. 1843
      Sol. 5 Jan. 1843, George Winn, J. P.

Andrews, William C. to Mary J. Terry   24 Dec. 1846
      Sol. 24 Dec. 1846, R. H. Simmons, J. P.

Andrews, William L. to Frances C. Mills   6 Oct. 1849
      Sol. 10 October 1849, Samuel W. Allen, J. P.

Apperson, William T. to Martha A. Howard   25 Dec. 1844
      Sol. 26 Dec. 1844, G. C. Stockard, M. G.

Armstrong, Elias J. to Maria A. Walker   10 Aug. 1842
      Sol. 12 Aug. 1842, C. P. Wing, M. G.

Armstrong, George D. to Elizabeth Gale   16 Dec. 1850
      Sol. 19 December 1850

Armstrong, James to Lucinda A. Hickman   31 Mar. 1848
      Sol. 2 April 1848

Armstrong, William O. to Mary E. Smith   18 Sept. 1838
      Sol. 20 Sept. 1838, James M. Arnell, Pastor, Zion Church

Armstrong, William T. to Myra E. Bingham   13 Aug. 1851
      Sol. 16 Aug. 1851

Arnold, George S. to Mary K. Mangrum   29 Dec. 1842
      Sol. 29 Dec. 1842, William Burn, M. G.

Arnold, Isaac N. to Sarah E. Lusk   28 Feb. 1850
      Sol. 28 Feb. 1850, J. T. Moss, M. G.

Arnold, James to Nancy A. Duke   12 June 1851
      Sol. 12 June 1851, J. B. Padgett, J. P.

Arnold, James W. to Jane Neely   6 Apr. 1848

Arnold, William to Ann Neely   23 Apr. 1849
      Sol. 25 April 1849, Coleman Goad, J. P.

Arthur, William L. to Elizabeth L. Cockrell   15 Aug. 1850
      Sol. 15 Aug. 1850, W. B. Gilham, M. G.

Ashton, James H. to Julia A. Butler   5 Sept. 1848

Ashton, John to Clara C. A. Parish   24 June 1852
      Sol. 7 July 1852, B. F. A. Burke, J. P.

Ashton, Thomas to Mary F. Brown   9 Jan. 1841
      Sol. 14 Jan. 1841, Alexander Johnson, J. P.

Ashworth, Elisha W. to Manerva A. True   31 July 1849

Ashworth, Washington to Nancy Mays   8 Dec. 1847
    Sol. 8 Dec. 1847, Washington Oakley

Askew, David O. to Elizabeth V. Boles   5 Nov. 1849
    Sol., Joseph Foster, J. P.

Askew, Joseph to Susan Brooks   28 Oct. 1841

Aydalotte, James P. to Martha P. Parten   7 Aug. 1845

Aydelotte, Samuel C. to Jane Fuzzell   27 July 1850
    Sol. 30 July 1850, Aroma Clark, J. P.

B

Babit, Harrison P. to Rachel T. Welch   21 May 1850
    Sol. 21 May 1850, William Mack, M. G.

Bailey, John H. to Nancy A. Turnbo   14 Dec. 1846
    Sol. 3 Dec. 1846, Alvis Williams , J. P.

Bailey, Peter C. to Rebecca P. Robson   26 June 1838
    Sol. 28 June 1838, Richard Stockard, J. P.

Baird, James H. to Permetia R. Williams   22 Jan. 1850
    Sol. 22 Jan. 1850, W. H. Baldridge, M. G.

Baird, James P. to Sarah E. Kinzer   16 Oct. 1850
    Sol. 16 Oct. 1850, D. K. Sowell, J. P.

Baird, John to Julia C. Young   11 Nov. 1844
    Sol. 12 Nov. 1844, Thomas W. Randle, M. G.

Baird, William D. to Mary J. C. Allen   31 Oct. 1849
    Sol. 31 Oct. 1849, Elias C. Frierson, J. P.

Baker, Daniel to Catherine Fogleman   27 Oct. 1841

Baker, Daniel to Elizabeth C. Mills   3 Dec. 1851
    Sol. 4 Dec. 1851, Asa Hardison, M. G.

Baker, Humphrey to Elizabeth Furr   3 Feb. 1840
    Sol. 4 Feb. 1840, H. W. Derryberry, J. P.

Baker, Richard B. to Nancy J. Blair   14 Dec. 1839

Baker, Thomas T. to Rachel Holly   22 May 1843
    Sol. 23 May 1843, Washington Oakley, J. P.

Baker, William A. to Dorcas E. Smoot   12 Feb. 1849
    Sol. 12 Feb. 1849 at residence of J. E. Williams at
    Williamsport, Tenn. by John B. Hamilton, J. P.

Baker, William A. to Sophia C. Jossey   19 Nov. 1851
    Sol. 19, November 1851

Balch, Samuel Y. to Edy T. Temple   5 Mar. 1839
    Sol. 7 Mar. 1839, William W. Coleman, J. P.

Baldridge, John A. to Margaret J. Adkins   29 July 1847
    Sol. 29 July 1847, Benjamin F. Alexander, M. G.

Baldridge, William R. to Mary E. Farney   17 Jan. 1849
    Sol. 18 Jan. 1849, James N. Edmiston, M. G.

Ball, Young A. to Mahala Roberson   17 Feb. 1844
    Sol. 20 Feb. 1844

Ballard, Thomas to Margaret Craig   4 Jan. 1842
    Sol. 4 Jan. 1842, Robert Thompson, M. G.

Barker, Alexander to Ann E. Johnston   19 Oct. 1842
    Sol. 19 Oct. 1842, A. T. Gray, J. P.

Barker, George to Maria L. Byers   12 Feb. 1846
    Sol. 12 Feb. 1846, Daniel Judd, L. E. of M. C.

Barker, William to Margaret E. McCain   23 Jan. 1851
    Sol. 23 Jan. 1851, E. Hanks, M. G.

Barley, James to Elizabeth Craig   10 Oct. 1843

Barlow, Thomas to Cretia Lawrence   24 Sept. 1840
    Sol. 24 Sept. 1840, William W. Coleman, J. P.

Barnes, John T. to Lavinia D. Blakely   12 Oct. 1843
    Sol. 12 Oct. 1843, Duncan Brown, V. D. M.

Barnes, John V. to Sarah M. Arnold   25 May 1843
    Sol. 25 May 1843, Berryman Hamblett, J. P.

Barnes, Thomas W. to Ellen H. Blakely   7 Oct. 1840
    Sol. 7 Oct. 1840, James M. Arnell, Pastor, Zion Church

Barnet, Isaac N. to Jane C. Walker   20 June 1842
    Sol. 21 June 1842, James H. Otey, Bishop of Tennessee

Barnett, James G. to Mahala V. Oliver   25 Nov. 1839
    Sol. 27 Nov. 1839, B. Gresham, J. P.

Barnett, Robert S. to Eliza M. Johnson   3 Feb. 1845
    Sol. John Mack, J. P.

Barnett, William M. to Mary Barnett   6 Jan. 1842

Barnhart, William J. to Judy Smith   7 Mar. 1846
    Sol. 7 March 1846, J. C. Spinks, J. P.

Barr, Isaac G. to Susan S. K. Coffman   9 Feb. 1852
    Sol. 2 Feb. 1852, W. B. Gilham, M. G.

Barrett, William T. to Nancy J. Beaty   9 Nov. 1847
    Sol. 9 Nov. 1847, Alfred Fleming, J. P.

Barron, Thomas to Temperance D. Dawson   10 Dec. 1844
       Sol. 11 Dec. 1844, D. Brown

Batchelor, John to Elizabeth Louder   31 Jan. 1843

Bateman, William L. to Flora L. T. Witherspoon   6 July 1847
       Sol. 7 July 1847, W. H. Baldridge, M. G.

Bates, James W. to Elizabeth Paul   22 May 1849
       Sol. 22 May 1849, James M. White, J. P.

Batey, Thomas H. to Delila Watson   20 Oct. 1851
       Sol. 21 Oct. 1851, Edward R. Puckett, J. P.

Baty, John J. to Maria Calahan   16 Aug. 1852
       Sol. 26 Aug. 1852, J. H. Burns, M. G.

Baughan, Elisha J. to Nancy Jordan   11 May 1848
       Sol. 11 May 1848, James M. White, J. P.

Bauguss, Robert J. to D. L. Partee   15 July 1852
       Sol. 15 July 1852, J. B. Hamilton, Methodist Minister

Beard, Abner to Esther L. Nelson   15 Sept. 1846
       Sol. 15 Sept. 1846, James Brownlow, M. G.

Beard, John to Emily D. Butt   1 Oct. 1838
       Sol. 3 Oct. 1838, Robert Campbell, J. P.

Beasley, John to Emily McKee   2 Nov. 1842
       Sol. 8 Nov. 1842, S. W. Akin, J. P.

Beasley, William to Matilda Fox   26 Nov. 1843
       Sol. 30 Nov. 1843, Peter Wrenn, J. P.

Beasley, William H. to Elizabeth Robertson   22 Dec. 1852
       Sol. 23 Dec. 1852, E. Hanks, M. G.

Beasley, Williamson F. to Nancy Beasley   1 Nov. 1841
       Sol. 4 Nov. 1841, Parke Street, J. P.

Beck, Willis H. to Sarah S. Richardson   24 Sept. 1849
       Sol. 25 Sept. 1849

Beckett, James to Marthy C. Perry   19 July 1850
       Sol. 25 July 1850, E. H. Hatcher

Bell, William R. to Sophronia S. Stockard   9 June 1846
       Sol. 9 June 1846, Joseph Brown

Benner, Henry E. to Mary Scruggs   20 Feb. 1838
       Sol. 20 Feb. 1838, H. H. Brown, E.M.E.C.

Bennett, Alexander to Elizabeth Stone   29 Nov. 1850
       Sol. 30 Nov. 1850, Jeremiah F. Holt, J. P.

Bennett, Oliver H. P. to Maria L. Orton   20 June 1844
       Sol. 20 June 1844, Finch P. Scruggs, M. G.

Berry, Archibald to Lucy Jordan   17 Mar. 1842
      Sol. 17 March 1842, John Herndon, J. P.

Berry, Joseph L. to Susan R. Salmon   24 Aug. 1842
      Sol. 24 Aug. 1842, G. W. Mitchell, M. G.

Biffle, John A. to Nancy J. Emerson   16 Oct. 1843
      Sol. 19 Oct. 1843, James M. Richardson

Biffle, Valentine to Elizabeth Koonce   14 Sept. 1841
      Sol. 14 Sept. 1841, Wilie Ledbetter, L. E. M.E.C.

Bigby, Thomas L. to Sarah Stringfellow   17 Sept. 1850
      Sol. 17 Sept. 1850, William Mack, M. G.

Biggers, Andrew H. to Elizabeth R. Bond   10 Nov. 1840
      Sol. Bradley Kimbrough

Biggers, William D. to Martha M. Flanikin   17 Nov. 1849
      Sol. 18 Nov. 1849, F. A. Burke, J. P.

Bigham, James to Elizabeth Hart   18 Oct. 1852
      Sol. 21 Oct. 1852

Bigham, Samuel H. to Mine J. Bird (or Baird) 23 Jan. 1850
      Sol. 24 Jan. 1850

Billington, James M. to Emily J. Hardison   1 Feb. 1851
      Sol. 6 Feb. 1851, Asa Hardison, M. G.

Bingham, Jesse J. to Mary A. C. York   27 Sept. 1849

Bird, John to Eleanor Kennedy   9 Dec. 1848
      Sol. 12 Dec. 1848, Edward R. Puckett, J. P.

Bizzell, Stephen to Lavina Childress   29 Mar. 1845
      Sol. March 29, 1845, R. A. Glenn, J. P.

Bizwell, Josiah A. to Parthena M. Slayden   3 Sept. 1840
      Sol. 3 Sept. 1840, E. Hanks, M. G.

Black, Allen to Catherine A. Nisbit   23 Mar. 1850
      Sol. 28 Mar. 1850, M. B. Molloy, M. G.

Black, John H. to Emaline E. Stubbins   21 Feb. 1838
      Sol. 21 Feb. 1838, Robert Campbell, J. P.

Blackburn, John A. to Rebecca A. Carter   7 Mar. 1849
      Sol. 8 March 1849

Blackwood, William P. to Nancy J. Grimes   4 Oct. 1843
      Sol. 5 Oct. 1843, G. W. Mitchell, M. G.

Blair, George H. to Harriet S. Hardin   17 Sept. 1847
      Sol. 22 Sept. 1847, W. C. Dunlap

Blair, George H. to America P. Hardin   20 Apr. 1852
      Sol. 4 May 1852, Milton H. Dyast, M. G.

Blair, James H. McL. to Mary E. F. S. T. Montgomery 28 Oct. 1844
    Sol. 30 Oct. 1844, D. Brown

Blair, Joseph to Martha Buckner   22 Dec. 1852
    Sol. 30 Dec. 1852, Thomas P. Stone, J . P.

Blair, Taylor A. to Nancy Butler   11 Jan. 1839
    Sol. 16 Jan. 1839, H. H. Brown, E.M.C.

Blake, William H. to Martha E. Moss   2 Nov. 1838
    Sol. 6 Nov. 1838, James M. Arnell, Pastor, Zion Church

Blake, William H. to Susan A. Brown   13 Jan. 1845
    Sol. 15 Jan. 1845, James M. Arnell, Zion Pastor

Blakely, John D. to Harriett W. Fettillo   7 Apr. 1852
    Sol. 8 Apr. 1852

Blalock, John D. to Martha Dalton   29 Dec. 1843
    Sol. 29 Dec. 1843, Hiram Anthony, J. P.

Blanks, Joseph to Rosannah Stephenson   10 Feb. 1846
    Sol. Feb. 10, 1846, John Brown, J. P.

Blanton, John H. to Sarah J. Nicholson   3 May 1847
    Sol. 5 May 1847, G. K. Perkins

Blanton, Wilson F. to Frances Lane   27 Apr. 1840
    Sol. 29 April 1840, William Davis, M. G.

Bledsoe, Enoch S. to Mary Ann Frierson   16 Jan. 1844
    Sol. 17 Jan. 1844, Thomas Kelsey, J. P.

Bledsoe, Watts to Martha A. Barnes   22 Apr. 1844
    Sol. 25 Apr. 1844, George R. Hoge, M. G.

Blocker, Samuel A. to Margaret J. Laird   23 Oct. 1839
    Sol. 23 Oct. 1839, H. H. Brown, E.M.E.C.

Blocker, Thomas P. to Julia A. Ferrell   22 June 1839
    Sol. 23 June 1839, George Gantt, M. G.

Blythe, Anderson M. to Martha J. Crawford   25 Feb. 1847
    Sol. 25 Feb. 1847, Parke Street, J. P.

Boaz, David to Esther T. Ruse   22 May 1838
    Sol. 23 May 1838, E. Hanks, M. G.

Bobo, Spencer S. to Margaret J. Williams   8 Oct. 1840
    Sol. 8 Oct. 1840, H. H. Brown, E.M.E.C.

Bogard, Alexander A. to Matilda A. Overstreet 1 Nov. 1849
    Sol. 1 Nov. 1849 at Mt. Pleasant, Henry Miller, J.P.

Boggs, James B. to Elizabeth Bryan   9 Aug. 1841
    Sol. 12 Aug. 1841, Andrew Scott, J. P.

Bomar, Davis to Caroline Trulove   8 June 1847

Bond (or Bone), John H. to Nancy G. Brown   20 Nov. 1851
     Sol. 20 Nov. 1851, Joseph Brown, M. G.

Bond, Thomas H. to Mary M. Banks   7 Sept. 1850
     Sol. 12 Sept. 1850, James B. Porter, M.G.

Booker, Albert to Ruth A. Johnson   17 Oct. 1843

Booker, Henry L. to Mary A. H. Porter   10 Nov. 1840
     Sol. 10 Nov. 1840, Joseph Sherman, M. G.

Booker, James S. to Priscilla Arnold   13 Nov. 1838
     Sol. 13 Nov. 1838, L. Jordan, J. P.

Booker, Joel S. to Ann C. Trulove   14 Oct. 1848
     Sol. 15 Oct. 1848, William R. Sharp, J.P.

Booker, John A. to Margaret Duncan   30 Sept. 1846
     Sol. 13 Oct. 1846, R. A. Glenn, J. P.

Booker, John T. to Mary Batey   13 Sept. 1848
     Sol. 15 Oct. 1848, R. A. Glenn, J. P.

Booker, William C. to Elizabeth Morriss   30 Sept. 1846
     Sol. 30 Sept. 1846, John Brown, J.P.

Boon, Alvin to Rebecca Wood   21 Feb. 1846
     Sol. 21 Feb. 1846, R. H. Simmons, J. P.

Boshears, James R. to Honor C. Weaver   21 Aug. 1852
     Sol. 22 Aug. 1852, Henry A. Miller, J.P.

Bouman, Wiley W. to Maria Witt   8 Apr. 1843
     Sol. 13 Apr. 1843, Park Street, J. P.

Bowden, Robert C. to Mary A. Baldridge   26 Jan. 1839
     Sol. 30 Jan. 1839, R. M. Galloway

Bowen, Achilles to Rebecca O. Helm   1 July 1850
     Sol. 4 July 1850, William Mack, M.G.

Bracken, A. F. to Elizabeth Dickey   7 Aug. 1843
     Sol. 7 Aug. 1843, Stephen Patterson, Rector, St. Peter's Church

Brackenridge, David to Nancy Overstreet   15 Sept. 1852
     Sol. 15 Sept. 1852, M. W. Gray, M.G.

Bradley, Wiley to Eliza A. Miller   12 Aug. 1840
     Sol. 13 Aug. 1840, R. H. Simmons, J. P.

Bradley, William R. to Leacy P. Watson   17 Jan. 1844
     Sol. 17 Jan. 1844, Park Street, J.P.

Bradshaw, William F. to Rebecca Pickard   30 Nov. 1842
     Sol. 1 Dec. 1842, C. Y. Hudson, J. P.

Branch, James G. to Sarah A. Uzzell   17 June 1840
  Sol. 18 June 1840, Alexander Johnson, J. P.

Branch, William M. to Mary A. Uzzell   27 Jan. 1841

Branden, John L. to Izora Hall   16 Mar. 1852
  Sol. 16 March 1852

Brantly, James H. to Martha Z. Arnold   16 Dec. 1851
  Sol. 16 Dec. 1851, William J. Strayhorn, J. P.

Brayman, Ira to Mary George   19 Nov. 1840
  Sol. 19 Nov. 1840, G. Tucker, M.G.

Brazier, William to S. E. Barker   5 Aug. 1852
  Sol. 7 Aug. 1852, E. W. Benson, M.G.

Briggs, John A. to Elvira Strayhorn   14 Oct. 1847
  Sol. 14 Oct. 1847, George S. Arnold

Brin, Charliton E. to Mary Sargent   14 Aug. 1848
  Sol. 14 Aug. 1848, A. T. Gray, J. P.

Brinn, James to Lucy Ann Sargent   17 Dec. 1843
  Sol. 19 Dec. 1843, E. Flocker, J. P.

Brin, William A. to Elizabeth C. Jaggers   31 Jan. 1843
  Sol. 2 Feb. 1843, E. Flocker, J. P.

Brock, James to Lucindy Davis   7 June 1852
  Sol. 7 June 1852, James H. Colburn, J.P.

Brock, Thomas to Jane Green   8 Jan. 1851
  Sol. 9 Jan. 1851, James H. Burns, M.G.

Brooks, Aaron H. to Narcissa A. Harris   24 Apr. 1838

Brooks, James T. to Malinda E. Priest   29 Apr. 1848

Brooks, Samuel to Jane Clendenin   22 July 1839

Brooks, Samuel T. to Patsy Young   5 Mar. 1850
  Sol. 5 March 1850, James A. Moore, J.P.

Brooks, William T. to Mary E. Dodson   3 Dec. 1845
  Sol. 3 Dec. 1845, W. H. Baldridge, M.G.

Brown, Alexander H. to Mary J. Hill   26 Mar. 1839
  Sol. 26 March 1839, Thomas Fielding Scott, V.D.M.

Brown, David C. to Sarah H. Witherspoon   4 Apr. 1844
  Sol. 4 Apr. 1844, James M. Arnell, Pastor, Zion Church

Brown David Y. to Winney Ellis   3 Apr. 1843
  Sol. 6 Apr. 1843, C. Y. Hudson, J. P.

Brown, Edward B. to Martha A. M. Perry   23 Apr. 1838
  Sol. April 24, 1838, H. H. Brown, E.M.E.C.

Brown, Ephraim to Celia Burrass   22 May 1852
    Sol. 23 May 1852, Ezra Hardison, J. P.

Brown, Gabriel to Hariet J. Miller   20 Dec. 1852
    Sol. 23 Dec. 1852, R. M. King, J. P.

Brown, Iley (?) to Nancy Strayhorn   4 Jan. 1847
    Sol. 5 Jan. 1847, W. H. Baldridge, M.G.

Brown, Irey E. to Sarah E. Brown   18 Apr. 1844
    Sol. 18 Apr. 1844, James M. Arnell, Zion Pastor

Brown, Irvin to Farthena Johnson   31 July 1839

Brown, James H. to Pellina J. Thurmond   23 Jan. 1851
    Sol. 23 Jan. 1851, Andrew Scott, J. P.

Brown, Jasper M. to Malinda Ingram   13 Apr. 1847
    Sol. 14 Apr. 1847, Hiram Anthony, J. F.

Brown, John to Sarah Ann Roy   2 Oct. 1851
    Sol. 2 Oct. 1851, R. G. Irvine, MG.

Brown, John J. to Ellen Howard   27 Dec. 1848

Brown, Joseph J. to Eliza S. Vestal   29 May 1852
    Sol. 30 May 1852, R. M. King, J. P.

Brown, McNeal to Eliza Vincent   9 Dec. 1846
    Sol. 10 Dec. 1846, J. G. Harris, J.P.

Brown, Mitchell to Sarah Lamb   10 Mar. 1840
    Sol. 12 Mar. 1840, R. H. Simmons, J.P.

Brown, Richard S. to Malinda A. Ament   6 Oct. 1845

Brown, Riley W. to Eliza Strayhorn   24 Nov. 1838
    Sol. 29 Nov. 1838, Wilie Ledbetter, E.M.E.C.

Brown, Robert to Elizabeth Farmer   22 Jan. 1849
    Sol. 26 Jan. 1849, William R. Sharp, J. F.

Brown, Robert to Elizabeth Collins   4 June 1852
    Sol. 6 June 1852, Ezra Hardison, J.P.

Brown, Thomas J. to Mary J. Flaniken   10 Feb. 1848
    Sol. 10 Feb. 1848, James G. Harris, J.F.

Brown, William to Delila Jackson   11 Nov. 1839
    Sol. 13 Nov. 1839, Thomas E. Kirkpatrick, M.G.

Brown, William to Sarah Gordon   7 May 1840
    Sol. 7 May 1840, Lewis G. Lanier, J.P.

Brown, William to Mary M. George   31 Dec. 1851
    Sol. 31 Dec. 1851, John B. Hamilton, M.G.

Brown, William D. to Mary O. Cokrell   31 Aug. 1847
    Sol. 1 Sept. 1847, James M. White, J.P.

Brown, William D. to Mary A. Smith   16 May 1850
    Sol. 16 May 1850, J. B. Padgett, J. P.

Brown, William H. to Emily E. Anthony   14 Jan. 1848
    Sol. 13 Jan. 1848, Joseph Brown, M.G.

Brown, William H. to Eliza A. Calhoun   5 Sept. 1850
    Sol. 5 Sept. 1850, William Mack, M.G.

Bruce, Joseph A. to Dizay K. Ellett   21 Feb. 1846
    Sol. 21 Feb. 1846, George S. Arnold, M.G.

Drummett, James to Mary Mangrum   21 June 1841

Bryant, Andrew D. to Sarah W. Hill   3 Jan. 1852
    Sol. 4 Jan. 1852, W. P. Modrall

Bryant, James J. to Martha A. Malone   20 June 1846

Bryant, Robert D. to Martha C. Jackson   19 Dec. 1849
    Sol. 20 Dec. 1849, F. A. Burk, J. P.

Bryant, Thomas S. to Nancy J. Bryant   15 Mar. 1852
    Sol. 18 March 1852, D. G. Moore, M.G.

Bryant, Wiley T. to Elizabeth S. Wallis   31 July 1851
    Sol. 31 July 1851, Aroma Clark, J. P.

Bryant, William R. to Sarah D. Anthony   4 Oct. 1841
    Sol. 7 Oct. 1841, Jonathan S. Hunt, J.P.

Bryant, William T. to Mary E. Hill   5 Jan. 1846
    Sol. 8 Jan. 1846, J. G. Harris, J. P.

Buckner, Alexander J. to Elizabeth Hilliard   30 Mar. 1847
    Sol. 30 March 1847, Joseph Herndon, J. P.

Bullion, John H. to Mary Ann Marlow   14 Oct. 1839
    Sol. 16 Oct. 1839, S. Whiteside, J.P.

Bullock, Aaron H. to Martha E. Hunter   26 Mar. 1849
    Sol. 1 April 1849, B. O. Wall, J. P.

Bumpass, Augustus to Malinda Collins   31 July 1852
    Sol. 31 July 1852, Thomas P. Stone

Bunter (?), William R. to America F. Miller   22 Apr. 1850
    Sol. 22 April 1850, J. M. White, J. P.

Burchett, William to Rebecca K. Thompson   9 Jan. 1846
    Sol., George W. Fly, J. P.

Burks, William to Frances Runyon   9 Oct. 1839
    Sol. 10 Oct. 1839, John B. Bond, J.P.

Burley, George to Mary A. Fitzgerald   30 Nov. 1843
    Sol. 30 Nov. 1843, Aaron Vestal, J.P.

Burnett, Richard D. to Elizabeth C. Brooks   5 May 1849
    Sol. 13 May 1849, J. Crafton, J.P.

Burney, Charles to Hanna Hale   21 Dec. 1842
    Sol. 22 Dec. 1842, Jones Daly, J.P.

Burnham, William to Mary Baker   7 Feb. 1849

Burnham, William to Elizabeth Page   4 Sept. 1850
    Sol. 4 Sept. 1850, M. F. Erwin, J.P.

Burns, George M. to Indianna S. Atkerson   2 Dec. 1850
    Sol. 5 Dec. 1850, J. B. Padgett, J.P.

Burns, Jesse to Nancy S. Fitzgerald   22 Feb. 1852
    Sol. 29 Jan. 1852, M. W. Gray, M. G.

Burns, Lawrence to Martha J. Fitzgerald   11 Dec. 1845

Burpo, George W. to Mary E. McNeely   2 Nov. 1850
    Sol. 3 Nov. 1850, R. A. Glenn

Burt, Charles H. to Margaret M. Stockard   6 Nov. 1848
    Sol. 14 Nov. 1848, G. W. Mitchell, M.G.

Butler, Ephriam to Martha A. Priest   12 Jan. 1847
    Sol. 13 Jan. 1847, M. B. Malloy, M.G.

Butler, Francis to Alzira J. Cross   2 Dec. 1845
    Sol. 2 December 1843 (?), P. P. Neely, M.G.

Butler, Isaiah W. to Eliza Young   4 Dec. 1849
    Sol. 4 Dec. 1849, F. A. Burke, J.P.

Butt, James M. to Martha A. Goad   13 Mar. 1851
    Sol. 13 March 1851, E. Hanks, M.G.

Butt, Josiah to Parthena Brooks   16 Aug. 1838
    Sol. 16 Aug. 1838, F. S. Ferguson, Ord. Elder, M.E.C.

Butt, William L. to Louisa J. Goad   4 Nov. 1848
    Sol. 5 Nov. 1848, R. G. Irvine, M.G.

Byers, M. W. to Susan W. Rodney (?)   15 Apr. 1850
    Sol. 16 Apr. 1850

Bynum, Robert to Mary Goad   5 Aug. 1844
    Sol. 6 Aug. 1844, Berryman Hamlett, J.P.

Byrum, William A. to Nancy A. Noles   25 Jan. 1842
    Sol. 27 Jan. 1842, James W. Matthews, J. P.

Cain, Samuel S. to Elizabeth Sellers (?)   11 Oct. 1843
    Sol. 11 Oct. 1843, Adam S. Riggs, M.G.

Calahan, Jackson to Mary Calahan .   29 Nov. 1850
    Sol. 1 Dec. 1850, F. A. Burke, J.P.

Caldwell, Andrew W. to Elinah J. Jones   31 July 1839
    Sol. 31 July 1839, G. C. Stockard, M.G.

Caldwell, David A. to Sarah Stratton   28 Nov. 1846

Caldwell, David A. to Louisa A. Moore   19 Dec. 1849
    Sol. 20 Dec. 1849

Caldwell, John S. to Sarah A. Jameson .   4 Nov. 1839
    Sol. 5 Nov. 1839, R. W. Morris, E.M.E.Ch.

Caldwell, Thomas S. to Harriet Tyner .   27 May 1846
    Sol. 27 May 1846, Joseph Herndon, J.P.

Calhoon, Milton A. to Rebecca J. Carter   13 Jan. 1840
    Sol. 22 Jan. 1840, J. P. Brown

Cameron, William D. to Mary J. Kusu .   29 Sept. 1845
    Sol. 1 Oct. 1845, William Mack, M.G.

Campbell, Alexander T. to Sarah M. Hughes   10 Dec. 1851
    Sol. 10 Dec. 1851, S. S. Yarbrough, M.G.

Campbell, Andrew J. to Sarah Gilliam   25 Jan. 1845
    Sol. 26 Jan. 1845, Samuel Wheatley, J.P.

Campbell, George W. to Martha A. Blackwell   2 June 1838
    Sol. 3 June 1838, W. W. Coleman, J.P.

Campbell, George W. to Ann Pullin   25 Aug. 1841

Campbell, Isaac A. to Nancy C. Blackwell   5 Oct. 1838
    Sol. 7 Oct. 1838, William W. Coleman, J.P.

Campbell, James H. to Sarah A. Hunt   19 Oct. 1843
    Sol. 19 Oct. 1843, Wade Barnett, Eld. C. C.

Campbell, John A. to Eliza Akin   2 June 1840
    Sol. 3 June 1840, E. Hanks, M.G.

Campbell, John J. to Julia J. Mack :   16 July 1839
    Sol. 19 July 1839, C. B. Porter, M.G.

Campbell, Robert B. to Naomi A. Kirby .   11 Nov. 1844

Campbell, Samuel S. to Emily E. Alexander   14 Oct. 1847
    Sol. 14 Oct. 1847, R. C. Garrison .

Campbell, William C. to Mary E. Sharp   2 July 1844
    Sol. 4 July 1844, G. C. Stockard, M.G.

Campbell, William W. to Mary Ann Harris — 10 Dec. 1847
    Sol. 12 Dec. 1847, William Mack, M.G.

Caperton, John C. to Julia A. Ferguson — 26 Aug. 1846
    Sol. 31 Aug. 1846, M. B. Molloy, M.G.

Caperton, Samuel B. to Susan J. Brown — 20 Nov. 1848
    Sol. 23 Nov. 1848, J. Crafton, J. P.

Caperton, William S. to Sarah H. Ferguson — 3 Jan. 1850
    Sol. 3 Jan. 1850, J. Crafton, J.P.

Capoots, Jeremiah to Nancy Johnson — 6 May 1846

Carr, James H. to Martha A. Kerr — 21 Apr. 1851
    Sol. 27 Apr. 1851, James A. Moore, J.P.

Carr, Nathaniel F. to Nancy C. Stone — 22 Dec. 1842
    Sol. 22 Dec. 1842, J. P. Campbell

Carigan, Allen to Beda Harris — 8 Sept. 1851
    Sol. 10 Sept. 1851, Aroma Clark, J. P.

Carrigan, James D. to Elizabeth J. Chaffin — 29 July 1843
    Sol. 30 July 1843, Park Street, J.P.

Carrigan, James D. to Martha J. Cooper — 11 Oct. 1848

Carrigan, Sample to Frances Timmons — 4 Feb. 1843
    Sol. 5 Feb. 1843, Parke Street, J.P.

Carrigan, William to Eliza Notgrass — 27 Feb. 1845
    Sol. 27 Feb. 1845, Berryman Hamlett, J.P.

Carter, B. Frank to Cynthia Rivers — 6 Apr. 1852
    Sol. 6 Apr. 1852 at Columbia before divers witnesses,
        James H. Otey, Bishop of Tennessee

Carter, John A. to Ann Sims — 14 Oct. 1841
    Sol. 16 Oct. 1841, H. A. McMacken, J.P.

Carter, Lewis C. to Lucinda Temple — 2 Sept. 1845
    Sol. 2 Sept. 1845, Joseph Foster, J.P.

Carter, Mary to Cordelia Thomas — 7 Aug. 1841
    Sol. 12 Aug. 1841, Andrew Scott, J.P.

Carter, Merry to Catha Thomas — 11 Jan. 1844
    Sol. 11 Jan. 1844, Andrew Scott, J.P.

Carter, Stephen H. to Mary T. Hanks — 25 Nov. 1848
    Sol. 26 Nov. 1848, Thomas Witherspoon, M.G.

Carter, William E. to Eliza A. Hill — 6 Nov. 1848
    Sol. 8 Nov. 1848, W. H. Baldridge, M.G.

Cartwright, Nelson to Elizabeth J. Norman — 16 Oct. 1841
    Sol. 16 Oct. 1841, William Horsley

·Casky, James A. To Almanza A. McDonald   5 Sept. 1849
    Sol. 6 Sept. 1849, W. H. Baldridge, M.G.

·Cason, William R. to Emira J. Chappell   19 Oct. 1843
    Sol. 19 Oct. 1843, Joseph E. Douglass, Elder, Methodist Church

Cathey, James to Nancy Currey   23 Sept. 1840
    Sol. 23 Sept. 1840, Robert Foster, J.P.

Cathey, James J. to Elizabeth Liles   30 Nov. 1843
    Sol. 14 Dec. 1843, John W. Kilpatrick

Cathey, William to Martha S. Kennedy   9 Dec. 1852
    Sol. 9 Dec. 1852, W. W. Coleman, J.P.

Catinna, Peter to Ellen M. Melchor   12 Nov. 1849
    Sol. 13 Nov. 1849 at house of Mr. Langham, John B. Hamilton,
              Elder, Methodist Church

Catron, Oliver P. to Susan Booker   20 Oct. 1845
    Sol. 21 Oct. 1845, James H. Otey

Caughorn, John W. to Martha E. Miller   19 Dec. 1849
    Sol. 20 Dec. 1849, A. T. Gray, J.P.

Caughran, James to Louisa P. Puckett   4 Dec. 1850
    Sol. 5 Dec. 1850, E. Hanks, M.G.

Causey, Z. to Nancy Wilson   22 Sept. 1847
    Sol. 22 Sept., 1847, R. A. Glenn, J.P.

Cauthen, William A. To Elizabeth Adkisson   23 Feb. 1839
    Sol. 28 Feb. 1839, James F. Adkins, J.P.

Cavender, Joseph W. To Sarah Pierce   19 Sept. 1838
    Sol. 19 Sept. 1838, Alexander R. Dickson, Elder, M.E. Church

Cavender, Silas S. to Permelia R. O. Andrews   10 Apr. 1848
    Sol. 13 Apr. 1848, G. S. Arnold, M.G.

Cavender, William to Harriet Liles   17 Jan. 1844
    Sol. 17 Jan. 1844, R. A. Goodgion, L.E.M.E. church

Cavenor, George to Sarah E. Agnew   20 June 1846
    Sol. 30 June 1846, J. G. Harris, J.P.

Cayce, George M. to Eliza A. Everett   17 Dec. 1851
    Sol. 18 Dec. 1851, M. B. Molloy, M.G.

Cayce, Henry to Mary Tomlin   20 Dec. 1838

Cecil, James H. to Julia E. Ingram   19 Oct. 1847
    Sol. 21 Oct. 1847, Richard P. Miles, Bishop of Nashville

Cecil, Samuel F. to Elizabeth W. McMurry   2 Oct. 1848
    Sol. 2 Oct. 1848, John F. Hughes

Chaffin, Green T. to Nancy A. Dowell   29 Aug. 1850
    Sol. 29 Aug. 1850; E. Hanks, M.G.

Chaffin, William G. to Amanda P. Atkinson   1 Nov. 1843
    Sol. 1 Nov. 1843, Joseph Sherman

Chalk, William R. to Frances O. Blackburn   24 Sept. 1838
    Sol. 27 Sept. 1938, Wilie Ledbetter, L.E.M.E.C.

Chancey, John J. to Mary Coughron   25 Dec. 1851
    Sol. 25 Dec. 1851

Chandler, James W. to Mary J. McRady   21 Nov. 1850
    Sol. 22 Nov. 1850

Chandler, John to Susan M. Cosby   4 July 1838
    Sol. 4 July 1838, William Harris, M.G.

Chandler, Shelby to Lorena M. M. Fitzgerald   23 Apr. 1850
    Sol. 24 Apr. 1850, E. Hanks, M.G.

Chandler, Thornton to Malinda Clemmons   9 Feb. 1841
    Sol. 10 Feb. 1841, E. Hanks, M.G.

Chapman, Calvin C. to Nancy E. Dunlap   19 Sept. 1849
    Sol. 21 Sept. 1849, R. C. Garrison

Chapman, James to Alfreda Davis   22 June 1852
    Sol. 22 June 1852, James H. Colburn, J.P.

Chappell, Thomas D. to Mary A. V. Lockridge   4 Jan. 1841
    Sol. 5 Jan 1841, William Davis, M.G.

Chappin, Samuel M. to Elizabeth T. McConnel   4 Dec. 1838
    Sol. 4 Dec. 1838, C. B. Porter, M.G.

Charter, John O. P. to Frances E. Helm   14 Oct. 1841
    Sol. 14 Oct. 1841, E. R. Osborne, E.C.C.

Chatham, Robert to Mahala Hood   13 Nov. 1841
    Sol. 16 Nov. 1841, Parke Street, J.P.

Chatham, Wiley to Mary Holcomb   23 June 1842
    Sol. 23 June 1842, J. H. Wooldridge, J.P.

Cheairs, Nathaniel F. to Susan P. McKissack   31 Aug. 1841
    Sol. 2 Sept. 1841, J. Burck Walker, M.G., M.E.Church

Cheatham, John A. to Sarah D. T. Carothers   21 July 1847
    Sol. 21 July 1847, Alfred Fleming, J.P.

Cheatham, Lewis R. to Mary E. Cheatham   11 Nov. 1850
    Sol. 12 Nov. 1850, W. H. Wilkes, M.G.

Cheatham, Thomas H. to Celia Fitzpatrick   20 Dec. 1848
    Sol. 21 Dec. 1848, F. A. Burke, J.P.

Cheek, Eli A. to Mary A. McKee   21 Feb. 1838
    Sol. 21 Feb. 1838, William Davis, M.G.

Cheek, Jesse A. to Thirzey E. Craig   15 Nov. 1840
    Sol. 25 Nov. 1840, William Davis, M.G.

Cherry, William C. to Eliza F. Thompson   3 Aug. 1848
    Sol. 4 Aug. 1848, W. D. F. Saurie, M.G.

Childers, Benjamin to Vina Lankston   25 May 1840

Childress, Jackson to Sarah Langston   6 Feb. 1843
    Sol. 7 Feb. 1843, R. A. Glenn, J.P.

Childress, Stephen W. to Adelia C. Patten   20 Sept. 1849
    Sol. 20 Sept. 1849, Edmond Dillahunty, Judge

Childress, William L. to Mary Hall   12 Nov. 1847
    Sol. 13 Nov. 1847, Hiram Anthony, J.P.

Choat, Robert S. to Harriet E. Dain   7 Jan. 1847
    Sol. 7 Jan. 1847, J. C. Spinks, J.P.

Choat, Thomas to Elizabeth Husband   14 Apr. 1842
    Sol. 14 Apr. 1842, H. A. McMackin, J.P.

Chriesman, David V. to Lydia A. Dunlap   6 Mar. 1841
    Sol. 7 Mar. 1841, Absalom Bostick, M.G.

Christopher, Benjamin F. to Ann M. Griffin   31 Dec. 1846
    Sol. 31 Dec. 1846, Parke Street, J.P.

Christopher, Smith H. to Ora D. Dyers   29 Apr. 1846
    Sol. 29 Apr. 1846, Samuel Wheatley, J.P.

Christopher, Townsend to Sarah J. Latta   6 Feb. 1841

Chumbly, Henry A. to Olivia A. Payne   13 Jan. 1851
    Sol. 14 Jan. 1851, J. B. Hamilton, Methodist Elder

Chumbly, John to Virginia E. Davis   15 Feb. 1849
    Sol. 15 Feb. 1849, J. Crafton, J.P.

Chumbly, Robert T. to Sarah Renfro   21 Dec. 1839

Chunn, Henry to Beda Shires   19 Nov. 1842

Chun, John to Maria Shires   18 Mar. 1846
    Sol. J. C. Spinks, J.P.

Chunn, Neely to Catherine Jackson   2 Aug. 1845

Church, Edmund F. to Naomi Cathey   19 July 1842
    Sol. 19 July 1842, Ishmael Stevens, J.P.

Church, James M. to Lena Elliott   29 July 1841
    Sol. 29 July 1841, Ishmael Stevens, J.P.

Church, Joshua P. to Mary J. Vestal   27 Oct. 1852

Church, Robert to Leasy J. Jack   22 Oct. 1845
        Sol. 23 Oct. 1845, Ishmael Stevens, J.P.

Church, Thomas H. to Nancy M. Bryan   12 May 1846

Clanton, Dudley to Lucinda Scott   25 May 1849
        Sol. 27 May 1849, Jeremiah F. Holt, J.P.

Clap, Henry to Susan Helton   11 Aug. 1840

Clark, Cyrus C. to Nancy C. Cooke   7 June 1850
        Sol. 7 June 1850 in District 14, Joseph Foster, J.P.

Clayton, William to Winney S. Payton   23 Feb. 1842
        Sol. 23 Feb. 1842, D. W. Fain

Clemons, William to Clarinda Johnson   27 July 1839
        Sol. 28 July 1839, E. Hanks, M.G.

Clendenin, John, to Emily J. Mayes   24 Sept. 1851
        Sol. 24 Sept. 1851

Clendenin, Samuel to Maria Mays   12 Apr. 1838
        Sol. Britain Garner

Cleveland, Jeremiah to Mary A. Stone   27 Oct. 1841
        Sol. 27 Oct. 1841, William Davis, M.G.

Clift, Abner to Mary J. Pillow   14 Aug. 1840

Clymore, John C. to Sarah Shires   1 Aug. 1838

Cobler (?), John M. to Eliza J. Moore   22 Oct. 1852
        Sol. J. O. Church

Coburn, Theophilus to Naomi Howard   28 Sept. 1852
        Sol. 29 Sept. 1852, James Brownlow, M.G.

Cochran, John W. to Mary Freeland   20 Jan. 1843
        Sol. 22 Jan. 1843, B. Gresham, J.P.

Cockran, William W. to Elizabeth T. Dillard   17 June 1850
        Sol. 18 June 1850, J. P. Hamilton, Methodist Minister

Cockrill, Benjamin F. to Sarah A. M. Dox   4 Dec. 1851
        Sol. 4 Dec. 1851, Joseph A. Wright, J.P.

Coffey, James J. to Ann E. Matthews   20 Feb. 1847
        Sol. 22 Feb. 1847, G. C. Stockard, M.G.

Coffey, John W. to Lydia F. Dallas   22 Jan. 1845
        Sol. 23 Jan. 1845, James M. Richardson, J.P.

Coffey, Landon H. to Martha Meece   6 May 1848

Coffey, Nathan to Euphance Stockard   8 Feb. 1848
      Sol, 10 Feb. 1848, J. T. Moss, M.G.

Coffey, William F, to Priscilla Howard   23 Dec. 1850
      Sol. 24 Dec. 1850, James Brownlow, M.G.

Cole, Pelmore to Elizabeth Garrigus   8 Sept, 1838

Coleburn, James C. to Rebecca E, Lanier   18 Feb, 1843
      Sol, 22 Feb. 1843, G. W. Mitchell, M.G., C.P. Church

Coleman, Albert G. to Nancy Kelly   7 Mar. 1842
      Sol, 9 Mar. 1842, Y. McFall, J.P.

Collart, John to Margaret McIntire   23 June 1847
      Sol, 24 June 1847, William Mack, M.G.

Collier, Albert W., to Dosha Bostick   24 Sept. 1839
      Sol. 24 Sept. 1839, H. H. Brown, E.M.E.C.

Collier, William H. to Mary J. Hight   12 July 1845

Collins, Cornelius C. to Sarah Green   30 Apr, 1842
      Sol. 1 May 1842, E. R. Freeman, J.P.

Collins, George W. to Elizabeth A. Hospered   22 June 1847
      Sol. 22 June 1847, J. C. Spinks, J.P.

Collins, Lycurgus to Margaret Young   18 May 1852
      Sol. 19 May 1852, John B. Hamilton, M.M.

Collins, Thomas to Mary Thomas   7 July 1841
      Sol. 12 July 1841, R. A. Glenn, J.P.

Collins, William to Lucinda Burch   25 Jan. 1844

Collins, William Thomas to Malinda McManus   20 May 1844
      Sol, 22 May 1844, George W. Johnston, J.P.

Compton, Albert S. to Susan M. Thompson   22 Oct. 1846
      Sol. 22 Oct. 1846, H. K. Shields, M.G.

Compton, Elisha S. to Mira Ann Rust   21 Oct. 1852
      Sol. 21 Oct. 1852, J. A. Wright

Compton, Felix to Emily G. Webster   6 July 1843
      Sol. 6 July 1843, Joseph Sherman, M.G.

Conkey, Z. to S. H. Thomas   24 May 1852
      Sol. 25 May 1852, Joseph Brown, M.G.

Conner, William R. to Martha Blocker   14 June 1852
      Sol. 14 June 1852, William W. Jossey, J.P.

Connor, George to Mary A. S. Ridley   26 Oct, 1842
      Sol. 27 Oct, 1842, James B. Porter

Cook, Albert B. to Matilda Blackburn
     Sol. 15 Feb. 1844, Park Street, J.P.   15 Feb. 1844

Cook, James A. to Elizabeth Parkin
     Sol. 4 May 1843, John Y. Faris, J.P.   4 May 1843

Cook, John M. to Mary A. Turbeville
     Sol. 16 Dec. 1841, Thomas W. Randle, M.G.   16 Dec. 1841

Cook, Noah to Sarah Gates (or Gotes)
     Sol. 28 Nov. 1846, Berryman Hamlett, J.P.   28 Nov. 1846

Cooke, Wilford W. to Nancy C. Gray
     Sol. 10 June 1840, William W. Coleman, J.P.   6 June 1840

Cooper, Albert G. to Elizabeth F. Webb
     Sol. 8 Apr. 1838, Willie Ledbetter, L.E.M.E.C.   2 Apr. 1838

Cooper, Benjamin H. to Judy Williams
     Sol. 7 Feb. 1851, James A. Moore, J.P.   7 Feb. 1851

Cooper, Charles L. to Tabitha Ostion
     Sol. 22 Aug. 1841, H. A. McMeckin, J.P.   19 Aug. 1841

Cooper, Edmund to Rebecca F. Pinkston
     Sol. 12 Dec. 1850, N. P. Modrell   12 Dec. 1850

Cooper, John A. to Sarah E. Law
     Sol. 15 May 1839, Philip Ball, M.G.   6 May 1839

Cooper, Lancaster D. to Martha Bobo
     Sol. 2 Mar. 1843, G. R. Hoge, M.G.   2 Mar. 1843

Cooper, M.D. to Mary A. Brown   24 June 1841
     Sol. 24 June 1841, James M. Arnell, Pastor, Zion Church

Cooper, Faris to Elizabeth J. Cooper
     Sol. 24 Sept. 1840, H. H. Brown, E.M.E.C.   24 Sept. 1840

Cooper, Samuel M. to Martha J. Kennedy
     Sol. 15 Aug. 1844, R. Stockard, J.P.   11 Aug. 1844

Cooper, William H. to Elizabeth Kersey
     Sol. 1 June 1846, John Brown, J.P.   1 June 1846

Cooper, W. W. to Eliza E. Tombs
     Sol. 12 July 1843, C. Y. Hudson, J.P.   10 July 1843

Copley, George W. to Mahala J. Nall
     Sol. 23 Sept. 1849, J. C. Oliphant, J.P.   22 Sept. 1849

Corben, Francis to Elizabeth Gorden
     Sol. 20 Apr. 1840, Lewis G. Lanier, J.P.   20 Apr. 1840

Costler, William D. to Nancy E. Scott   1 July 1843

Covey, Elijah W. to Elizabeth F. Fitzgerald   26 May 1841
     Sol. 27 May 1841, Alfred Fleming, J.P.

Cowen, Arthur B. to Amanda M. Dickson   29 Nov. 1841
     Sol. 30 Nov. 1841, G. W. Mitchell, M.G.

Cox, Jesse J. to Rebecca A. C. D. Pogue   11 Feb. 1852
     Sol. 12 Feb. 1852, Andrew Akin, J.P.

Cox, Samuel F. to Hannah A. Bain   11 July 1851
     Sol. 15 July 1851, Asa Hardison, M.G.

Craig, Charles K. to Elizabeth C. Lindsey   26 Oct. 1849
     Sol. 30 Oct. 1849, James C. Moore

Craig, Gazuaway to Julia A. Carothers   3 Mar. 1841
     Sol. 4 Mar. 1841, G. C. Stockard, M.G.

Craig, John to Sarah H. Gilliam   23 Jan. 1838
     Sol. 23 Jan. 1838, William Davis, M.G.

Craig, Joseph M. to Nancy M. Gilliam   20 Mar. 1844
     Sol. 21 March 1844, B. Gresham, J.P.

Craig, Samuel S. to Nancy E. Lindsey   29 Nov. 1842
     Sol. 1 Dec. 1842, Jones Dailey, J.P.

Craig, William to Lotty Johnson   2 June 1838
     Sol. 6 June 1838, Richard Stockard, J.P.

Crandford, William J. to Elizabeth Scott   18 Aug. 1851
     Sol. 18 Aug. 1851, Aroma Clark, J.P.

Cranford, Benjamin F. to Mahala Stuart   20 July 1847
     Sol. 21 July 1847, Park Street, J.P.

Cranford, William F. to Manerva Dyer   22 July 1840

Cranford, William to Nancy A. Cochran   12 Jan. 1843
     Sol. 12 Jan. 1843, Joseph Herndon, J.P.

Crawford, James S. to Martha J. Renfro   28 Jan. 1841
     Sol. 28 Jan 1841, Parke Street, J.P.

Crawford, Luke B. to Delila E. Swyny   13 Jan. 1842
     Sol. Laban Jordan, J.P.

Crawford, Wesley to Susan J. Powell   27 Aug. 1851
     Sol. 28 Aug. 1851, Asa Hardison, M.G.

Crawley, William C. to Eliza M. Vaught   18 Feb. 1845
     Sol. 19 Feb. 1845, William H. Wilkes, M.G.

Crenshaw, Charles to Elizabeth C. Blackman   22 Mar. 1845
     Sol. 23 Mar. 1845, E. Hanks, M.G.

Crews, James F. to Mary A. M. Nichols   7 Dec. 1842
     Sol. 7 Dec. 1842, George L. Arnold, M.G.

Crews, Joseph A. to Elizabeth Bryant   9 Dec. 1850
        Sol. 11 Dec. 1850, F. A. Burke, J.P.

Crews, Wesley E. to Nancy W. Collier   23 Jan. 1840
        Sol. 23 Jan. 1840, J. N. Dills, J.P.

Crippen, Samuel M. to Elizabeth G. Dunahoo   22 Sept. 1846
        Sol. 22 Sept. 1846, Samuel Wheatley, J.P.

Crockett, Joseph H. to Eliza F. White   26 July 1851
        Sol. 20 July 1851, Edward C. Slater, M.G.

Crosby, Thomas J. to Mary E. Dobbins   11 Sept. 1850
        Sol. 12 Sept. 1850

Cross, Edwin O. to Eliza J. Bond   20 June 1843
        Sol. 21 June 1843, C. R. Harris, M.G.

Cross, John F. to Mary J. Lanier   11 Nov. 1850
        Sol. 12 Nov. 1850, Henry A. Miller, J.P.

Cross, Robert to Elizabeth Smith   15 Nov. 1838
        Sol. 15 Nov. 1838

Culver, James to Mary A. Culver   12 Feb. 1851
        Sol. 12 Feb. 1851, R. A. Glenn, J.P.

Cumpton, James to Eleanor Young   27 Dec. 1842
        Sol. 27 Dec. 1842, Park Street, J.P.

Cunningham, William J. to Adeline S. Harris   16 Sept. 1847
        Sol. 17 Sept. 1847, William Mack, M.G.

Curry, John to Vina Wirick   4 Apr. 1839
        Sol. 4 Apr. 1839, Robert Foster, J.P.

Curtis, Benjamin F. to Elizabeth A. Fogleman   3 Jan. 1844
        Sol. 4 Jan. 1844, D. R. Gant, M.G.

                          D

Dabney, William W. to Sallie E. Sedberry   17 May 1850
        Sol. 20 June 1850, B. H. Ragsdale

Daimwood, Henry B. to Eliza J. Gullett   26 Feb. 1840
        Sol. 27 Feb. 1840, Parke Street, J.P.

Dallas, Robert B. to Elizabeth Richardson   12 July 1843
        Sol. 25 July 1843, James Brownlow, M.G.

Dalton, Lacy W. to Mary H. Dixon   3 Nov. 1840
        Sol. 3 Nov. 1840, G. Tucker, M.G.

Daniels, James C. to Mary A. Sneed   11 June 1846
        Sol. 11 June 1846, C. Cooke, J.P.

Daniels, Samuel M. to Mary Baker   6 June 1849
        Sol. 6 June 1849, M. H. Mays, J.P.

Dark, Stephen, to Mary J. Rutledge   28 Oct. 1841
     Sol. 28 Oct. 1841, Berryman Hamlett, J.P.

Dark, Stephen to Mary A. Taylor   12 Mar. 1846
     Sol. 15 Mar. 1846, E. Hanks, M.G.

Daugherty, Samuel H. to Mary Carrigan   20 Nov. 1851
     Sol. 20 Nov. 1851, Joseph A. Wright, J.P.

Davidson, Calvin to Malinda Anglin   3 July 1841
     Sol. Britain Garner

Davidson, John D. to Mary D. Pipkin   29 June 1848
     Sol. 6 July 1848, A. T. Gray, J.P.

Davidson, John F. to Mary M. Davidson   23 Dec. 1845
     Sol. 24 Dec. 1845 at house of Colonel Edward Chaffin by
James H. Otey

Davis, Alexander H. to Margaret K. Matthews   17 Dec. 1838
     Sol. 19 Dec. 1838, R. M. Galloway

Davis, David to Louisa Stacy   11 Jan. 1844
     Sol. 11 Jan. 1844, Hiram Anthony, J.P.

Davis, Eliphas R. to Maria A. Black   4 Mar. 1841
     Sol. 8 Mar. 1841, J. A. Duncan, J.P.

Davis, Henry W. to Sarah Robison   31 Jan. 1849

Davis, James to Margaret Whiteside   25 Aug. 1842

Davis, James O. to Sarah A. Gooding   9 Apr. 1846
     Sol. 9 Apr. 1846, Philip P. Neeley, M.G.

Davis, John D. to Margaret Williams   15 Mar. 1851
     Sol. 16 Mar. 1851

Davis, John T. to Louisa J. McMeen   19 Aug. 1851
     Sol. 21 Aug. 1851, M.B. Molloy, M.G.

Davis, Lemuel M. to Elizabeth H. Baker   21 Dec. 1841
     Sol. 21 Dec. 1841, Andrew Scott, J.P.

Davis, Nelson to Julia Ann Blanton   2 Mar. 1840
     Sol. 4 Mar. 1840, William Davis, M.G.

Davis, Samuel to Amelia Lunn   15 Dec. 1846
     Sol. 15 Dec. 1847, Samuel W. Akin, J.P.

Davis, William T. to Mary M. Mangrum   28 Aug. 1849
     Sol. 28 Aug. 1849, James M. White, J.P.

Davis, Wootson D. to Mary Susan Nevils   10 Oct. 1839
     Sol. 10 Oct. 1839, R. H. Simmons, J.P.

Downey, James C. to Nancy M. Temple   8 May 1840
     Sol. 12 May 1840, Powhatan Gordon, J.P.

Dawson, Jesse A. to Mary E. Ward   14 Apr. 1847
      Sol. 14 Apr. 1847, John F. Hughes

Dawson, Orris P. to Sarah C. Witherspoon   10 Oct. 1844
      Sol. 11 Oct. 1844, E. Hanks, M.G.

Deal, William M. to Elizabeth McFarland   12 Sept. 1850
      Sol. 12 Sept. 1850, Andrew Scott, J.P.

Dean, Alexander to Catherine Clark   7 Aug. 1850
      Sol. 12 Aug. 1850, John Glenn, J.P.

Deaton, James B. to Margaret M. Croner   18 Dec. 1839
      Sol. 19 Dec. 1839

Debman, Bartlett to Sarah Neeley   25 Dec. 1840
      Sol. 25 Dec. 1840, Absalom Bostick, M.G.

DeLannay, James L. to Sarah C. Napier   26 July 1841
      Sol. 27 July 1841, Joseph Sherman, M.G.

Denham, Thomas to Mary A. Bond   2 July 1838
      Sol. 5 July 1838, G. W. Mitchell, M.G.

Denham, Thomas to Tempe Hunter   2 Apr. 1840
      Sol. 2 Apr. 1840, Richard Stockard, J.P.

Denham, Thomas to Nancy Mills   7 Feb. 1852
      Sol. 7 Feb. 1852, Joseph M. White, J.P.

Derryberry, David L. to Malinda D. Hardison   8 Jan. 1846
      Sol. 8 Jan. 1846, Joshua K. Speer, M.G.

Derryberry, David L. to Sarah Brown   22 July 1847
      Sol. 27 Aug. 1847, R. A. Glenn, J.P.

Derryberry, Jacob to Martha Wade   27 Jan. 1847
      Sol. 28 Mar. 1847, R. A. Glenn, J.P.

Derryberry, James L. to Sarah A. Hardison   27 Feb. 1838
      Sol. 1 Mar. 1838, Joshua K. Speer, M.G.

Derryberry, John T. to Phoebe C. Speer   9 Feb. 1842
      Sol. 10 Feb. 1842, R. A. Glenn, J.P.

Derryberry, Joseph H. to Averilla W. Stanfield   23 Feb. 1841

Derryberry, Joshua to Elizabeth C. Bain   2 Mar. 1846
      Sol. 2 Mar. 1846, J. C. Spinks, J.P.

Derryberry, Levi C. to Eliza E. Robinson   19 Dec. 1840
      Sol. 22 Dec. 1840, C. Cooke, J.P.

Derryberry, Sopley A. to Elizabeth C. Kincaid   17 Sept. 1844
      Sol. 17 Sept. 1844, John Brown, J.P.

Deveser, Booker to Frances E. Lindsey   4 Jan. 1847
    Sol. 7 Jan. 1847, Alvis Williams, J.P.

Devasure, William R. to Lucinda A. Green   9 Oct. 1848

Dew, James C. to Parthena Black   20 Nov. 1848
    Sol. 21 Nov. 1848, C. D. Elliott, M.G.

Dial, Robert to Elizabeth Rust   11 Feb. 1845
    Sol. 11 Feb. 1845, Alfred Fleming, J.P.

Dial, Robert to Nancy J. Barnett   24 July 1852
    Sol. 25 July 1852, James H. Burns, M.G.

Dickens, A. J. M. to Sarah Smith   13 Apr. 1850
    Sol. 14 Apr. 1850, John E. Williams, J.P.

Dickerson, Caleb J. to Ann T. Phillips   17 Oct. 1842
    Sol. 20 Oct. 1842, Philip P. Neeley, M.G.

Dickey, James W. to Elizabeth Jane Kimes   6 Feb. 1845
    Sol. by J. T. Faris, J.P.

Dickey, John E. to Margaret J. Gray   10 Jan. 1842
    Sol. 11 Jan. 1842, Thomas Kelsey, J.P.

Dickey, Samuel G. to Sophronia Warfield   23 Sept. 1839
    Sol. 24 Sept. 1839, T. E. Kirkpatrick, M.G.

Dickey, Samuel L. to Catherine H. Stockard   26 Mar. 1845
    Sol. 26 March 1845, G. W. Mitchell, M.G.

Dickey, William E. to Frances J. Bingham   26 Nov. 1846
    Sol. 26 Nov. 1846, James N. Edmiston, M.G.

Dickie, James R. to Frances Hutson   20 May 1839
    Sol. 23 May 1839, James Calhoon

Dickson, Alexander R. to Hannah Nixon   31 Jan. 1838
    Sol. 6 Feb. 1838, Wilie Ledbetter, L.E.M.E.C.

Dickson, Alexander R. to Margaret A. Spence   8 July 1845

Dickson, Ephrium M. to Sarah J. Massie   22 Dec. 1849
    Sol. 22 Dec. 1849, W. B. McKee

Dickson, L. F. to Frances Martin   6 Nov. 1844
    Sol. 12 Nov. 1844, Wade Barrett, Elder in C. Ch.

Dickson, Milton M. to Emaline Pickard   15 Nov. 1839
    Sol. 17 Nov. 1839, G. W. Mitchell, M. G.

Dickson, William G. to Mary T. Davis   30 June 1851
    Sol. 1 July 1851, F. A. Burke, J.P.

Dicky, Thomas P. to Mary J. McKannon   31 Dec. 1850
    Sol. 2 Jan. 1851, James F. Jordan, J.P.

Dicus, J. W. to Frances Cox   24 Mar.1852
    Sol. 24 March 1852, Andrew Akin, J.P.

Dillard, Richard M. to Mildred A. Hunt   5 Dec. 1848
    Sol. 7 Dec. 1848, A. G. Kelley, M.G.

Dillehay, John T. to Mary J. Harris   7 Dec. 1850
    Sol. 12 Dec. 1850, Edward R. Puckett, J.P.

Dillehay, John W. to Elizabeth Sewell   16 Jan. 1846
    Sol. 18 Jan. 1846, Alfred Fleming, J.P.

Dillehay, John W. to Louisa Murphey   31 March 1852
    Sol. 4 Mar. 1852, J. A. Wright, J.P.

Dillehay, Marcus G. to Mary Lancaster   22 Dec. 1842
    Sol. 22 Dec. 1842, B. Gresham, J.P.

Dixon, Samuel H. to Ann C. White   25 Feb. 1847

Dobbins, Archibald S. to Mary P. Dawson   2 Feb. 1850
    Sol. 3 Feb. 1850, William S. Langdon, Minister,
          Cumberland Presbyterian Church

Dobbin, David W. to Eliza Lockridge   11 Nov. 1840
    Sol. 12 Nov. 1840, William Davis, M.G.

Dobbin, John J. to Ann R. A. Chappell   22 Feb. 1841
    Sol. 23 Feb. 1841, J. B. Walker, M.G.

Dobbin, William A. to Ellis J. Lockridge   18 Sept. 1843
    Sol. 19 Sept. 1843, William Burn

Dockery, Hiram to Margaret Finch   6 Oct. 1846

Dockery, James M. to Martha E. Puckett   22 July 1841
    Sol. 22 July 1841, R. S. Bigham, J.P.

Dockery, William R. to Sarah Southern   22 Dec. 1841
    Sol. 23 Dec. 1841, Ishamel Stevens, J.P.

Dockry, Hiram to Martha Griffin   29 Apr. 1841
    Sol. 29 Apr. 1841, George R. Hoge, M.G.

Dodson, Beverly P. to Nancy Fitzgerald   6 Nov. 1839
    Sol. 6 Nov. 1839, James P. Adkins, J.P.

Dodson, David to Nancy Fitzgerald   26 May 1848
    Sol. 27 May 1848, Coleman Goad, J.P.

Dodson, Elias to Isabella Baldridge   3 Jan. 1844
    Sol. 3 Jan. 1844, H. B. Warren

Dodson, Elisha to Elizabeth Galloway   28 Feb. 1838
    Sol. 29 Feb. 1838, R. W. Morris, E.M.P. Church

Dodson, James E. to Mary J. Dodson   10 Aug. 1843
    Sol. 10 Aug. 1843, E. Hanks, M.G.

Dodson, James N. to Mary Wilkes   4 Jan. 1838
     Sol. 4 Jan. 1838, E. Hanks, M.G.

Dodson, John A. to Maria Studivant   19 June 1840

Dodson, Lazarus to Gilla Clements   10 Dec. 1838
     Sol. 11 Dec. 1838, E. Hanks, M.G.

Dodson, Marion L. to Martha Fitzgerald   24 Sept. 1852
     Sol. 25 Sept. 1852, M. P. Erwin, J.P.

Dodson, Monroe A. to Elizabeth A. Shaw   13 Sept. 1847
     Sol. 15 Sept. 1847, Daniel Judd, L.E.M.C.

Dodson, Presley E. to Mary Smith   11 Aug. 1839
     Sol. 11 Aug. 1839, James Adkins, J.P.

Dodson, Raleigh to Lucinda M. Witherspoon   3 Nov. 1841
     Sol. 3 Nov. 1841, Ishamel Stevens, J.P.

Dodson, Raleigh W. to Ann A. Alderson   27 Feb. 1850
     Sol. 27 Feb. 1850, E. Hanks, M.G.

Dodson, Riley to Matilda Rutledge   21 Dec. 1847

Dodson, Thomas A. to Sarah E. Moore   28 Aug. 1844
     Sol. 29 Aug. 1844, E. Hanks, M.G.

Dodson, Thomas A. to Mary A. Whitaker   5 Feb. 1851
     Sol. 17 Feb. 1851, Joseph Foster, J.P.

Dodson, Washington P. to Harriett A. Witherspoon   24 July 1841
     Sol. 29 July 1841, W. H. Baldridge, M.G.

Dodson, William to Sarah Smith   10 Feb. 1841
     Sol. 11 Feb. 1841, R. Stochard, J.P.

Dodson, William R. to Eliza C. Overton   24 Sept. 1840

Dodson, W. D. to Sirena P. Fitzgerald   21 June 1852
     Sol. 22 June 1852, James H. Colburn, J.P.

Doe, Augustus to Nancy C. Stanfield   30 Dec. 1841
     Sol. 30 Dec. 1841, Joseph Sherman, M.G.

Dolton, Isom to Mary Renfro   28 July 1846
     Sol. 28 July 1846, Samuel Wheatley, J.P.

Donaldson, Alfred R. to Martha Perry   19 June 1852
     Sol. 20 June 1852, William H. Wilks, M.G.

Donaldson, Andrew J. to Marinda Rains   24 Jan. 1838
     Sol. James M. Grimes

Donelson, Samuel to Eliza Easten   14 Mar. 1838

Dooley, Isaac M. to Susan Moore   31 Jan. 1838
    Sol. 1 Feb. 1838, T. E. Kirkpatrick, M.G.

Dooley, James M. to Louisa M. Maxwell   9 Jan. 1838
    Sol. 10 Jan. 1838, Thomas Fielding Scott, V.D.M.

Dooley, Madison W. to Susan C. (?) Wilson   8 Jan. 1838

Dooley, Madison W. to Mary E. Tranum   27 Jan. 1842
    Sol. 27 Jan. 1842, Samuel Wheatley, J.P.

Dooley, Martin F. to Mary Ann Joyce   8 Mar. 1838
    Sol. 8 Mar. 1838, T. E. Kirkpatrick, M.G.

Dooley, William A. to Sarah J. Joyce   11 Jan. 1843
    Sol. 14 Jan. 1843, Thomas Kelsey, J.P.

Dooley, William H. to Mary M. Holcomb   29 Sept. 1841
    Sol. 30 Sept. 1841, James Smith, J.P.

Dorch, Willis R. to Elizabeth J. Morris   19 July 1851
    Sol. 20 July 1851, E. Hanks, M.G.

Dorten, Alvin to Gracy Kersy   20 Nov. 1849
    Sol. 21 Nov. 1849

Douglass, David to Mary R. Malone   14 June 1845

Douglass, Samuel J. to Martha M. Powell   30 Nov. 1840
    Sol. Britain Garner

Dowd, Benjamin F. to Alpina M. Williams   9 July 1850
    Sol. 11 July 1850, J. B. Hamilton

Dowdy, Henry to Malady Stokes   29 Dec. 1842
    Sol. 1 Jan. 1843, G. C. Stockard, M.G.

Dowdy, Samuel to Mary McMillan   18 Nov. 1846
    Sol. 18 Nov. 1846, J. T. Moss, M.G.

Dowell, John F. to Jane McCormick   13 Sept. 1848

Dowell, William B. to Phoebe E. Lane   30 Sept. 1850
    Sol. 30 Sept. 1850, T. N. McKee, M.G.

Downey, Richard to Martha A. Gillham   25 Jan. 1842
    Sol. 25 Jan. 1842, George R. Hoge, M.G.

Doyle, Patrick B. to Cynthia Barnes   14 Nov. 1845

Drake, James L. to Mary D. Patterson   6 Oct. 1852
    Sol. 7 Oct. 1852, M. B. Molloy, M.G.

Draper, Jarrett W. to Isabella Thomas   13 Aug. 1838
    Sol. 15 Aug. 1838, Andrew Scott, Acting J.P.

Draper, William to Elizabeth Emerson   3 June 1847
    Sol. 3 June 1847, James M. Richardson, J.P.

Dugger, Almern S. to Maria M. Grasnett (or Gravvett) 2 Dec. 1846
    Sol. 3 Dec. 1846, Andrew Scott, J.P.

Dugger, James A. to Narcissa P. Richardson   9 Nov. 1839
    Sol. 14 Nov, 1839, Joseph Brown, M.G.

Dugger, Jeremiah to Elizabeth F. Moore   9 Jan. 1845

Dugger, Jonathan H. to Elizabeth J. Moore   24 Apr. 1852
    Sol. 25 Apr. 1852, F. A. Burke, J.P.

Dugger, Joseph to Elizabeth McConnel   12 Feb. 1849

Dugger, Silas to Nancy Robinson   29 Dec. 1846
    Sol. 29 Dec. 1846, Joshua K. Speer, M.G.

Dugger, William W. to Mary Ann Howard   10 July 1841
    Sol. 11 July 1841, R. A. Glenn, J.P.

Dugger, Willie to Rachel A. Faris   9 Dec. 1844

Duke, Burley J. to Jane F. Trousdale   9 Oct. 1838
    Sol. 11 Oct. 1838, G. W. Mitchell, M.G.

Duke, Green to Exaline Nichols   6 July 1846
    Sol. 9 July 1846, Berryman Hamlett, J.P.

Duke, Green E. to Martha J. Collins   23 May 1840

Duke, Green E. to Mary J. Manual   25 Sept. 1850
    Sol. 25 Sept. 1850, Asa Hardison, M.G.

Duke, Henry to L. L. Woodward   2 Feb. 1844

Duke, William to Margaret Vandike   4 Apr. 1844
    Sol. 4 Apr. 1844, James M. Arnell, Zion Pastor

Duke, William G. to Susannah Ray   2 June 1838
    Sol. 6 June 1838, S. Whiteside, J.P.

Duke, William G. to Katherine Ray   26 Dec.1843

Duncan, Joseph G. to Parthena Jackson   22 Nov. 1848
    Sol. 23 Nov. 1848, William R. Sharp, J.P.

Dungan, Allen to Jane Holmes   1 Oct. 1838
    Sol. 2 Oct. 1838, E. Hanks, M.G.

Dunham, Hiram M. to Caroline M. Smith   18 May 1848
    Sol. 21 May 1848, Rev. W. P. Canders

Dunlap, James S. to Mary A. Bingham   16 Oct. 1848

Dunn, John W. to Nancy E. Mills   13 Oct. 1847
    Sol. 13 Oct. 1847, Hugh C. Harrison, J.P.

Dunn, Renklin (?) to Frances Rennel (?)   27 Dec. 1851
     Sol. 28 Dec. 1851, W. R. H. Mack, J.P.

Durham, Thomas to Margaret Kerr   23 Dec. 1847
     Sol. 23 Dec. 1847, O. A. Mabry, M.G.

Dyas, Alexander J. to Sarah B. Jackson   21 Oct. 1841
     Sol. 21 Oct. 1841, Joseph Sherman, M.G.

Dycas, William to Francina Wier   7 Oct. 1839
     Sol. 8 Oct. 1839, S. Whiteside, J.P.

Dyer, William F. to Margaret Cranford   22 July 1840
     Sol. 29 July 1840, C. Cooke, J.P.

E

Eagle, Alexander to Eliza Furlow   25 Aug. 1838
     Sol. 26 Aug. 1838, Robert P. Lockridge, J.P.

Eagle, Philip to Sarah Swaim   4 Nov. 1840

Eagle, William H. to Rosetta Minter   24 May 1843
     Sol. 25 May 1843, Joseph Sherman, J.P.

Easley, James to Mary J. Perry   28 Aug. 1843
     Sol. 28 Aug. 1843, G. W. Mitchell, M.G.

Easley, William H. to Josephine Partee (or Porter) 2 Sept. 1847
     Sol. 3 Oct. 1847, James M. White, J.P.

Eddlemon, John W. to Louisa R. Jones   30 Aug. 1843
     Sol. 30 Aug. 1843, John B. Bond, J.P.

Edgar, Henry to Annis Moten   21 Mar. 1842
     Sol. 21 Mar. 1842, Ishamel Stevens, J.P.

Edgar, Joshua N. to Martha W. Wolland   14 Nov. 1848
     Sol. 30 Nov. 1848, B. D. Wall, J.P.

Edgin, John W. to Nancy Daniel   22 Aug. 1851
     Sol. 26 Aug. 1851, R. Baker, J.P.

Edgin, Nathan A. to Abba J. Litten   8 Jan. 1851
     Sol. 8 Jan. 1851, R. Baker, J.P.

Edmiston, James N. to Margaret M. Dixon   4 Jan. 1849
     Sol. 4 Jan. 1849, G. C. Stockard, M.G.

Edmiston, John to Charlotte A. Barnes   28 Dec. 1842
     Sol. 29 Dec. 1842, James M. Granberry

Edmiston, Samuel D. to Easther A. Gatland   16 Jan. 1839
     Sol. 17 Jan. 1839, John B. Bond, J.P.

Edmiston, Samuel H. to Matilda Harrison   21 Mar. 1842

Edwards, George W. to Ellen J. Han   25 Jan. 1838
     Sol. 25 Jan. 1838, F. G. Ferguson, M.G.

Edwards, Green T. to Paralee Z. Taylor   13 Mar. 1841
     Sol. 13 Mar. 1841, William W. Coleman, J.P.

Edwards, John A. to Margaret V. Stewart   24 Sept. 1851
     Sol. 25 Sept. 1851, J. B. Hamilton, Elder, M.E.C.

Edwards, Obadiah to Letha Dodson   21 Dec. 1842
     Sol. 21 Dec. 1842, E. Hanks, M.G.

Edwards, Philemon to Susan E. McMeen   12 Feb. 1838
     Sol. 15 Feb. 1838, R. W. Morris, E.M.P. Church

Edwards, Redman G. to Mary E. Scott   21 Dec. 1839
     Sol. 24 Dec. 1839, H. H. Brown, E.M.E.C.

Edwards, Silas to Nancy Alderson   27 Oct. 1838
     Sol. by Robert Campbell, J.P.

Edwards, William to Mary O. Walker   14 May 1839
     Sol. 15 May 1839 Thomas F. Scott, V.D.M.

Edwards, William to Mahaly Montgomery   13 Sept. 1850
     Sol. 13 Sept. 1850, Jeremiah F. Holt, J.P.

Edwards, William C. to Ursula E. Kennemore   6 Mar. 1839
     Sol. 6 Mar. 1839, Andrew Scott, J.P.

Edwards, William C. to Narcissa L. Johnson   24 Dec. 1846
     Sol. 24 Dec. 1846, John Mack, J.P.

Egnew, George R. to Ruth E. Holden   21 Sept. 1850
     Sol. 22 Sept. 1850, W. B. Gilham, M.G.

Elam, Edward B. to Susan J. Maddox   3 Jan. 1842

Elliott, Andrew J. to Louisa L. Tynnell   7 Mar. 1851
     Sol. 9 Mar. 1851, Edward C. Slater, Methodist, M.G.

Elliott, Hamilton M. to Elizabeth A. Jones   5 May 1840
     Sol. 5 May 1840, G. C. Stockard, M.G.

Elliott, Wright W. to Mary A. Hooper   6 Jan. 1838
     Sol. 6 Jan 1838, Thomas Fielding Scott, V.D.M.

Ellis, Hutson to Harriet Davis   21 Apr. 1848
     Sol. 21 Apr. 1848, G. W. Johnson, J.P.

Ellis, Robert B. to Maria Morris   20 June 1846
     Sol. 21 June 1846, J. T. Moss, M.G.

Ellis, Thomas J. to Martha E. Swan   26 Dec. 1846
     Sol. 27 Dec. 1846, G. W. Mitchell, M.G.

Elmore, Thomas to Martha A. Caldwell   1 Dec. 1842
    Sol. 1 Dec. 1842, Adam G. Riggs, M.G.

Elmore, William to Jane Galmore   12 Dec. 1849
    Sol. 13 Dec. 1849, J. T. Faris, J.P.

Embrey, Willis B. to Emily Frierson   2 Sept. 1847
    Sol. 2 Sept. 1847, James M. Arnell, Zion Pastor

Emby, Wiley S. to Nancy P. Wells   9 Oct. 1852
    Sol. 10 Oct. 1852, S. S. Yarbrough, M.G.

Emerson, Benjamin R. to Permelia Bazzell   8 July 1839

Emerson, James H. to Rebecca R. Dallas   9 Jan. 1843
    Sol. 12 Jan. 1843, James M. Richardson, J.P.

Emerson, James H. to Susan Galbraith   2 Sept. 1844
    Sol. 8 Sept. 1844, James Brownlow, M.G.

Emerson, Reuben T. to Anna Richardson   24 Mar. 1838
    Sol. 28 Mar. 1838, Philip Ball, M.G.

Engle, John A. to Margaret E. Frierson   10 Nov. 1852
    Sol. 11 Nov. 1852, William Mack, M.G.

English, Thomas H. to Mary A. Marshall   31 Dec. 1844
    Sol. 31 Dec. 1844, George G. Arnold, Elder, Methodist Church

Ennis, George R. to Mary M. Toumbs   3 Mar. 1849
    Sol. 4 Mar. 1849, N. F. Modrall, M.G.

Ephlin, Michael W. to Derinda Baley   31 Aug. 1840
    Sol. 1 Sept. 1840, G. W. Mitchell, M.G.

Eppes, Peter to Mary Mayberry   18 Sept. 1838
    Sol. Britain Garner

Epps, Freeman to Louisa Wilson   21 Dec. 1841

Erwin, John A. to Priscilla L. Erwin   24 Oct. 1838
    Sol. 25 Oct. 1838, Wilie Ledbetter, L.E.M.E.C.

Erwin, Lycungus to Selatha Hawkins   18 Aug. 1841
    Sol. 18 Aug. 1841, Robert Foster, J.P.

Erwin, Martin P. to Laura Blackman   6 May 1852
    Sol. 6 May 1852, John E. Hamilton, Methodist Minister

Erwin, Robert G. to Frances Chappell   16 Oct. 1845
    Sol. 16 Oct. 1845, William H. Wilkes, M.G.

Erwin, William D. to Julia A. Kinzer   21 Aug. 1850
    Sol. 21 Aug. 1850, W. B. Walker

Erwin, William H. to Jemima A. Smith   19 Aug. 1844

Estes, Coleman C. to Elizabeth M. Matthews   20 Feb. 1840
    Sol. 20 Feb. 1840, Hugh Shaw

Estes, William W. to Mary S. Trousdale   24 July 1844
    Sol. 25 July 1844, James N. Edmiston

Evans, Daniel to Emily D. Johnson   29 May 1849
    Sol. 29 May 1849, D. G. Moore, M.G.

Evans, James R. to Sarah Miller   7 Oct. 1844
    Sol. 8 Oct. 1844, Park Street, J.P.

Evans, Jesse E. to Martha J. Amis   18 Dec. 1845
    Sol. 19 Dec. 1845, D. Judd, L.E.

Evans, William H. to Louisa J. Russ   8 Jan. 1840

Evans, William J. to Elizabeth K. Allen   18 Dec. 1849
    Sol. 19 Dec. 1849, E. Hanks, M.G.

Everett, George F. to Mary E. Caldwell   17 Sept. 1849
    Sol. 18 Sept. 1849, Park Street, J.P.

Everett, James E. to Isabella Stamps   7 Jan. 1846
    Sol. 8 Jan. 1846, Hugh C. Harrison, J.P.

Everet, William to Elizabeth C. Sowell   16 Aug. 1848
    Sol. 16 Aug. 1848, Russell Eskew, M.G.

Ewing, Samuel D. to Jane E. Hill   3 June 1844
    Sol. 6 June 1844, Robert C. Garrison, Pres. Minister

F

Faires, Jackson J. to Lavina Fullen   5 Jan. 1847

Fairis, John to Sophia Cannon   18 July 1849

Faires, Thomas C. to Margaret J. Fleming   31 Dec. 1850
    Sol. 31 Dec. 1850, W. R. H. Mack, J.P.

Fariss, Samuel to Eliza English   19 Dec. 1838
    Sol. 20 Dec. 1838, S. Whiteside, J.P.

Fariss, William H. to M. J. Stockard   15 Jan. 1850
    Sol. 17 Jan. 1850

Farley, John H. to Mary Jane Holden   3 May 1852
    Sol. 3 May 1852, J. H. Colburn, J.P.

Farney, John to Eliza Ament   17 Mar. 1839
    Sol. 17 Mar. 1839, Thomas Fielding Scott, V.D.M.

Farrar, Edmund W. to Harriet A. Kerchival   6 June 1838
    Sol. 6 June 1838, F. G. Ferguson, ord. eld. M.E.C.

Farrar, William to Martha M. Nicholson   17 June 1840

Fergerson, Arthur to Jane Scruggs   12 July 1838
      Sol. 12 July 1838, F. G. Ferguson, ord.eld.M.E.C.

Ferguson, David S. to Nancy Thurmond   13 Apr. 1839

Ferguson, Granvile M. to Elizabeth Waldrum   10 Nov. 1849
      Sol. 11 Nov. 1849, J. M. White, J.P.

Ferguson, Isaac H. to Eliza J. Bovers   3 Aug. 1844
      Sol. 4 Aug. 1844, W. G. Owen, M.G.

Ferrell, William H. to Mary Ann Marien   1 Jan. 1838
      Sol. 2 Jan. 1838, T. E. Kirkpatrick, M.G.

Fielder, Jason Y. to Alice E. Kinzer   15 Dec. 1847
      Sol. 16 Dec. 1847, Thomas Kelsey, J.P.

Fielder, Jason Y. to Sarah E. Estes   2 Oct. 1851
      Sol. 2 Oct. 1851, J. B. Hamilton, Elder, M.E.C.

Fields, Abraham to Virginia Thurmond   31 Oct. 1846

Fields, James to Sarah J. Dockery   28 Sept. 1846

Fields, Stephen P. to Elizabeth Sharp   6 Jan. 1847

Fields, William H. to Martha Slayden   17 Jan. 1843
      Sol. 17 Jan. 1843, E. Hanks, M.G.

Finch, Kuble T. to Caroline Wall   2 Jan. 1847
      Sol. 3 Jan. 1847, Ishmael Stevens, J.P.

Finch, Sylvester to Mary C. Dansbee   12 Mar. 1845
      Sol. 12 Mar. 1845, Washington Oakley, J.P.

Finch, Turner to Sarah Letsinger   19 Aug. 1841
      Sol. 19 Aug. 1841, William W. Coleman, J.P.

Findly, Andrew to L. B. Ament   30 June 1849
      Sol. 2 July 1849, William Mack, M.G.

Finley, Josiah B. to Harriett Jackson   8 Oct. 1842

Fisher, John to Mildred Stratton   14 Feb. 1842

Fisher, William P. to Sarah P. Tate   13 Feb. 1844

Fitzgerald, Beverly A. to Roana E. Harbison   16 Sept. 1845
      Sol. 18 Sept. 1845, W. H. Baldridge, M.G.

Fitzgerald, Carroll G. to Frances H. Thompson   29 Nov. 1851
      Sol. 30 Nov. 1851, W. H. Baldridge, M.G.

Fitzgerald, David L. to Martha A. Shannon — 4 Nov. 1847

Fitzgerald, David S. to Martha A. Shannon — 4 Nov. 1847
    Sol. 4 Nov. 1847, E. Hanks, M.G.

Fitzgerald, Dolphin L. to Cerena A. Walker — 31 Aug. 1852
    Sol. 1 Sept. 1852, E. R. Puckett, J.P.

Fitzgerald, Duton (?) E. to Adaline Sowell — 18 Sept. 1851
    Sol. 18 Sept. 1851, W. W. Coleman, J.P.

Fitzgerald, Edmund to Sarah E. Louder — 3 Aug. 1845

Fitzgerald, Garrett to Frances E. Fitzgerald — 24 July 1849
    Sol. 26 July 1849, E. Hanks, M.G.

Fitzgerald, George W. to Gustavus D. Brown — 23 June 1852
    Sol. 24 June 1852, E. Hanks, M.G.

Fitzgerald, James E. to Mary J. Willis — 27 Dec. 1848

Fitzgerald, James M. to Manerva Thompson — 29 Nov. 1851
    Sol. 30 Nov. 1851, W. H. Baldridge, M.G.

Fitzgerald, Jesse H. to Susan J. Dodson — 9 Apr. 1840

Fitzgerald, John to Nancy Fitzgerald — 6 Sept. 1844

Fitzgerald, John to Elizabeth K. Morris — 11 Dec. 1845
    Sol. 11 Dec. 1845, James P. Porter, M.G.

Fitzgerald, John N. to Mary A. Lowder — 7 Feb. 1849
    Sol. 8 Feb. 1849, T. Hanks, M.G.

Fitzgerald, John W. to Nancy C. Collins — 26 Aug. 1846
    Sol. 27 Aug. 1846, J. T. Moss, M.G.

Fitzgerald, Moses C. to Louisa M. Sparkman — 6 Sept. 1848
    Sol. 6 Sept. 1848, Daniel Judd, L.E.M.E.C.

Fitzgerald, Polk L. to Delila Figg — 8 Oct. 1844
    Sol. 8 Oct. 1844, Ishamel Stevens, J.P.

Fitzgerald, Thomas to Cynthia Fisher — 16 May 1842
    Sol. 16 May 1842, Aaron Vestal, J.P.

Fitzgerald, William A. to Joycy Fitzgerald — 9 Oct. 1839
    Sol. 9 Oct. 1839, James P. Adkins, J.P.

Fitzpatrick, A. J. to Lucinda Tidwell — 19 Aug. 1846
    Sol. 20 Aug. 1846, Alfred Fleming, J.P.

Fitzpatrick, Benjamin F. to Sarah M. Brown — 24 Mar. 1847
    Sol. 25 Mar. 1847, Alfred Fleming, J.P.

Fitzpatrick, Samuel J. to Martha F. Bryant   10 Feb. 1849
     Sol. 13 Feb. 1849, F. A. Burk, J.P.

Flanigan, George B. to Margaret H. Erwin   6 Sept. 1852
     Sol. 6 Sept. 1852, G. C. Stockard, M.G.

Fleming, James A. to Sarah L. Frierson   26 Feb. 1845
     Sol. 27 Feb. 1845, James M. Arnell, Zion Pastor

Fleming, James S. to Louisa G. Gee   17 Feb. 1847
     Sol. 17 Feb. 1847, James M. Arnell

Fleming, Thomas S. to Catherine L. Jones   5 Jan. 1847
     Sol. 7 Jan. 1847, James M. Arnell, Zion Pastor

Fleming, William S. to Frances M. Stephenson   3 Sept. 1839
     Sol. 5 Sept. 1839, James M. Arnell

Flowers, Basley J. to Rebecca Cooper   21 Oct. 1848
     Sol. 24 Oct. 1848, Coleman Goad, J.P.

Flowers, James H. to Martha M. Stacy   6 July 1850
     Sol. 7 July 1850, Edward R. Puckett, J.P.

Flowers, John to Mary Stivers   17 July 1848
     Sol. 18 July 1848, Edward A. Puckett, J.P.

Flowers, William to James Catherine Johnson   6 Sept. 1841
     Sol. 9 Sept. 1841, H. A. McMackin, J.P.

Fly, Andrew J. to Hannah E. Kinzer   5 Oct. 1850
     Sol. 6 Oct. 1850, J. B. Hamilton, Methodist Elder

Fly, John to Cyrina Webb   30 Aug. 1839
     Sol. Britain Garner

Fly, John to Sarah L. McCoy   25 Nov. 1847
     Sol. 25 Nov. 1847, Washington Oakley, J.P.

Fly, John L. to Eliza Richards   26 Dec. 1851
     Sol. 28 Dec. 1851, R. Baker, J.P.

Fly, Joseph L. to Margaret R. Maddux   27 Mar. 1847
     Sol. 8 April 1847, G. W. Fly, Esquire

Fly, William H. to Mary J. Kinzer   9 Oct. 1849
     Sol. 11 Oct. 1849, D. R. Sowell, J.P.

Folsom, William B. to Nancy Kittrell   5 Dec. 1846
     Sol. 17 Dec. 1846, Parke Street, J.P.

Fonville, Jeremiah to Frances Smith   19 Sept. 1842
     Sol. 22 Sept. 1842, R. A. Glenn, J.P.

Ford, Richard L. to Sally G. Booker   16 Dec. 1851
     Sol. 17 Dec. 1851, William Mack, M.G.

Forehand, David to Matilda Robertson   21 Jan. 1841

Forehand, John W. to Martha Jamison   20 Oct. 1847
    Sol. 20 Oct. 1847, James M. White, J.P.

Forgusson, Abel to Sarah Arnold   9 Oct. 1838
    Sol. 9 Oct. 1838, William E. Davis, M.G.

Forsyth, John L. to Mary A. Weaver   3 Feb. 1840
    Sol. 4 Feb. 1840, William Davis, M.G.

Fortune, John to Jane Duncan   12 Jan. 1846
    Sol. 20 Jan. 1846, Adam S. Riggs, M.G.

Foster, Andrew J. B. to Nancy S. Jones   14 Sept. 1852
    Sol. 15 Sept. 1852, S. S. Yarbrough, M.G.

Foster, Benjamin C. to Frances G. Robinson   1 June 1846
    Sol. 1 June 1846, E. Blocker, J.P.

Foster, Bennet T. to Jane H. Meachim   10 Apr. 1839

Foster, Henry to Susan J. Stephenson   20 Nov. 1839
    Sol. 21 Nov. 1839, Robert Hardin, M.G.

Foster, Isaac M. to Christina H. Demonbreun   5 Dec. 1838
    Sol. 6 Dec. 1838, J. F. Campbell, M.G.

Foster, John to Julia A. Boaz   17 Oct. 1842

Foster, John O. to Rebecca E. Eply   27 July 1846
    Sol. 27 July 1846, J. C. Spinks, J.P.

Foster, Jonathan A. to Ann E. Moore   29 June 1847
    Sol. 29 June 1847, Alfred Fleming, J.P.

Foster, Luthur C. to Mary E. Witherspoon   29 Jan. 1851
    Sol. 29 Jan. 1851, E. Hanks, M.B.

Foster, Richard to Polly Mills   14 Apr. 1845
    Sol. 15 Apr. 1845, Parke Street, J.P.

Foster, Richard P. to Martha Campbell   17 Feb. 1845
    Sol. 17 Feb. 1845, W. J. Strayhorn, J.P.

Foster, Richard S. to Sarah A. Fleming   26 Dec. 1848
    Sol. 26 Dec. 1848, W. R. H. Mack, J.P.

Foster, Solomon to Martha Lancaster   28 Oct. 1848
    Sol. 28 Oct. 1848, Ezra Hardison, J.P.

Foster, Sylvanus J. to Sarah A. Love   2 July 1849
    Sol. 3 July 1849, W. H. Baldridge, M.G.

Foster, William H. to Sarah Goad   21 Dec. 1841
    Sol. 22 Dec. 1841, William Harris, M.G.

Foster, Willison to Rebecca E. Harberson   30 Sept. 1841
    Sol. 5 Oct. 1841, W. H. Baldridge

Fox, Austin to Martha J. Petty   27 Nov. 1851
    Sol. 30 Nov. 1851

Fox, Hugh A. to Ann W. Blackman   15 July 1851
    Sol. 17 July 1851, D. G. Moore, M.G.

Fox, John M. to Rachel Fox   1 Nov. 1838
    Sol. 1 Nov. 1838, Ishamel Stevens, J.P.

Fox, Joseph to Frances E. Hight   1 Sept. 1846
    Sol. 19 Sept. 1846, E. Hanks, M.G.

Frank, James S. to Sarah F. Emerson   13 Sept. 1842
    Sol. 15 Sept. 1842, John McKelvey, Methodist Minister

Franklin, P. G. to Martha A. E. Houston   10 Aug. 1846
    Sol. 11 Aug. 1846, P. P. Neeley, M.G.

Frankum, Edward to Elizabeth Barnhead   28 May 1840
    Sol. 28 May 1840, Robert Foster, J.P.

Frankum, William W. to Martha A. Goodman   4 Mar. 1841
    Sol. 4 Mar. 1841, H. A. McMackin, J.P.

Fraser, John A. to Amantha Butts   25 Mar. 1852
    Sol. 25 Mar. 1852, E. Hanks, M. G.

Freeland, James to Mary Morton   19 Nov. 1842
    Sol. 20 Nov. 1842, B. Gresham, J.P.

Freeland, James B. to Harriet E. Cockran   24 Mar. 1841
    Sol. 24 Mar. 1841, N. P. Modrall, M.G.

Freeland, James B. to Martha A. Weatherly   23 Jan. 1849
    Sol. 23 Jan. 1849, Park Street, J.P.

Freeland, Joseph K. to Mary J. Griffin   12 June 1850
    Sol. 13 June 1850, W. B. Gilham, M.G.

Freeland, Newton J. to Elizabeth Weatherly   4 Sept. 1850
    Sol. 4 Sept. 1850, James M. White, J.P.

Freeland, William to Patsy Wright   26 Feb. 1839
    Sol. 28 Mar. 1840, William Davis, M.G.

Freeman, Anderson to Sarah Goder   29 Oct. 1845

Freeman, David S. to Margaret A. Foster   11 July 1850
    Sol. 14 July 1850

Freeman, David S. to Sarah J. Chapman   25 Jan. 1851
    Sol. 26 Jan. 1851

Freeman, Joel W. to Mary J. Wilson   26 Feb. 1848
     Sol. 27 Feb. 1848, L. W. Johnson, J.P.

Freeman, William F. to Nancy T. Hickman   20 June 1849
     Sol. 21 June 1849, James Gibson, M.G.

Frierson, Benjamin R. to Jannette J. Blakely   11 June 1839

Frierson, James H. to Mary Frierson   29 Apr. 1839
     Sol. 29 Apr. 1839, James M. Arnell, Pastor, Zion Church

Frierson, James M. to Martha G. H. Dawson   19 Feb. 1849

Frierson, John D. to Mary J. Craig   13 Feb. 1851
     Sol. 20 Feb. 1851

Frierson, John W. to Ruth M. T. Brank   16 June.1840
     Sol. 16 June 1840, James M. Arnell, Pastor, Zion Church

Frierson, John W. to Alice E. Stephenson   15 Apr. 1852
     Sol. 15 Apr. 1852

Frierson, Madison S. to Mary E. Smith   22 Jan. 1839
     Sol. 24 Jan. 1839, James M. Arnell, Pastor, Zion Church

Frierson, Samuel W. to Eliza M. Gant   22 Dec. 1840
     Sol. 22 Dec. 1840, Joseph Sherman, M.G.

Frierson, Willis R. to Mary A. Goodloe   26 Sept. 1851
     Sol. 29 Sept. 1851, William Mack, M.G.

Furgeson, Arthur to Caroline Scott   27 July 1848
     Sol. 27 July 1848, E. Hanks, M.G.

Furgerson, Jackson to Mary J. Mills   7 Oct. 1843

Furgeson, James J. to Mary J. Furgeson   13 May 1847
     Sol. 13 May 1847, Thomas Kelsey, J.P.

Furgerson, William F. to Lucretia Robinson   25 Apr. 1848
     Sol. 26 Apr. 1848, William J. Strayhorn, J.P.

Fussell, Archibald to Abby Carrigan   25 Sept. 1839
     Sol. 25 Sept. 1839, Parke Street, J.P.

G

Galbraith, Green M. to Mary J. Smith   4 July 1850
     Sol. 4 July 1850, G. C. Stockard, M.G.

Galbreath, John to Blanche Derryberry   27 Dec. 1845
     Sol. 27 Dec. 1845, J. C. Spinks, J.P.

Galbreath, Joseph H. to Jane McGowen   29 Dec. 1840

Gale, James F. to Mary F. Fleming   23 Dec. 1846
     Sol. 23 Dec. 1846, James M. Arnell, Zion Pastor

Galloway, Francis L. to Jane E. Martin   9 Nov. 1847
    Sol. 9 Nov. 1847, J. K. Boyer, M.G.

Galloway, John to Edney S. Cragg   10 Oct. 1839
    Sol. 11 Oct. 1839, E. Hanks, M.G.

Galloway, Moses to Irene Gilbreath   8 Dec. 1838

Galloway, Sherwood to Mariah L. Wood   10 Jan. 1844
    Sol. 11 Jan. 1844, R. G. Irvine, M.G.

Galloway, Uriah to Sarah J. Fitzgerald   4 July 1848
    Sol. 4 July 1848, J. W. Irwin, L.E.M.E.C.

Galloway, William to Amanda M. Johnson   10 Dec. 1845
    Sol. 10 Dec. 1845, P.P.Neely, M.G.

Gambill, William M. C. to Jane E. Tate   29 June 1846
    Sol. 2 July 1846

Gantt, George to Sarah T. Blakely   11 Nov. 1844

Gantt, George to Sarah J. Hammer   12 Mar. 1850
    Sol. 13 Mar. 1850, William Mack M.G.

Gantt, George H. to Martha A. Alderson   28 Aug. 1849
    Sol. 28 Aug. 1849, M. H. Mayes, J.P.

Gantt, James S. to Nancy Forgey   13 Sept. 1843
    Sol. 14 Sept. 1843, C. H. Baldridge, M.G.

Gant, John J. to Martha J. Cocke   3 Jan. 1838
    Sol. 3 Jan. 1838, F. G. Ferguson, M.G.

Gardner, James P. to Nancy E. Folk   2 Jan. 1844
    Sol. 2 Jan. 1844, A. L. P. Green, M.G.

Gardner, John M. to Martha S. Foster   30 Mar. 1843
    Sol. 5 Apr. 1843, Joseph Foster, J.P.

Garner, Renfro to Dolly Roach   16 Dec. 1847

Garner, Renfro to Sarah Y. Byrd   3 Nov. 1852
    Sol. 5 Nov. 1852, Fleming, J.P.

Garratt, Edward to Mary E. Pickens   2 Apr. 1851
    Sol. 3 Apr. 1851, F. A. Burke, J.P.

Garrett, James A. to Sarah Thomas   14 Feb. 1846

Garrett, John J. to Mahala A. Ingram   13 Feb. 1851
    Sol. 13 Feb. 1851, F. A. Burk, J.P.

Garrett, Larkin to Clarymondie Emerson   30 Jan. 1850
    Sol. 30 Jan. 1850, F. A. Burke, J.P.

Garrett, Milton to Mary Tarwater   3 Dec. 1852
    Sol. 4 Dec. 1852, Thomas P. Stone, J.P.

Garrett, Stephen I. to Eliza Baley   30 Dec. 1844
    Sol. 9 Jan. 1845, W. J. Garrett, M.G.

Garrett, Thomas to Mary Ratliff   9 Jan, 1850
    Sol. 9 Jan. 1850, F. A. Burk, J.P.

Garrett, William H. to Louisa Oliver   31 Aug. 1831
    Sol. 2 Sept. 1838, R. F. Denham, J.P.

Garrett, William R. to Manerva Brown   6 Apr. 1848
    Sol. 11 Apr. 1848, Henry H. Fry, M.G.

Garrison, Robert C. to Martha Buchanan   1 Apr. 1839
    Sol. 3 Apr. 1839, Robert Hardin, M.G.

Garten, Philip to Christina S. Hofman   13 Nov. 1849
    Sol. 15 Nov. 1849, A. T. Gray, J.P.

Garton, John to Mary A. Hoge   7 Jan. 1839
    Sol. 8 Jan. 1839, George Gantt, M.G.

Gary, John W. to Eliza J. Graham   24 Nov. 1845
    Sol. 26 Nov. 1845, Robert C. Garrison, M.V.D.

Gaskill, Evans to Sarah E. Cathey   25 Mar. 1840
    Sol. 25 Mar. 1840, Ishmael Stevens, J.P.

Gaskill, Robert J. to Margaret Fox   12 Jan. 1848
    Sol. 13 Jan. 1848, Daniel Judd of M.E. Church

Gates, John W. to Martha L. McNeeley   18 July 1842
    Sol. 18 July 1842, J. C. Spinks, J.P.

Gibson, Henry C. to Mary Ann Johnson   5 July 1845

Gibson, John to Nancy Hubbell   24 Aug. 1841

Gibson, John to Mary Pearse   9 Sept. 1850
    Sol. 9 Sept. 1850, J. F. Holt, J.P.

Gibson, Joseph W. to Louisa J. Dillehay   7 Dec. 1850
    Sol. 19 Dec. 1850, Edward R. Puckett, J.P.

Gibson, Stanford E. to Zilpha J. Grimes   27 Mar. 1849
    Sol. 27 Mar. 1849, Robert D. Rickets, J.P.

Gibson, Thomas to Mary A. F. Clanton   21 July 1841
    Sol. 22 July 1841, R. Stockard, J.P.

Gibson, William to Lucretia Clanton   19 Mar. 1844
    Sol. 19 Mar. 1844, J. Y. Moss

Gidcomb, Thomas C. to Margaret Hood   2 Feb. 1852
    Sol. 2 Feb. 1852, R. Baker, J.P.

Gifford, Franklin to Rebecca Davis   29 Jan. 1846
  Sol. 29 Jan. 1846, Hiram Anthony, J.P.

Gifford, Gideon to Susan Vaughn   23 Oct. 1839
  Sol. 24 Oct. 1839, B. Gresham

Gifford, Robert A. to Albina Brown   2 Apr. 1845
  Sol. 3 Apr. 1845, J. G. Harris, J.P.

Gilbraith, James to Tempe Blalock   7 Jan. 1845
  Sol. 9 Jan. 1845, J. G. Harris, J.P.

Gilbreath, Absalom M. to Emily E. Morrow 27 Nov. 1852
  Sol. 1 Dec. 1852, James Brownlow, M.G.

Gilbreath, John to Elizabeth Stacy   9 Jan. 1850
  Sol. 10 Jan. 1850, Edward R. Puckett, J.P.

Giliam, Stephen M. to Nancy M. Campbell 3 June 1846
  Sol. 25 June 1846, E. Hanks, M.G.

Gill, John to Elizabeth Grimes   4 Nov. 1845
  Sol. 6 Nov. 1845, O. A. Mabrey, M.G.

Gill, William C. D. to Rachel J. Kilcrease 20 Nov. 1850
  Sol. 20 Nov. 1850, William Mack, M.G.

Gillespie, D. C. to R. M. E. Crews   5 Dec. 1842
  Sol. 5 Dec. 1842, G. L. Arnold, M.G.

Gillespie, N. C. to Mary A. H. Dillard 12 Dec. 1842
  Sol. 13 Dec. 1842, G. C. Stockard, M.G.

Gillham, Isaac A. to Hannah S. Foster 22 Dec. 1841

Gillham, James G. to Susan Sanders   24 May 1841
  Sol. 27 May 1841, Samuel Whiteside, J.P.

Gilliam, Edward H. to Cynthia C. Dyer 6 July 1848
  Sol. 6 July 1848, A. Clark, J.P.

Gillum, Charles W. to Rebecca F. Byers 8 Nov. 1851
  Sol. 10 Nov. 1851, Aroma Clark, J.P.

Gilmer, Jeremiah to Henrietta Adkisson 17 Jan. 1849
  Sol. 18 Jan. 1849, G. C. Stockard, M.G.

Gilpin, John to Eliza State   5 Oct. 1850
  Sol. 7 Oct. 1850

Ginger, John B. to Nancy L. London   5 Feb. 1847

Ginger, Nimrod F. to Mary A. London 13 May 1850
  Sol. 14 May 1850

Givens, Andrew J. to Mary A. Law   18 Oct. 1848
    Sol. 19 Oct. 1848, Aroma Clark, J.P.

Givens, William to Ann M. Crafton.   15 Nov. 1838
    Sol. 15 Nov. 1838, William Harris, M.G.

Gleess, William to Mary Douglass   29 Dec. 1851
    Sol. 29 Dec. 1851, J. B. Padgett, J.P.

Glenn, John to Martha J. Lockridge   22 June 1846
    Sol. 25 June 1846, M. B. Molloy, M.G.

Glenn, Robert A. to Margaret J. Hurd   11 July 1843

Goad, Abraham to Mary M. Atkerson   3 Dec. 1851
    Sol. 3 Dec. 1851, J. B. Padgett, J.P.

Goad, James R. to Mary A. Toumbs.   28 July 1849
    Sol. 28 July 1849, W. A. Wilkes, M.G.

Goad, Joel to Louisa A. Bynum   28 July 1849
    Sol. 1 Aug. 1849, Coleman Goad, J.P.

Goad, John C. to Louisa Witham   8 Dec. 1847
    Sol. 8 Dec. 1847, W. F. F. Saurie (?), M.G.

Goad, Lewis to Margaret M. Moore   16 Jan. 1840

Goad, Richard to Mary G. Beckum   10 Oct. 1843
    Sol. 10 Oct. 1843, Aaron Vestal, J.P.

Goad, Robert to Caroline Harris   31 Dec. 1845
    Sol. 31 Dec. 1845, E. Hanks, M.G.

Goad, Robert M. to Sarah E. Godwin   27 Feb. 1851
    Sol. 2 Mar. 1851, B. R. Gant, M.G.

Goad, William to Elizabeth Perry   10 Oct. 1842
    Sol. 10 Oct. 1842, J. Bills, J.P.

Godwin, Aaron S. to Mildred H. S. Lawson   17 Sept. 1846

Godwin, George to Elizabeth C. Moore   25 Jan. 1842
    Sol. 27 Jan. 1842, E. Hanks, M.G.

Godwin, James S. to Letha Bridges   11 Aug. 1842
    Sol. 11 Aug. 1842, William Burn, M.G.

Godwin, John J. S. to Rachel L. B. Church   23 Nov. 1852
    Sol. 25 Nov. 1852, John M. Vestal, M.G.

Goins, Isaac M. to Mary Adkison   29 July 1841
    Sol. James Caughron, J.P.

Goodgion, Alexander W. to Mary Stone   14 Oct. 1839
    Sol. 15 Oct. 1839, Wilie Ledbetter, L.E.M.E.C.

Goodgion, Hezekiah to Rhoda Bernam   28 Mar. 1838

Goodloe, Harvel H. to Mary A. Buckner   24 Nov. 1848
    Sol. 26 Nov. 1848, G. W. Mitchell, M.G.

Goodloe, Henry G. to Mary E. Cecil   25 Oct. 1852
    Sol. 25 Oct. 1852, M. W. Gray, M.G.

Goodman, Haden H. to Susan Dale   28 Aug. 1840

Goodman, Jackson G. to Violet D. Brown   25 Oct. 1851
    Sol. 26 Oct. 1851, William J. Strayhorn, J.P.

Goodwin, George B. to Louisa H. Minter   24 Dec. 1845
    Sol. 25 Dec. 1845, W. H. Wharton

Gordon, James C. to Susan A. Lockridge   20 Nov. 1848

Gordon, John W. to Kesiah H. Williams   25 Dec. 1850
    Sol. 26 Dec. 1850, James Brownlow, M.G.

Gordon, Lee to Nancy Thompson   29 Dec. 1838
    Sol. 2 Jan. 1838, James Calhoon

Gordon, Landon L. to Martha M. Cheek   7 Aug. 1850
    Sol. 8 Aug. 1850, Ezra Hardison, J.P.

Gordon, Neal M. to Martha J. Harris   12 Nov. 1841
    Sol. 18 Nov. 1841, H. Bryson

Gordon, Stanford to Nancy Williams   20 Feb. 1838
    Sol. 21 Feb. 1838, John R. Bond, J.P.

Gordon, William to Frances Lavender   27 Jan. 1847
    Sol. 27 Jan. 1847, John Brown, J.P.

Gosselin, Peter C. to Francis C. Houson   31 May 1838
    Sol. 31 May 1838, H. H. Brown, E.M.E.C.

Graham, Green to Elizabeth McCutcheon   30 May 1838
    Sol. 30 May 1838, H. H. Brown, E.M.E.C.

Graham, Samuel L. to Frances E. Charter   12 Mar. 1846
    Sol. 12 Mar. 1846, William Mack, M.G.

Graham, William to Mary Jane Potete   13 July 1842
    Sol. 13 July 1842, R. H. Timmons, J.P.

Grant, Joseph to Mary C. Mitchell   1 July 1851

Graves, Alexander to Martha H. Fuller   10 Mar. 1847
    Sol. 10 Mar. 1847, Alfred Fleming, J.P.

Graves, Harrison A. to Rachel Bond   18 Jan. 1845
    Sol. 18 Jan. 1845, P. P. Neely, M.G.

Gray, Andrew T. to Mary E. White   17 Dec. 1845
     Sol. 18 Dec. 1845, Thomas Kelsey, J. P.

Gray, James to Nancy Robertson   20 Sept. 1838
     Sol. 20 Sept. 1838, Ishmael Stevens, J.P.

Gray, Pinkney C. to Mary A. Cook   14 Jan, 1852
     Sol. 15 Jan. 1852, D. G. Moore, J. P.

Gray, Sampson D. to Margaret J. Bill   11 Jan. 1843
     Sol. 11 Nov. 1843, George Ninon, J.P.

Gray, Thomas W. to Leanna W. Jackson   19 Oct. 1852
     Sol. 19 Oct. 1852, E. W. Benson, M.G.

Gray, William to Gracy Kearsey   17 Feb. 1840

Green, Barzilla H. to Minerva A. Alford   30 Oct. 1844
     Sol. 31 Oct. 1844, John Mack, J.P.

Green, George to Anna Brawley   3 Feb. 1841
     Sol. 12 Feb. 1841, James W. Matthews, J.P.

Green, John to Frankee Kernel   29 Nov. 1851
     Sol. 30 Nov. 1851

Green, John B. to Sallie N. Walker   7 Jan. 1847
     Sol. 7 Jan. 1847, at James Walker's by James H. Otey, Bishop
                                     ot Tennessee

Green, John M. to Elizabeth Thomason   13 Dec. 1841
     Sol. 14 Dec. 1841, L. A. Nichols

Green, Samuel R. to Eliza Hott   21 Apr. 1841

Green, Sherwood to Nancy B. Harwood   1 July 1844
     Sol. 1 July 1844, G. W. Mitchell, M.G.

Green, W. E. B. to Mary A. E. Jacobs   29 Jan. 1852
     Sol. 29 Jan. 1852, E. Hanks, M.G.

Green, Wiley B. to Catherine Green   2 May 1850
     Sol. 3 May 1850

Green, Wiley B. to Susan Brock   16 Aug. 1851
     Sol. 20 July 1851, John T. Moss, M.G.

Greenpatrick, Samuel to Elizabeth E. Wells   7 Jan. 1851
     Sol. 7 Jan. 1851, F. A. Burke, J.P.

Greer, Thompson to Frances Walker   24 Jan. 1844
     Sol. 25 Jan. 1844, Joseph Foster, J.P.

Gresham, Isaac to Olivia A. Vincent   7 Apr. 1846
     Sol. 17 Apr. 1846, Hiram Anthony, J.P.

Griffin, Nathaniel E. to Rowena E. Jossey   17 Sept. 1850

Griffis, Wiley P. to Julia Stroud   14 Apr. 1846
     Sol. 16 Apr. 1846, Joseph Brown, M.G.

Griffith, Samuel S. to Adna W. Morgan   7 Mar. 1842
     Sol. 9 Mar. 1842, Justice Williams, J.P.

Grigsby, Miles G. to Sarah A. Emerson   18 Jan. 1840
     Sol. 23 Jan. 1840, Philip Ball, M.G.

Grigsby, William to Celina F. Hatcher   11 June 1849

Grimes, Henry A. to Elizabeth Evans   20 Feb. 1838
     Sol. 22 Feb. 1838, Richard Stockard, J.P.

Grimes, Henry M. to Martha J. Guinn   29 Mar. 1838

Grimes, Jesse B. to Arseneth Dullion   20 Mar. 1843

Grimes, John C. to Evelina B. Kenedy   28 Oct. 1846
     Sol. 29 Oct. 1846, J. C. Sparkman, M.G.

Grimes, John L. to Sarah C. Rickets   16 Nov. 1848
     Sol. 16 Nov. 1848, D. A. Mabrey, M.G.

Grimes, Levi C. to Margaret E. Ricketts   22 Dec. 1842
     Sol. 22 Dec. 1842, R. Stockard, J.P.

Grimes, Lewis W. to Harriet E. Blackwood   18 Oct. 1841
     Sol. 20 Oct. 1841, G. W. Mitchell, M.G.

Grimes, Nathan W. to Harriet I. Lindsey   11 Jan. 1845
     Sol. 12 Jan. 1845, J. M. Gordon, J.P.

Grimes, Nathaniel W. to Martha J. Craig   24 Jan. 1852
     Sol. 29 Jan. 1852, Jeremiah F. Holt, J.P.

Grimmett, Hodge to Mary J. Jones   1 Nov. 1849
     Sol. 2 Nov. 1849

Grisham, Wilis H. to Cynthia L. Griffin   22 Sept. 1843
     Sol. 25 Sept. 1843, James M. Richardson

Guest, David to Martha Wilson   2 Aug. 1852

Gullett, Robert J. to Nancy G. Frank   30 Apr. 1840
     Sol. 30 Apr. 1840, Samuel Wheatley, J.P.

Gunn, Henry to Martha J. Brooks   3 Nov. 1841
     Sol. 3 Mar. 1841, William Harris, M.G.

Gunnel, John R. to Martha Sherrod   8 Dec. 1847
     Sol. 8 Dec. 1847, Washington Oakley, J.P.

Gunner, William to Dorothy A. Welch   26 Dec. 1842
    Sol. 26 Dec. 1842

Gunter, John F. to Margaret Wood   15 Aug. 1842
    Sol. 18 Aug. 1842, Thomas Kelsey, J.P.

Gunter, John W. to Permelia E. Ware   11 Jan. 1843
    Sol. 18 Jan. 1843, R. A. Glenn, J.F.

Gustine, Frederick W. to Sallie W. Smith   20 Jan. 1852

Gurst, James L. to Emily I. Hill   18 Dec. 1839
    So. 18 Dec. 1839, B. H. Hubbard, M.G., M.E.Church

H

Hackney, Franklin to Sarah Coffey   9 Jan. 1843

Hackney, Joseph to Margaret Mulherin   4 Apr. 1843
    Sol. 4 Apr. 1843, D. Y. Moss

Haddox, Dr. John to Mary L. Holland   22 Sept. 1849
    Sol. 25 Sept. 1849, Act (?) Cunningham, M.G.

Hadley, Ruffin C. to Mary E. Smith   4 Oct. 1847
    Sol. 13 Oct. 1847, James M. Richardson, J.P.

Hale, Edward C. to Elizabeth London   11 Sept. 1845
    Sol. 14 Sept. 1845, James Brownlow, M.G.

Hale, Samuel to Sarah J. Burnett   5 Dec. 1848
    Sol. 10 Dec. 1848, J. Crafton, J.P.

Hale, Stephen E. to Nancy Jordan   1 Oct. 1841

Hall, Claudius B. to Salina J. Garland   19 Nov. 1845
    Sol. 20 Nov. 1845, Joseph Sherman, M.G.

Hall, Thomas K. to Martha A. Johnson   24 Sept. 1838
    Sol. 6 Oct. 1838, Andrew Scott, J.P.

Haly, William N. to Jane B. Mangrum   3 Feb. 1852
    Sol. 4 Feb. 1852, W. B. Gilham, M.G.

Hambrick, William J. to Matilda Tanner   15 Mar. 1843
    Sol. 16 Mar. 1843, B. Gresham, J.P.

Hamilton, Andrew to Rebecca J. Payton   26 Apr. 1843
    Sol. 26 Apr. 1843, Adam S. Riggs, M.G.

Hamlett, William C. to Missouri A. Thurmond   19 Feb. 1851
    Sol. 20 Feb. 1851, Thomas Hudspeth, M.G.

Hammer, Austin M. to Ann Eliza Anthony   26 Aug. 1847
    Sol. 28 Aug. 1847, F. G. Smith

Hammond, Anderson to Margaret Warren   22 Dec. 1842
     Sol. 22 Dec. 1842, Ishmael Stevens, J.P.

Hammons, Gabriel to Adelaide Shaw   7 Apr. 1842

Hamric, John to Lydia Fleming   28 Sept. 1842
     Sol. 28 Sept. 1842, James M. Richardson, Esquire

Harbison, Alexander to Maria V. Charles   7 Dec. 1844
     Sol. 10 Dec. 1844, C. H. Baldridge, M.G.

Harbison, David F. to Malinda F. Mays   5 Oct. 1847
     Sol. 7 Oct. 1847, B. F. Alexander, M.G.

Harbison, John to Lavina Bunch   21 Sept. 1846
     Sol. 24 Sept. 1846, Benjamin F. Alexander, M.G.

Harbison, Matthew to Caroline Galloway   28 Nov. 1839
     Sol. 28 Nov. 1839, James P. Adkins, J.P.

Harbison, Wesley to Mary D. Godwin   23 Dec. 1839

Hardeman, Thomas to Elizabeth A. Smith   2 Oct. 1845
     Sol. 6 Oct. 1845 in Mt. Pleasant, John S. Watt

Hardin, Martin to Nancy Toumbs   22 Oct. 1845

Hardison, Charles to Martha M. Derryberry   26 Mar. 1838
     Sol. 4 Apr. 1838, Joshua K. Speer, M.G.

Hardison, Ezra to Mary Clark   28 Jan. 1851
     Sol. 28 Jan. 1851, Asa Hardison, M.G.

Hardison, George W. to Elizabeth Melton   10 Feb. 1851
     Sol. 13 Feb. 1851, Asa Hardison

Hardison, George W. to Rebecca J. Dugger   27 Feb. 1851
     Sol. 27 Feb. 1851

Hardison, Hardy to Mary A. Derryberry   2 Mar. 1842
     Sol. 7 Mar. 1842, R. A. Glenn, J.P.

Hardison, James to Catherine S. Galbreath   12 July 1847
     Sol. 15 July 1847, J. C. Spinks, J.P.

Hardison, Lewis W. to Elizabeth A. Turner   23 Apr. 1845
     Sol. 24 Apr. 1845, Joshua K. Speer, M.G.

Hardison, Simon to Mary Dugger   17 Sept. 1851

Hardison, William C. to Emily H. Derryberry   27 Nov. 1848
     Sol. 28 Nov. 1848, Asa Hardison, M.G.

Hardister, Thomas T. to Mary A. Harris   25 Sept. 1844
     Sol. 26 Sept. 1844, John T. Moss

Hardy, Augustus W. to Sarah E. Whitaker   9 Dec. 1846
     Sol. P.F.Neeley

Hardy, G. W. to Poliner I. Whitaker   21 Aug. 1844
     Sol. 22 Aug. 1844, William H. Wilkes, M.G.

Here, Daniel to Priscilla Childress   21 Nov. 1844

Hargis, Abram S. to Ilila Bobo   27 Oct. 1841
     Sol. 27 Oct. 1841, John W. Ray, M.G.

Hargrove, John to Mahaly A. Bates   10 Mar. 1851
     Sol. 10 Mar. 1851, Hugh C. Harrison, J.P.

Hargrove, Levi to Letta Kincaid   14 Mar. 1850
     Sol. 14 Mar. 1850, L. W. Hardison, J.P.

Harlan, Benjamin to Sarah A. Harlan   11 Oct. 1844
     Sol. 14 Oct. 1844, William Mack, M.G.

Harlan, John to Priscilla T. Hunter   3 Dec. 1838

Harmon, Albert A. to Sarah Turner   25 Dec. 1841
     Sol. 27 Dec. 1841, R. H. Simmons, J.P.

Harrington, Philip Whitwell to Cyperessa Harrington   21 Feb. 1842

Harris, Adlai O. to Mary Wormeley   24 Apr. 1838

Harris, Andrew J. to Martha P. Mays   21 Dec. 1846
     Sol. 24 Dec. 1846, Washington Oakley, J.P.

Harris, Barrett to Comfort J. Carter   25 Dec. 1850
     Sol. 25 Dec. 1850, J. B. Padgett, J.P.

Harris, Benjamin R. to Martha W. Lawrence   16 Dec. 1839
     Sol. 18 Dec. 1839, H. H. Brown, E.M.E.C.

Harris, Daniel M. to Minerva White   28 July 1844
     Sol. 29 July 1844, William W. Coleman, J.P.

Harris, Edward to Salina Harris   30 Dec. 1852
     Sol. 30 Dec. 1852, J. H. Gregory, J.P.

Harris, Henry to Jane C. Henderson   22 Nov. 1845
     Sol. 27 Nov. 1845, J. K. Boyce, M.G.

Harris, James G. to Susan A. Hill   4 Dec. 1847
     Sol. 9 Dec. 1847, John McKelvey, M.G.

Harris, James M. to Martha J. Gray   21 Feb. 1852
     Sol. 22 Feb. 1852

Harris, Jeptha to Sophia Wantland   8 Nov. 1845
     Sol. 9 Nov. 1845, G. Hanks, J.P.

Harris, John to Ann Lortch   27 Nov. 1848
    Sol. 27 Nov. 1848, E. Hanks, M.G.

Harris, John B. to Elizabeth E. Sessom   24 Sept. 1838
    Sol. 25 Sept. 1838, S. Whiteside, J.P.

Harris, Jonathan to Diana Shires   18 Jan. 1849
    Sol. 18 Jan. 1849, Asa Hardison

Harris, Matthew to Mahala Langston   27 Sept. 1842
    Sol. 3 Oct. 1842, R. A. Glenn, J.P.

Harris, Nathaniel G. to Elizabeth D. Adkisson   20 Oct. 1840

Harris, Nathan W. to Eliza Alderson   18 Dec. 1849
    Sol. 19 Dec. 1849, J. W. Irwin

Harris, Nathan W. to Polena L. Gray   22 May 1851
    Sol. 22 May 1851, John W. Irvine

Harris, Neil (?) to Julia A. Jordan   18 Sept. 1843

Harris, Thomas A. to Sarah H. Cooper   10 May 1847
    Sol. 12 May 1847, F. P. Neely, M.G.

Harris, Wiley to Alita Butts   2 Aug. 1851
(Returned 19 July 1852 without indorsement. New ones issued
  came day...John B. Padgett, C.C.)

Harris, Wiley to Paladira Butts   19 July 1852
    Sol. 22 July 1852, J. H. Gregory, J.P.

Harrison, A. M. to Elizabeth Loftin   8 July 1844
    Sol. 9 July 1844, Parke Street, J.P.

Harrison, Hugh C. to Eliza Patterson   13 Jan. 1841

Hart, Richard C. H. to Almira Shaw   9 Oct. 1843
    Sol. 10 Oct. 1843, G. W. Mitchell, M.G.

Hart, William to Malinda C. Smith   18 Nov. 1844
    Sol. 19 Nov. 1844, G. C. Stockard, M.G.

Hart, William R. to Martha Akin   21 Sept. 1838

Harwell, James M. to Amanda L. Knott   1 Jan. 1850
    Sol. 2 Jan. 1850, G. C. Stockard, M.G.

Hassell, Arten, to Martha Gardner   18 Dec. 1845
    Sol. 18 Dec. 1845, Washington Oakley, J.P.

Hassell, John to Lavina Folk   31 Mar. 1841
    Sol. 31 Mar. 1841, Berryman Hamlett, J.P.

Hassell, Jordan to Sarah G. O'Neel   5 Feb. 1838
    Sol. 6 Feb. 1838, Berryman Hamlett, J.P.

Hassell, William to Rebecca C. Parke   18 Nov. 1839
    Sol. 21 Nov. 1839, George R. Hoge, M.G.

Hatcher, John R. to Matilda J. Hatcher   15 Jan. 1844
    Sol. 18 Jan. 1844, B. R. Gant, M.G.

Hate, John to Sarah Williams   20 June 1840
    Sol, 20 June 1840, Samuel Wheatley, J.P.

Hatfield, George W. to Ann J. Lawhorn   31 May 1849
    Sol. 31 May 1849, Robert A. Young

Hawkins, Henry to Elizabeth Stephens   19 Aug. 1842
    Sol. J. C. Spinks, J.P.

Hawkins, John C. to Louisa Hudspeth   8 Oct. 1844

Hay, James F. to Martha C. Duncan   14 Oct. 1851
    Sol. 15 Oct. 1851

Haynes, Calvin M. to Mary Ann Briggs   6 Oct. 1847
    Sol. 6 Oct. 1847, George S. Arnold, M.G.

Haynes, Randal M. to Caledonia B. White   20 Aug. 1844
    Sol. 20 Aug. 1844, Finch F. Scruggs, M.G.

Haynes, Tilmon to Jane Waggoner   23 Aug. 1841
    Sol. 24 Aug. 1841, Robert Thompson, J.P.

Hays, Charles R. to Rebecca Walker   26 Jan. 1843
    Sol. 26 Jan. 1843, C. Cook, J.P.

Hays, Samuel D. H. to Tanny N. Smith   20 Mar. 1849
    Sol. 20 Mar. 1849, William R. Sharp, J.P.

Head, John to Elizabeth Pipkins   26 May 1840
    Sol. 2 June 1840, Jonathon S. Hunt, J.P.

Head, William to Martha Pipkin   19 Aug. 1843
    Sol. 20 Aug. 1843, George R. Hoge, M.G.

Hedgepeth, Bious to Mary Waldrum   10 Apr. 1839
    Sol. 10 Apr. 1839, Isaac Moore

Hedgepeth, Bryant to Levisa Warren   12 Feb. 1847
    Sol. 12 Feb. 1847, G. W. Fly, Esquire

Helm, George W. to Eliza L. Horsley   14 Nov. 1849
    Sol. 16 Nov. 1849, John B. Hamilton, E.M.E.C.

Helm, Jerome B. to Jemima A. Turney   12 Oct. 1841
    Sol. 12 Oct. 1841, James M. Arnell

Helmick, John to Ruth A. Adkisson   22 Nov. 1851
    Sol. 23 Nov. 1851, G. W. Mitchell, M.G.

Henderson, Andrew to Susan Quarles   12 July 1838
     Sol. 12 July 1838, Andrew Scott, Acting J.P.

Henderson, Andrew to Martha Scott   13 Aug. 1844
     Sol. 14 Aug. 1844, G. C. Stockard, M.G.

Henderson, Edward N. to Sarah E. Baldridge   31 Oct. 1839
     Sol. 31 Oct. 1839, G. C. Stockard, M.G.

Henderson, James T. to Jane C. Davidson   10 June 1852
     Sol. 11 June 1852, Andrew Scott, J.P.

Henderson, Michael B. to Sarah J. Goodrum   22 June 1847
     Sol. 22 June 1847, G. C. Stockard, M.G.

Henderson, William S. to Sarah A. Davis   21 Aug. 1848
     Sol. 22 Aug. 1848, J. K. Boyce, M.G.

Henderson, Wilson to Matilda Hill   22 Oct. 1840
     Sol. 22 Oct. 1840, William W. Cockran

Henderson, Wilson to Matilda Thompson   20 Aug. 1851
     Sol. 21 Aug. 1851, G. C. Stockard, M.G.

Hendley, George S. H. to Elvria E. Foster   17 Jan. 1838
     Sol. 18 Jan. 1838, R. W. Morris, E.M.F. Church

Henson, Martin to Mildred Watson   26 Jan. 1848

Herndon, Benjamin F. to Caroline M. Yates   23 May 1838
     Sol. H. H. Brown, E.M.E.C.

Herrin, William to Dorcas Kinzer   13 Nov. 1849
     Sol. 15 Nov. 1849, A. T. Gray, J.P.

Hess, John to Martha E. Coffey   13 Oct. 1852
     Sol. 14 Oct. 1852, F. A. Burk, J.P.

Hickman, Andrew J. to Mary Galbreath   6 May 1845
     Sol. 15 May 1845, Andrew Scott, J.P.

Hickman, Edward T. to Mary A. M. Williams   1 Oct. 1849
     Sol. 2 Oct. 1849, Andrew Scott, J.P.

Hickman, James R. to Mary A. Williams   16 Aug. 1849
     Sol. 16 Aug. 1849, Andrew Scott, J.P.

Hickman, Jesse K. to Mary A. Weatherford   21 Sept. 1847
     Sol. 23 Sept. 1847, Andrew Scott, J.P.

Hicks, Milton C. to Charlotte E. Jones   23 Feb. 1849
     Sol. 23 Feb. 1849, Henry Harris, J.P.

Hicks, William to Elizabeth Turner   9 May 1840
     Sol. 10 May 1840, C. Cooke, J.P.

Hight, George C. to Minerva Deal   2 Sept. 1847

Hight, Goodman S. to Sarah A. Rust   15 Dec. 1847

Hight, Oliver to Sarah N. Gaskill   25 May 1848
    Sol. 25 May 1848, Daniel Judd, L.E. of M.E. Church

Hill, Asbey to Mary McRay   5 Dec. 1844
    Sol. 5 Dec. 1844, G. W. Mitchell, M.G.

Hill, Ashley to Maria T. Jennings   3 Nov. 1840
    Sol. 3 Nov. 1840, Thomas Kelsey

Hill, Benjamin F. to Susan M. Ingram   20 Oct. 1847
    Sol. 21 Oct. 1847, Richard I. Miles, Bishop of Nashville

Hill, James W. to Gabrilla Haynes   12 Feb. 1841
    Sol. 15 Feb. 1841, Andrew Scott, J.P.

Hill, James W. to Caroline Barnett   10 Apr. 1846

Hill, James W. to Aley P. Nickins   25 July 1851

Hill, John B. to Mary J. McMurry   30 Jan. 1844
    Sol. 1 Feb. 1844, J. F. Campbell

Hill, John W. to Susanna Rail   11 Nov. 1840
    Sol. by Britain Garner

Hill, Josiah B. to Louisa H. Jennings   11 Nov. 1840
    Sol. 11 Nov. 1840, Hugh Shaw, V.D.M.

Hill, Spencer H. to Mary E. Robarson   1 Jan. 1844
    Sol. 2 Jan. 1844, Joseph Foster, J.P.

Hilliard, A. W. to Margaret E. Odil   3 Jan. 1846
    Sol. 3 Jan. 1846, F. F. Neeley

Hilliard, Beverly G. to Elizabeth O. Stanfield 15 Dec. 1847
    Sol. 15 Dec. 1847, W. D. F. Saurie, M.G.

Hilliard, John to Sarah Pickard   24 Oct. 1840
    Sol. 25 Oct. 1840, Hugh Shaw

Hilton, Edward to Malvina Jane Craig   21 July 1841
    Sol. 21 July 1841, Alfred Fleming, J.P.

Hinson, Green to Sarah Clark   24 May 1838

Hinson, John, of Giles County, to Nancy R. K. W. Stewart
                      20 Feb. 1845

Hobbs, Thomas J. to Jane C. Coffey   30 Oct. 1852
    Sol. 3 Nov. 1852, F. A. Burk, J.P.

Hobbs, William H. to Louisa J. Kerr   10 Feb. 1849
        Sol. 13 Feb. 1849, F. A. Burk, J.P.

Hobson, Jeremiah to Frances Akin   9 Mar. 1841
        Sol. 10 Mar. 1841, Wilie Ledbetter, L.E.M.E.C.

Hofman, E. C. to Mary J. Russell   23 Nov. 1852
        Sol. 23 Nov. 1852, D. G. Moore, M.G.

Holcomb, David G. to Mary F. Simmons   3 Jan. 1846
        Sol. 4 Jan. 1846, C. Cooke, J.P.

Holcomb, Isaac M. to Amanda Truelove   27 Nov. 1847
        Sol. 28 Nov. 1847, L. W. Hardison, J.P.

Holcomb, Pleasant M. to Olivia V. Wilkins   13 Dec. 1851
        Sol. 14 Dec. 1851, Aroma Clark, J.P.

Holcomb, Thomas J. to Elizabeth M. Crawford   3 Apr. 1838
        Sol. Labon Jordan, J.P.

Holden, Eli C. to Nancy Long   24 Mar. 1851
        Sol. 26 Mar. 1851, Mark W. Gray

Holden, Norflet R. to Minerva C. Perry   31 Mar. 1846
        Sol. 2 Apr. 1846, F. F. Neeley, M.G.

Holland, John T. to Elizabeth A. Hanks   22 July 1840
        Sol. 22 July 1840, E. Hanks, M.G.

Holland, Smith W. to Elizabeth J. Smith   11 Sept. 1843
        Sol. 12 Sept. 1843, E. Gresham, J.P.

Holmes, John to Jackey R. Evans   5 Oct. 1846

Holmes, Samuel H. to Mary A. Shaw   7 Feb. 1842
        Sol. 10 Feb. 1842, G. W. Mitchell, M.G.

Holmes, William O. to Mary A. Johnson   8 Feb. 1844
        Sol. 11 Feb. 1844, Ishmael Stevens, J.P.

Holt, Jeremiah F. to Margaret J. Ball   20 Oct. 1845
        Sol. 12 Oct. 1845, George W. Johnston, J.P.

Holt, Jordan C. to Rebecca Foster   10 Jan. 1843
        Sol. 10 Jan. 1843, E. R. Osborne, E.C.C.

Holt, William L. to Lucy A. M. Taylor   19 Sept. 1848
        Sol. 19 Sept. 1848, Jonathan S. Hanks, J.P.

Hommel, Peter to Margaret Bolton   31 Mar. 1851
        Sol. 3 Apr. 1851, E. Hanks, M.G.

Hommel, William to Sarah Batin   3 Aug. 1852
        Sol. 5 Aug. 1852, E. Hanks, M. G.

Hood, David to Permelia Dodson   13 Dec. 1838
    Sol. 13 Dec. 1838, H. H. Brown, E.M.C.

Hood, David K. to Martha J. Kinzer   15 July 1840
    Sol. 19 July 1840, Joseph E. Douglas

Hood, Marcus L. to Parthena Mills   1 Jan. 1839
    Sol. L. Jordan, J.P.

Hood, Spencer S. to Julia A. Stallings   3 Jan. 1838
    Sol. 4 Jan. 1838, George R. Hoge, M.G.

Hord, Reuben to Parthena Vestal   7 Dec. 1844

Horsford, John to Cordelia Usery   9 Nov. 1842

Howell, John O. to Eliza J. McManus   13 Dec. 1844
    Sol. 13 Dec. 1844, G. W. Johnston, J.P.

House, Thomas to Susan Y. Poyner   30 Nov. 1843
    Sol. 30 Nov. 1843, M. Fitzgerald, J.P.

Houser, Augustus H. to Elizabeth Kinzer   21 Feb. 1849
    Sol. 22 Feb. 1849, A. T. Gray, J.P.

Houser, Henry D. to Stena Caysa Hoten   21 Aug. 1839
    Sol. 22 Aug. 1839, Thomas Kelsey, J.P.

Houser, Henry G. to Sarah E. L. Alexander   8 Apr. 1850
    Sol. 18 Apr. 1850, John B. Padgett, J.P.

Houser, Jacob to Priscilla Shaddon   5 Apr. 1838
    Sol. 5 Apr. 1838, Berryman Hamlett, J.P.

Houston, Appolonius to Nancy Bridges   9 Oct. 1844
    Sol. 9 Oct. 1844, E. Blocker, J.P.

Houston, Moses W. to Julia S. Toler   4 Jan. 1838
    Sol. 4 Jan. 1838, F. G. Ferguson, M.G.

Houston, Russel to Grizelda Polk   4 June 1844
    Sol. 4 June 1844, James H. Otey

Howard, Isaac L. to Sarah M. Wheatley   22 Dec. 1848
    Sol. 28 Dec. 1848, Park Street, J.P.

Howard, James to Naomi Nelson   23 Jan. 1844
    Sol. 24 Jan. 1844, James Brownlow, M.G.

Howard, James D. to Elizabeth K. T. McDonald   5 Sept. 1849
    Sol. 6 Sept. 1849, W. H. Baldridge, M.G.

Howard, Spencer L. to Harriet S. McCormack   7 Apr. 1848
    Sol. 9 Apr. 1848, M. B. Molloy, M. G.

Howard, Spincer L. to Saley Shannon   20 Jan. 1851
     Sol. 22 Jan. 1851, W. H. Baldridge, M.G.

Howard, Thomas to Ann L. Howard   3 Feb. 1851
     Sol. 4 Feb. 1851, J. W. Westmoreland, J.P.

Howard, Thomas R. to Margaret Hunter   14 Jan. 1845
     Sol. 14 Jan. 1845, G. C. Stockard, M.G.

Howard, William F. G. to Eleanor Steele   9 Apr. 1840
     Sol. 9 Apr. 1840, A. Smith, M.G.

Howard, William H. to Emily B. Matthews   16 Jan. 1844

Howell, Brinkley J. to Winfrey J. Roberts   12 Dec. 1850
     Sol. 12 Dec. 1850, R. G. Irwin, M.G.

Howell, George W. To Elizabeth R. Davis   25 Mar. 1852
     Sol. 25 Mar. 1852, E. Hanks, M.G.

Howell, Jesse F. to Sarah E. McManus   21 Jan. 1851
     Sol. 22 Jan. 1851, J. F. Holt, J.P.

Hubbard, David to Susan E. Smithers   16 Jan. 1848
     Sol. 16 Jan. 1848, J. O. Church, M.G.

Hubbell, James B. to Tirzah E. Bell   22 Mar. 1842

Hubbell, William B. to Harriet Garrett   13 Mar. 1849
     Sol. 13 Mar. 1849, Andrew Scott, J.P.

Hubble, Napoleon B. to Mary J. Garrett   23 Dec. 1839

Hucksba, Thomas J. to Eliza A. Lathan   16 Aug. 1849
     Sol. 16 Aug. 1849, William Mack, M.G.

Huckaty, A. to Elizabeth Truelove   12 Feb. 1844
     Sol. 12 Feb. 1844, Park Street, J.P.

Huckaby, John F. to Martha M. Williams   18 Dec. 1847
     Sol. 19 Dec. 1847, Parke Street, J.P.

Huckaby, Thomas L. to Eliza C. Blocker   28 July 1847
     Sol. 29 July 1847, Joseph Foster, J.P.

Huckaby, William H. to Martha Kinzer   10 Mar. 1849
     Sol. 11 Mar. 1849, A. T. Gray, J.P.

Hudson, Joseph F. to Cyprissa Harrington   10 June 1843
     Sol. 11 June 1843, C. Y. Hudson, J.P.

Hudspeth, James to Sarah Fage   7 Feb. 1839
     Sol. 7 Feb. 1839, Ishmael Stevens, J.P.

Hudspeth, Richard B. to Margaret Young   31 Aug. 1842
     Sol. 31 Aug. 1842, Joseph Brown, M.G.

Hudspeth, Thomas to Sarena White   31 July 1849
     Sol. 31 July 1849

Hudspeth, William to Elizabeth McKaskill   9 July 1840
     Sol. 9 July 1840, Ishmael Stevens, J.P.

Huey, James H. to Elizabeth P. Moore   23 Mar. 1841

Huey, Thomas to Elizabeth A. Ritchie   13 June 1844
     Sol. 13 June 1844, Hiram Anthony, J.P.

Huggins, Luke to Mary A. Tanner   5 June 1843
     Sol. 6 June 1843, B. Gresham, J.P.

Hughes, J. M. to L. K. Zellner   7 Feb. 1844
     Sol. 8 Feb. 1844, Berryman Hamlett, J.P.

Hughes, John L. to Martha E. Howard   14 Oct. 1850
     Sol. 16 Oct. 1850, Joseph Brown, R.M.G.

Hughes, Nathaniel to Mary Lee   26 Dec. 1842

Hughes, Robert M. to Annie C. Howell   25 Oct. 1848
     Sol. 25 Oct. 1848, E. Hanks, M.G.

Hughes, William H. to Zuluka Kittrell   13 Oct. 1849
     Sol. 14 Oct. 1849, A. G. Kelly, M.G.

Hull, Rowland to Susan Renfro   7 June 1845
     Sol. 8 June 1845, George W. Johnston, J.P.

Humphrey, David to Jane Angland   16 Dec. 1845
     Sol. 17 Dec. 1845, Washington Oakley, J.P.

Humphrey, John to Harriet Cunningham   17 May 1844

Humphreys, Joseph to Amanda Cunningham   30 Dec. 1847

Hunter, J. Henry to Caroline R. Tindall   3 Jan. 1843
     Sol. 5 Jan. 1843, A. L.F.Green, M.G.

Hunter, James M. to Mary A. McConico   17 Dec. 1844
     Sol. 18 Dec. 1844, E. Hanks, M.G.

Hunter, Jacob H. to Mary A. Sedberry   5 June 1851
     Sol. 5 June 1851, E. B. Slater, M.G.

Hunter, John to Sarah Gibson   11 Nov. 1839
     Sol. 12 Nov. 1839, William W. Grimes, M.G.

Hunter, John S. to Margaret E. Johnston   15 June 1841
     Sol. 17 June 1841, G. W. Mitchell, M.G.

Hunter, John S. to Eliza A. Jennings   7 Dec. 1848
    Sol. 8 Dec. 1848, Samuel D. Baldwin, Methodist Minister

Hunter, Thomas J. to Mary M. Reese   15 Jan. 1842
    Sol. 16 Jan. 1842, Joseph H. Wilkes, J.P.

Hunter, William K. to Jennette W. Blakely   20 Dec. 1843

Hussell, Zebulon to Sarah Gardner   15 May 1843
    Sol. 15 May 1843, Washington Oakley, J.P.

Hustin, Paul to Sarah M. Rains   9 Nov. 1843
    Sol. 9 Nov. 1843, George Ninon, J.P.

Hutchcraft, James to Martha Powell   26 June 1840

I

Irvin, James to Ahn Hargrove   17 Nov. 1841
    Sol. 19 Nov. 1841, R. A. Glenn, J.P.

Irvine, James D. to Mary L. Walker   3 Jan. 1839
    Sol. 3 Jan. 1839, H. H. Brown, E.M.C.

Irwin, John W. to Sarena Sellers   4 June 1838
    Sol. 13 June 1838, William W. Coleman, J.P.

Irwin, John W. to Amanda Witherspoon   19 Jan. 1846
    Sol. 21 Jan. 1846, W. H. Baldridge, M.G.

Irwin, William to Delilah A. Gary   23 Nov. 1847

Irwin, William M. to Frances A. Moss   30 Nov. 1852
    Sol. 30 Nov. 1852, M. W. Gray, M.G.

Isbell, James to Elizabeth A. Branch   4 Sept. 1840
    Sol. 8 Sept. 1840, Joseph Sherman, M.G.

J

Jack, Robert D. to Louisa J. McKnight   22 June 1844
    Sol. 23 June 1844, W. H. Baldridge

Jackson, Andrew to Nancy W. Hays   3 Nov. 1840
    Sol. 11 Nov. 1840, Parke Street, J.P.

Jackson, Burwell A. to Caroline A. Hull   6 Jan. 1846
    Sol. 11 Jan. 1846, G. L. Arnold, M.G.

Jackson, David to Sarah J. Kittrell   4 Jan. 1841

Jackson, Joseph F. to Tincy J. Loftin   11 Oct. 1851
    Sol. 12 Oct. 1851, Ephraim Davis, J.P.

Jackson, Joseph T. to Martha E. Bryant   8 Feb. 1847
     Sol. 10 Feb. 1847, John McKelvey, Methodist Minister

Jackson, Richard C. to Sarah E. Daimwood   16 July 1850
     Sol. 16 July 1850, William R. Sharpe, J.P.

Jackson, Robert to Barbary G. Sharp   13 May 1850
     Sol. 16 May 1850

Jaggers, James D. to Mary M. W. Pillow   7 Apr. 1847
     Sol. 7 Apr. 1847, A. T. Gray, J.P.

James, Henry M. to Hannah Nelson   7 Oct. 1846
     Sol. 8 Oct. 1846, James Brownlov, M.G.

Jameson, Hosea to Jane Witt   18 Jan. 1841
     Sol. 19 Jan. 1841, William Davis, M.G.

Jameson, William A. to Mary E. Kirby   19 Dec. 1849
     Sol. 19 Dec. 1849, E. Hanks, M.G.

Jamison, John T. to Mary A. Green   26 Nov. 1849
     Sol. 29 Nov. 1849, E. Hanks, M.G.

Jarrett, John N. to Mary C. Fly   1 Jan. 1852
     Sol. 1 Jan. 1852

Jarrett, Obadiah A. to Maria A. Fleming   24 Dec. 1852

Jennings, James W. to Jane Nelson   21 Sept. 1852
     Sol. 21 Sept. 1852, G. W. Mitchell, M.G.

Jennings, Robert H. to Amanda J. Stockard   22 Aug. 1844
     Sol. 22 Aug. 1844, G. W. Mitchell, M.G.

Job, William to Margaret Jane Rankin   2 May 1846

Job, William to Margaret J. Rankin   14 Nov. 1846
     Sol. 15 Nov. 1846, Parke Street, J.P.

Johnson, Abner to Martha L. Chamberline   2 Apr. 1845

Johnson, Aidorn to Sarah Riggins   23 Sept. 1841

Johnson, Brittain G. to Rachel S. Oakley   9 Jan. 1843

Johnson, Cader to Nancy McCormick   30 Nov. 1850
     Sol. 1 Dec. 1850

Johnson, Chapman to Frances E. Dodson   19 Dec. 1842
     Sol. 21 Dec. 1842, E. Hanks, M.G.

Johnson, Edward C. to Mary Jettun   14 Nov. 1842
     Sol. 15 Nov. 1842, F. Zollicoffer, J.P.

Johnson, H. A. to Frances J. Tidwell   12 Nov. 1847
    Sol. 14 Nov. 1847

Johnson, Harvey to Winnifred Slayden   18 Nov. 1848
    Sol. 22 Nov. 1848, B. D. Wall, J.P.

Johnson, Henry to Nancy Reives   24 Dec. 1845
    Sol. 24 Dec. 1845, D. Judd, L.E.

Johnson, Henry T. to Martha A. Payton   9 Mar. 1844
    Sol. 10 Mar. 1844, Andrew Scott, J.P.

Johnson, John to Eleanor Kittrell   6 Oct. 1838

Johnson, John to Sarah Huff   10 Dec. 1838
    Sol. 11 Dec. 1838, W. L. Williams, J.P.

Johnson, John to Sophia Cunningham   12 Feb. 1839
    Sol. 12 Feb. 1839, Thomas Kelsey, J.P.

Johnson, John to Mary Beaver   18 Jan. 1843
    Sol. 18 Jan. 1843, Andrew T. Gray, J.P.

Johnson, John to Elizabeth Watson   22 Oct. 1845
    Sol. 23 Oct. 1845, J. C. Griffith, J.P.

Johnson, John J. to Sarah J. Harris   20 Dec. 1851
    Sol. 23 Dec. 1851

Johnson, Joseph A. to Witmuth H. Malone   10 Nov. 1847
    Sol. 11 Nov. 1847, Joseph Brown, M.G.

Johnson, L. J. to Louisa Slayden   24 Oct. 1845

Johnson, Lucius F. to Malessa A. Hubble   5 June 1851
    Sol. 5 June 1851, F. T. Moss, M.G.

Johnson, Marshall to Catherine Holcum   26 June 1852
    Sol. 27 June 1852, R. A. Glenn, J.P.

Johnson, Moore to Malinda Gray   28 Nov. 1839
    Sol. 28 Nov. 1839, Robert Hill, J.P.

Johnson, Mordecai to Mary C. Willis   3 Feb. 1849
    Sol. 4 Feb. 1849

Johnson, Moses to Mary Fielder   29 May 1838
    Sol. 29 May 1838, W. W. Coleman, J.P.

Johnson, Richard to Frances N. Amis   18 Apr. 1848

Johnson, Stanmore to Cornelia J. Long   5 Oct. 1846
    Sol. 5 Oct. 1846, Aliois Williams, J.P.

Johnson, Thomas to Mary M. Murphey   4 Jan. 1842
    Sol. 11 Jan. 1842, E. R. Osborne, E.C.C.

Johnson, Thomas B. to Cynthia P. Johnson   13 July 1850
     Sol. 14 July 1850

Johnson, William to Mary Johnson   11 May 1839
     Sol. 12 May 1839, Samuel Wheatley, J.P.

Johnson, William to Betsy King   25 May 1839
     Sol. 25 May 1839, Thomas Kelsey, J.P.

Johnston, Charles L. to Nancy R. McCafferty   22 Dec. 1849
     Sol. 23 Dec. 1849, Jeremiah F. Holt, J.P.

Johnston, David W. to Mary Gibson   20 Nov. 1844
     Sol. 21 Nov. 1844, J. N. Gordon, J.P.

Johnston, George W. to Nancy W. Andrews   21 Apr. 1846
     Sol. 23 Apr. 1846, James Brownlow, M.G.

Johnston, James to Sarah J. Ruddle   13 Feb. 1843
     Sol. 14 Feb. 1843, J. Hunter, M.G.

Johnston, John to Caroline Gooding   1 Sept. 1842
     Sol. 1 Sept. 1842, Thomas Randle, M.G.

Johnston, John C. to Martha A. V. Knott   10 Feb. 1841
     Sol. 11 Feb. 1841, G. W. Mitchell, M.G.

Johnston, Martin H. to Gracy M. Turnbo   13 Sept. 1842
     Sol. 14 Sept. 1842, J. O. Griffith, J.P.

Johnston, Samuel O. to Malinda G. Oakley   30 Aug. 1844
     Sol. 5 Sept. 1844, G. W. Fly, J.P.

Johnston, Thomas F. to Eliza M. Parr   31 Aug. 1842
     Sol. 1 Sept. 1842, William H. Crafford, M.G.

Johnston, William to Martha Maxwell   30 June 1840
     Sol. 30 June 1840, S. Whiteside, J.P.

Johnston, William to Adeline Stewart   11 Dec. 1844
     Sol. 11 Dec. 1844, Hugh C. Harrison, J.P.

Johnston, Dr. William R. to Martha A. E. Franklin   25 Oct. 1852
     Sol. 26 Oct. 1852, E. C. Slater, M.G.

Joice, Robert C. to Nancy C. Walker   14 Dec. 1842
     Sol. 14 Dec. 1842, J. C. Spinks, J.P.

Jones, Daniel to Flora Armstrong   23 Feb. 1838

Jones, David C. to Nancy S. Pickard   3 Nov. 1838
     Sol. 15 Nov. 1838, James Calhoon

Jones, George W. to Martha L. Tanner   9 Aug. 1851
     Sol. 9 Aug. 1851, J. W. Westmoreland, J.P.

Jones, James to America A. Dodson   26 Nov. 1847
      Sol. 26 Nov. 1847, Benjamin F. Alexander, M.G.

Jones, James J. to Martha A. Williams   22 Apr. 1843
      Sol. 23 Apr. 1843, Powhatan Gordon, J.P.

Jones, James P. to Mary A. Roberts   9 Aug. 1849
      Sol. 9 Aug. 1849, J. F. Holt, J.P.

Jones, James P. to Rebecca E. Jones   20 Jan. 1851
      Sol. 21 Jan. 1851, J. F. Holt, J.P.

Jones, Jesse to Sarah A. Moore   27 Feb. 1845
      Sol. 27 Feb. 1845, Hiram Anthony, J.P.

Jones, Jonathan to Mary Harmon   4 Oct. 1838
      Sol. 4 Oct. 1838, John B. Bond, J.P.

Jones, John J. to Samella Atkinson   31 Mar. 1851
      Sol. 1 Apr. 1851, J. O. Church

Jones, John N. B. to Mary Ann A. Stephens   26 Apr. 1845
      Sol. 28 Apr. 1845, Isaac N. Bills, J.P.

Jones, Nathaniel W. to Ann M. Cooper   27 Apr. 1840
      Sol. 27 Apr. 1840, Joseph McMurry, J.P.

Jones, Robert B. to Mary J. Sessoms   23 Feb. 1842

Jones, Samuel H. to Sarah Jane Bingham   9 Dec. 1845
      Sol. 11 Dec. 1845, Andrew T. Gray, J.P.

Jones, Seburn to Sarah Stephens   14 Jan. 1841
      Sol. 14 Jan. 1841, Isaac N. Bills, J.P.

Jones, Wilie to Sarah J. Dodson   18 Dec. 1839
      Sol. 19 Dec. 1839, E. Hanks, M.G.

Jones, William I. (or J.) to Harriet J. Miller   10 Dec. 1844
      Sol. 11 Dec. 1844, Henry Miller, M.G.

Jones, William J. to Nancy Hanks   2 Dec. 1841
      Sol. 4 Dec. 1841, William Harris, M.G.

Jones, William K. to Mary E. Harlan   18 June 1850
      Sol. 18 June 1850, J. B. Hamilton, Methodist Minister

Jordan, Benjamin B. to Rachel McCrory   23 Dec. 1847
      Sol. 23 Dec. 1847, Thomas Kelsey, J.P.

Jordan, Edward J. to Martha A. Jennings   31 Jan. 1844
      Sol. 31 Jan. 1844, A. T. Gray, J.P.

Jordan, Edward to Mary A. Cockrell   17 Dec. 1845
      Sol. 17 Dec. 1845, F. P. Neely, M.G.

Jordan, James B. to Ann Wood   29 May 1852
     Sol. 30 May 1852, E. C. Slater, M.G.

Jordan, James F. to Permelia F. Lickey   16 Feb. 1842
     Sol. 17 Feb. 1842, Thomas Kelsey, J.P.

Jordan, John A. to Elizabeth Biggers   24 June 1851
     Sol. 26 June 1851, James M. White, J.P.

Jordan, Stephen to Christiana A. Foster   15 Aug. 1845
     Sol. 20 Aug. 1845, W. H. Baldridge, M.G.

Journey, Edmund to Phebe Foster   24 June 1846
     Sol. 25 June 1846, E. Hanks, M.G.

Journey, Flavius J. to Eliza A. Foster   11 Feb. 1852
     Sol. 11 Feb. 1852, D. G. Moore, M.G.

Journey, Thomas to Louisa J. Taylor   23 Dec. 1845
     Sol. 24 Dec. 1845, E. Hanks, M.G.

Joyce, John H. to Eliza G. Joyce   12 Dec. 1844
     Sol. 18 Dec. 1844, G. W. Mitchell, M.G.

Judd, Nelson P. to Martha A. Pittillo   17 May 1849
     Sol. 17 May 1849, M. B. Molloy, M.G.

Julian, Thomas F. to Mary Walker   8 Mar. 1839
     Sol. 8 Mar. 1839, James C. Adkins, J.P.

K

Kannon, William B. to Frances J. Hughes   10 Dec. 1851
     Sol. 11 Dec. 1851, Robert B. Wear, M.G.

Kearney, William B. to Jane Smith   7 Oct. 1841
     Sol. 10 Oct. 1841, John Hunter, M.G.

Keel, David to Patsy Smith   20 Sept. 1838
     Sol. 20 Sept. 1838, James Adkins, J.P.

Kellam, Thomas J. to Nancy J. Cathcart   4 Feb. 1839
     Sol. 5 Feb. 1839, A. Smith, M.G.

Kelsey, Samuel L. to Ophelia J. Butler   15 Jan. 1846
     Sol. 15 Jan. 1846, A. T. Gray, J.P.

Kelsey, Thomas to Sarah Butler   20 Dec. 1842
     Sol. 20 Dec. 1842, A. T. Gray, J.P.

Kennedy, Andrew to Martha S. Reaves   16 Dec. 1839
     Sol. 17 Dec. 1839, Robert Hardin, M.G.

Kennedy, John M. to Elizabeth Tom   14 June 1838
     Sol. 14 June 1838, B. D. Neal

Kennemore, Grant A. to Emily London   26 Aug. 1844

Kercheval, Vance G. to Ann L. Thompson   18 Feb. 1847
    Sol. P. P. Neely

Kerr, Andrew to Lavina Nelson   3 Mar. 1841
    Sol. 3 Mar. 1841, J. B. Walker, M.G., M.E.Church

Kerr, John B. to Priscilla A. Warden   9 Dec. 1843
    Sol. 12 Dec. 1843, Hiram Anthony, J.P.

Kerr, Thomas B. to Mary A. Warden   9 Dec. 1839
    Sol. Wade Barrett, Elder, C. Ch.

Kerr, William H. to Arkansas Leonard   3 Dec. 1847
    Sol. 5 Dec. 1847, James G. Harris, J.P.

Kerr, William N. to Emaline Campbell   24 Feb. 1843
    Sol. 28 Feb. 1843, Wade Barrett, Eld. C. C.

Kersey, Claiborn to Mary Whitted   8 June 1846
    Sol. 9 June 1846, Henry A. Miller, J.P.

Killingsworth, John W. to Margaret J. Fitzpatrick   25 Aug. 1849
    Sol. 30 Aug. 1849, F. A. Burke, J.P.

Kilpatrick, James M. to Harriet Smith   17 Mar. 1843

Kilpatrick, Thomas J. to Sarah G. Dickey   18 July 1839
    Sol. 18 July 1839, Thomas Fielding Scott, V.D.M.

Kincaid, Calvin to Martha Chumbly   17 Apr. 1852
    Sol. 18 Apr. 1852, John Glenn, J.P.

King, Carver D. to Lucy A. Voorhies   29 June 1842
    Sol. 30 June 1842, C. P. Wing, M.G.

King, Eli to Amanda Buckner   25 July 1851
    Sol. 27 July 1851, G. W. Mitchell, M.G.

King, Levi to Manerva W. Jennings   13 Aug. 1850
    Sol. 13 Aug. 1850, W. H. Baldridge, M.G.

King, Richard M. to Elizabeth Campbell   13 May 1846
    Sol. 14 May 1846, Philip P. Neely, M.G.

King, William H. to Tabitha Bostwick   16 Dec. 1851
    Sol. 16 Dec. 1851, John B. Hamilton, Methodist Elder

Kingston, Samuel W. to Emma White   23 Nov. 1852
    Sol. 21 Nov. 1852, R. G. Irwin, M.G.

Kinnard, David M. to Ophelia E. H. Polk   6 Sept. 1847
    Sol. 9 Sept. 1847, W. H. Baldridge, M.G.

Kinzer, John W. to Elizabeth Lusk   11 Jan. 1842

Kinzer, John W. to Martha P. Witherspoon   28 July 1846

Kirby, W. G. to Mary A. Hill   13 Feb. 1844
    Sol. 14 Feb. 1844, W. H. Baldridge, M.G.

Kirkman, Alfred L. to Edna Hammons   10 Apr. 1845

Kirkpatrick, W. C. to Mary Warfield   5 Sept. 1846
    Sol. 6 Sept. 1846, William Nix, M.G.

Kittrell, John P. to Cassander H. Briggs   15 Sept. 1847
    Sol. 17 Sept. 1847, George S. Arnold, M.G.

Klyce, James H. to Mary C. Pickard   15 Feb. 1851
    Sol. 16 Feb. 1851, Sam Dickson, J.P.

Knight, George W. to Pelina M. Taylor   17 Oct. 1840
    Sol. 22 Oct. 1840, Jonathon S. Hunt, J.P.

Kuhn, Edward to Eliza A. Wilson   10 Feb. 1846
    Sol. 12 Feb. 1846, William Mack, M.G.

Kuhn, Thomas W. to Eloira N. Nelson   1 Nov. 1842
    Sol. 1 Nov. 1842, Thomas W. Randle, M.G.

L

Ladd, Noble E. to Virginia Oliphant   27 Jan. 1846
    Sol. 27 Jan. 1846, W. H. Baldridge, M.G.

Lamaster, William H. to Mary A. Hill   6 Jan. 1848
    Sol. 6 Jan. 1848, James G. Harris, J.P.

Lamb, Drury to Elizabeth P. Rustin   6 July 1852
    Sol. 6 July 1852, B. R. Gant, M.G.

Lamb, Wilie R. to Mary C. Blocker   3 Apr. 1839

Lambert, John to Evaline Payton   19 Feb. 1848

Lancaster, Charles A. to Margaret Galloway   25 Nov. 1841
    Sol. 25 Nov. 1841, Alfred Fleming, J.P.

Lancaster, Elisha to Melinda Henderson   16 Nov. 1843
    Sol. 16 Nov. 1843, Isaac N. Bills, J.P.

Lancaster, Washington W. to Adaline Vaughan.   19 Dec. 1844
    Sol. 20 Dec. 1844, W. J. Gant, M.

LANE or LOVE note: In the old records Lane and Love appear to be
identical and it was very difficult to separate them. We suggest
that researchers for those two names look at listings for both Lane
and Love.

Lane--see note on preceding page

Lane, James C. to Sarah J. Hottshoser   25 Sept. 1838
    Sol. 27 Sept. 1838, Robert Foster, J.P.

Lane, James W. to Phebe E. Barfield   10 Jan. 1844
    Sol. 11 Jan. 1844, J.P. Campbell

Lane, Joel to Susannah H. Carter   5 Apr. 1847
    Sol. 14 Apr. 1847, R. W. Meacham

Lane, John to Mary Cates   13 April 1840

Lane, Samuel C. to Mary E. Lemaster   3 May 1847
    Sol. 6 May 1847, Rev. G. K. Perkins

Langham, Thomas to Emma Goodson   19 Oct. 1847
    Sol. 19 Oct. 1847, A. R. Dickson, Eld. Meth.Ch.

Langley, William to Eliza Bryson   20 Nov. 1838
    Sol. 20 Nov. 1838, H. H. Brown, E.M.E.C.

Langly, John to Sarah C. Montgomery   4 Apr. 1850
    Sol. 5 Apr. 1850, James Calhoun

Lanier, Hardin to Hannah Wilson   28 July 1841
    Sol. 28 July 1841, Andrew Scott, J.P.

Lanier, Lewis F. to Margaret A. Alderson   5 July 1849
    Sol. 5 July 1849, in the presence of near 400 persons at
    residence of James R. Shelton by John B. Hamilton, Traveling
    Elder, M.E.C.

Lanier, Robert P. to Louisa J. Dillard   5 Nov. 1850
    Sol. 6 Nov. 1850, G. C. Stockard, M.G.

Lasley, John H. to Elizabeth Thompson   6 Oct. 1840
    Sol. 7 Oct. 1840, G. W. Mitchell, M.G.

Latta, John to Lucretia Slayden   19 May 1842
    Sol. 20 May 1842, E. Hanks, M.G.

Latta, John to Angeline E. Gant (or James)   15 Dec. 1847

Latty, Calvin to Minta Mitchell   26 May 1842
    Sol. 26 May 1842, Berryman Hamlett, J.P.

Lattimer, Robert S. to Malinda C. Malone   12 Oct. 1840

Lattin, John Y. to Margaret H. Tilman   13 Apr. 1843
    Sol. 13 Apr. 1843, Adam J. Riggs, M.G.

Lauhorn, William to Ellen Stockard   30 May 1843
    Sol. 1 June 1843, G. W. Mitchell, M.G.

Lavender, Charles to Adaminter Cruse   6 Dec. 1838
    Sol. 6 Dec. 1838, H. H. Brown, E. M. C.

Lavender, John S. to Nancy Carter   3 Aug. 1842

Lavender, Nicholas to Mary Potts   30 Mar. 1852
    Sol. 30 Mar. 1852, R. Baker, J.P.

Law, Burrel C. to Mary A. Jones   15 Apr. 1841
    Sol. 15 Apr. 1841, Benony Grisham, J.P.

Law, Stephen W. to Mary A. Dyer   12 Jan. 1842
    Sol. 8 Jan. 1842, Alfred Fleming, J.P.

Lawson, Alphonis L. to Hester J. McBride   23 July 1845
    Sol. 26 July 1845, A. T. Gray, J.P.

Lee (or Fu), Stephen to Roda Langham   11 July 1850
    Sol. 11 July 1850, J. B. Hamilton

Leeper, William H. to Mary L. S. Davidson   1 Apr. 1852
    Sol. 8 Apr. 1852

Leetch, Robert G. to Sarah H. Tillow   4 Jan. 1847
    Sol. 6 Jan. 1847, A. H. Hanah, J.P.

Leftwich, G. G. to Annie E. MacKey   29 Aug. 1848

Leftwich, John W. to Martha Gantt   26 Sept. 1850
    Sol. 26 Sept. 1850, J. B. Hamilton, Meth. Eld.

Leigh, James to Mary P. Sellers   5 Jan. 1852
    Sol. 8 Jan. 1852, E. Hanks, M.G.

Lester, Benjamin L. to Elizabeth P. Martin   9 May 1839
    Sol. 9 May 1839, Allen Richardson

Lester, James C. to Minerva Laird   23 Nov. 1839
    Sol. 23 Nov. 1839, Joseph Herndon, J.P.

Lester, Thomas M. to Elizabeth P. Pate   11 May 1839
    Sol. 11 May 1839, E. Hanks, M.G.

Lester, William R. to Ruth Arnold   3 Jan. 1846
    Sol. Hiram Anthony, J.P.

Lewallen, Joseph to Elizabeth P. Dew   3 Dec. 1849
    Sol. 3 Dec. 1849, J. F. Jordan, J.P.

Liggitt, John C. to Sarah E. Hardison   22 Dec. 1852
    Sol. 23 Dec. 1852, Charles Hardison, J.P.

Liles, Manus W. to Nancy Hines   11 Jan. 1844
    Sol. 11 Jan. 1844, George Ninon, J.P.

Lincoln, Anthony to Jane Roberts   9 Jan. 1845
      Sol. 9 Jan. 1845, William Mack, M.G.

Lindsey, Caleb, to Littice McManus   19 Jan. 1842
      Sol. 20 Jan. 1842, L. A. Nichols

Lindsey, David to Eliza Steward   7 Oct. 1840
      Sol. 8 Oct. 1840, R. Stockard, J.P.

Lindsey, Jackson to Catherine McManus   28 Jan. 1850
      Sol. 28 Jan. 1850

Linom, William J. to Martha J. Strayhorn 3 Sept. 1849
      Sol. 5 Sept. 1849, S. C. Dickson, M.G.

Lipscomb, George to Mary C. Erwin   18 June 1838
      Sol. 21 June 1838, Wilie Ledbetter, L.E.M.E.C.

Little, Joseph M. to Rebecca J. Turbeville 15 Aug. 1852
      Sol. 18 Aug. 1852, E. C. Slater, M.G.

Little, Josiah M. to Mary A. Turbaville   7 Nov. 1848
      Sol. 7 Nov. 1848, William Mack, M.G.

Littlefield, John to Elizabeth J. Kercheval 13 Dec. 1843
      Sol. 14 Dec. 1843, Joseph Sherman, M.G.

Litton, Wesley to Permelia A. Baker   26 July 1849
      Sol. 26 July 1849, John P. Oliphant, J.P.

Lockhart, William M. to Malinda McKnight 1 Oct. 1844
      Sol. 6 Oct. 1844, Ishmael Stevens, J.P.

Lockridge, C. H. to Mary A. E. Foster   14 June 1844
      Sol. 14 June 1844, John P. Campbell, M.G.

Lockridge, Wesley D. to Olivia P. Lane   13 Apr. 1852
      Sol. 15 Apr. 1852, M. B. Molloy, M.G.

Loftin, John to Eliza Hays   13 Aug. 1846
      Sol. 13 Aug. 1846, Samuel Wheatley, J.P.

Loftin, Shadrack to Sarah Freeland   4 Feb. 1845
      Sol. 5 Feb. 1845, Samuel Wheatley, J.P.

Loftin, Thomas to Mary Loftin   3 June 1847
      Sol. 3 June 1847, Samuel Wheatley, J.P.

Logan, James W. to Margaret C. Vanhook   7 Feb. 1843
      Sol. 7 Feb. 1843, James M. Arnell, Zion Pastor

Lomax, Obadiah to Sarah J. Aydlott   6 Oct. 1849
      Sol. 7 Oct. 1849

Lomax, Obadiah A. to Manerva Murphy   7 Sept. 1850
     Sol. 8 Sept. 1850, F. A. Burke, J.P.

Lomax, Robert W. to Edna B. Aydelotte   7 Mar. 1850
     Sol. 7 Mar. 1850, F. A. Burke, J.P.

Long, Lemuel to Zocky M. Martin   24 Oct. 1842
     Sol. 24 Oct. 1842, Jones Daley, J.P.

Long, Willis E. to Elizabeth Dansen (or Dawson)   15 Nov. 1852

Looney, Abraham M. to Susan K. Todd   26 Nov. 1844
     Sol. 27 Nov. 1844, Joseph Sherman

Looney, Benjamin F. to Rachel C. Knott   16 Jan. 1850
     Sol. 29 Jan. 1850, J. W. Westmoreland, J.P.

Looney, Robert F. to Louisa M. Crafford   2 Nov. 1847
     Sol. 2 Nov. 1847, Philip P. Neely, M.G.

Louder, Elisha E. to Emily Fitzgerald   13 Nov. 1844
     Sol. 14 Nov. 1844, Powhatan Gordon, J.P.

Louder, William I. F. to Saphronia Hawkins   17 July 1844
     Sol. 18 July 1844, Powhatan Gordon, J.P.

Lourence, Thomas to Sarah Watson   9 Oct. 1847
     Sol. 10 Oct. 1847, A. T. Gray, J.P.

Love--see Lane also. Also see note on page 67

Love, Thomas K. to Jane Love   26 Nov. 1838
     Sol. 27 Nov. 1838, Richard Anderson, J.P.

Love, W. D. to E. A. Byrum   5 Feb. 1844
     Sol. 7 Jan. 1844, G. Cathey, J.P.

Lovel, William to Margaret P. Fitzgerald   26 Oct. 1844
     Sol. 26 Oct. 1844, Park Street, J.P.

Lovett, John to Mary E. Burpo   18 Dec. 1838

Lovett, Thomas D. to Mary P. Hardison   11 July 1843
     Sol. 11 July 1843, Joshua K. Speer, M.G.

Lowder, Edward C. to Sarah E. Blackburn   12 July 1848
     Sol. 13 July 1848, John D. Oliphant, J.P.

Lowrance, Josiah N. to Jane E. Baldridge   5 June 1849
     Sol. 17 June 1849, G. C. Stockard, M.G.

Lowry, George W. to Rebecca Hart   31 Mar. 1841
     Sol. 31 Mar. 1841, L. A. Nichols

Lowsey, Giles to Eliza Stamps   24 Nov. 1849
     Sol. 28 Nov. 1849, J. Crafton, J.P.

Luckett, George W. to Mary L. Wilkes   8 Apr. 1850
     Sol. 8 Apr. 1850, A. T. Gray, J.P.

Luckett, John to Martha Rainey   2 Apr. 1850
     Sol. 2 Apr. 1850, James F. Jordan, J.P.

Luckett, Samuel to Lucinda Lawrence   10 Jan. 1849
     Sol. 11 Jan. 1849, A. T. Gray, J.P.

Lumpkins, Jackson to Mary Shelby   9 Mar. 1839
     Sol. 14 Mar. 1839, William W. Coleman, J.P.

Lumsden, George T. to Elizabeth C. Derryberry 22 Jan. 1848
     Sol. 25 Jan. 1848, James G. Harris, J.P.

Lunn, Peter to Zibbi Lunn   19 Dec. 1846

Lunn, William to Martha A. Thompson   7 July 1845
     Sol. 7 July 1845, Samuel W. Akin, J.P.

Lusk, William I. to Hannah Kinzer   26 Dec. 1846
     Sol. 31 Dec. 1846, D. K. Hood, J.P.

Lynn, James W. to Sarah H. Kerr   20 Oct. 1840
     Sol. 21 Oct. 1840, G. C. Stockard, M.G.

M

Maberry, Joseph I. to Nancy Ricketts   3 Nov. 1841
     Sol. 4 Nov. 1841, R. Stockard, J.P.

Mabrey, Willis to Eliza Carroll   26 Nov. 1845
     Sol. 28 Nov. 1845, Henry A. Miller, J.P.

Mack, James W. to Eliza Ann Smith   13 Sept. 1849
     Sol. 13 Sept. 1849, G. C. Stockard, M.G.

Mack, John W. D. La Fletcher to Sarah N. Murphey 1 May 1843
     Sol. 2 May 1843, F. S. Ferry, M. G.

Mack, J. W. D. T. F. to Mary J. Murphy   12 Sept. 1850
     Sol. 12 Sept. 1850, G. C. Stockard, M. G.

Mack, William R. H. to Margaret A. Campbell 19 Sept. 1838
     Sol. 19 Sept. 1838, C. B. Porter, M. G.

Madden, Count A. to Sarah J. Johnson   28 Jan. 1843
     Sol. 29 Jan. 1843, Park Street, J.P.

Madden, Count A. to Emaline Daimwood   26 Mar. 1845
     Sol. 27 Mar. 1845, Park Street, J.P.

Madden, Gardiner to Elizabeth Renfro   3 Nov. 1852
     Sol. E. Davis, J.P.

Maddox, George W. to Mary J. Moore   1 May 1852
     Sol. 2 May 1852

Maddux, William W. to Lucy A. Byrd   6 Apr. 1850
     Sol. 10 Apr. 1850

Magers, Samuel to Matilda Bynum   2 Nov. 1839
     Sol. 7 Nov. 1839, Joseph McMurry, J.P.

Malloy, Milton B. to Matilda J. Hill   19 Nov. 1839
     Sol. 21 Nov. 1839, W. H. Baldridge

Malone, Newton J. to Juliet E. Kercheval   30 Mar. 1841
     Sol. 31 Mar. 1841, H. Shaw

Malugen, George W. to Margaret E. Malugen   22 Feb. 1849
     Sol. 23 Feb. 1849, R. Baker, J.P.

Mangrum, George W. C. to Margaret E. Jameson   20 Dec. 1849
     Sol. 20 Dec. 1849, E. Hanks, M.G.

Mangrum, James to Mariah Caruthers   2 March 1848
     Sol. 5 March 1848, Hugh C. Harrison, J.P.

Mangrum, John J. to Aurilla A. Rountree   11 Dec. 1839
     Sol. 11 Dec. 1839, E. Hanks, M.G.

Mangrum, William D. to Ruth L. Hilliard   4 Aug. 1842
     Sol. 4 Aug. 1842, Thomas W. Randle, M.G.

Marlar, John R. to Elizabeth R. Culbertson   29 June 1847
     Sol. 29 June 1847

Marr, Nicholas to Sarah A. Perkins   7 July 1847
     Sol. 7 July 1847, James M. White, J.P.

Marsh, (or Mack), Leonard J. to Sarah B. Scribner   24 Apr. 1843
     Sol. 25 Apr. 1843, F. Zollicoffer, J.P.

Marshall, Gilbert to Martha Kennedy   3 July 1839
     Sol. 3 July 1839, Robert Hardin, M.G.

Martin, Caswell C. to Elizabeth J. Smith   27 Apr. 1852
     Sol. 28 Apr. 1852, G. W. Fly, J.P.

Martin, George M. to Mary H. Porter   10 May 1852
     Sol. 11 May 1852, William Mack, M.G.

Martin, William P. to Sarah North   19 May 1843
     Sol. 19 May 1843, Joseph Sherman, J.P.

Masker, Lewis to Margaret Grisham   4 Dec. 1852

Massie, Samuel M. W. to Sarah A. E. J. Spencer   4 Aug. 1842
    Sol. 4 Aug. 1842, G. W. Mitchell, J.P.

Matthews, David R. to Elizabeth Whitaker   6 Oct. 1847
    Sol. 7 Oct. 1847

Matthews, Joseph A. to Louisa J. Galloway   16 July 1846
    Sol. 16 July 1846, J. K. Boyce, M.G.

Matthews, Robert R. to Mary E. Galloway   9 Jan. 1844
    Sol. 11 Jan. 1844, Alfred Fleming, J.P.

Matthews, Samuel S. to Ann M. Coleburn   5 Jan. 1841
    Sol. 7 Jan. 1841, Hugh Shaw, V.D.M.

Matthews, Thomas S. to Mary A. Black   11 Feb. 1843
    Sol. 15 Feb. 1843, James H. Otey

Matthews, William D. to Martha J. Hanno (?)   22 Jan. 1844

Maury, William P. to Catherine E. Early   30 Nov. 1847

Maxey, B. T. to Martha J. Hamilton   28 Sept. 1841
    Sol. 30 Sept. 1841, Justice Williams, M.G.

Maxwell, David S. to Derinda A. Amis   9 Sept. 1852
    Sol. 9 Sept. 1852, William D. Wear, M.G.

Maxwell, G. W. C. to Eliza A. Dixon   23 July 1846
    Sol. 23 July 1846, W. H. Baldridge, M.G.

Maxwell, Jesse W. E. to Ruth M. Hill   4 Oct. 1842
    Sol. 5 Oct. 1842, J. P. Campbell

Maxwell, William L. to Mary M. Napier   17 May 1841
    Sol. 18 May 1841, Joseph Sherman, M.G.

Mayberry, Abram to Mary Dean   31 Oct. 1840

Mayes, James H. to Mary E. Fly   13 Aug. 1849
    Sol. 15 Aug. 1849, R. Baker, J.P.

Mayes, John W. to Cornelia Maguire   8 July 1846
    Sol. 8 July 1846, James M. Arnell, Zion Pastor

Mayes, William D. to Martha J. Porter   19 Dec. 1848
    Sol. 19 Dec. 1848, James M. Arnell, Zion Pastor

Mayfield, James F. to Nancy E. Brown   4 Jan. 1849
    Sol. 8 Jan. 1849, R. A. Glenn, J.P.

Mays, Isaac to Polly Edwards   22 Feb. 1845
    Sol. 23 Feb. 1845, Washington Oakley, J.P.

Mays, Jesse O. to Margaret A. McCracken   16 Sept. 1839
    Sol. 17 Sept. 1839, Joseph Carle, Methodist Minister

Mays, Samuel F. to Mary M. Porter   9 Nov. 1847
    Sol. 9 Nov. 1847, William Mack, M.G.

Mays, Stewart to Elizabeth J. Purty   28 Dec. 1848
    Sol. 28 Dec. 1848, J. D. Oliphant, J.P.

Mays, William F. to Delilah Mays   10 Apr. 1847

McAdams, Thomas J. to Jane N. Revier   19 July 1838
    Sol. 26 July 1838, G. W. Mitchell, M.G.

McAdoo, Samuel to Elizabeth Good   13 March 1847
    Sol. 14 March 1847, Berryman Hamblett, J.P.

McAdoo, William to Anna C. Horsley   22 June 1848
    Sol. 22 June 1848, W. D. F. Saurie, M.G.

McAfee, Jacob to Elizabeth Taylor   22 Feb. 1838
    Sol. 22 Feb. 1838, F. S. Perry, M.G.

McAfee, Nabe (?) M. to Malinda Cheek   7 March 1850
    Sol. 7 March 1850, Ezra Hardison, J.P.

McAfee, Redin to Jephia Cheek   21 Sept. 1843
    Sol. 21 Sept. 1843, J. G. Harris, J.P.

McAfee, Redin to Nancy B. Garrett   24 Sept. 1850
    Sol. 24 Sept. 1850, Henry Harris, J.P.

McBraftin (?), John to Martha Tidwell   9 Nov. 1850
    Sol. 11 Nov. 1850, B. H. Ragsdale

McBride, James to Martha J. Jaggers   11 Jan. 1843
    Sol. 11 Jan. 1843, Joseph Foster, J.P.

McBride, James F. to Sarah H. Jones   14 Dec. 1846
    Sol. 15 Dec. 1846, Thomas Kelsey, J.P.

McBride, James J. to Frances H. Charter   25 Nov. 1847
    Sol. 25 Nov. 1847, William I. Strayhorn, J.P.

McBride, Jessie S. to Martha J. McBride   17 Dec. 1844
    Sol. 25 Dec. 1844, E. Blocker, J.P.

McBride, John P. to Emily S. Lawson   21 July 1845
    Sol. 22 July 1845, Joseph Foster, J.P.

McBride, William S. to Rosannah Kinzer   6 Mar. 1839
    Sol. 12 Mar. 1839, Thomas Kelsey, J.P.

McCafferty, Jenkin G. to Mary S. Kinnimore   9 Nov. 1847
    Sol. 10 Nov. 1847, James Gibson

McCafferty, William G. to Nancy Kennemore   4 July 1839
    Sol. 4 July 1839, Andrew Scott, J.P.

McCallum, Austin J. to Ann E. Thompson   25 Feb. 1851
    Sol. 11 March 1851, B. F. Alexander, M.G.

McCallum, Thomas M. to Mahala Brooks   23 Oct. 1845
    Sol. 23 Oct. 1845, R. W. Morris, M.G.

McCandless, John R. to Sallie A. Farrar   18 Sept. 1849
    Sol. 1 Sept. 1849, William Mack, M.G.

McCearley, James to Elizabeth McClain   29 Sept. 1838
    Sol. 30 Sept. 1838, Berryman Hamlett, J.P.

McClain, John to Jane Lindsey   21 Dec. 1844

McClain, William to Mary A. Coleman   27 July 1839
    Sol. 30 July 1839, R. Stockard, J.P.

McClanahan, Ditter M. to Valera A. Blackburn   19 Apr. 1842
    Sol. 21 Apr. 1842, B. N. Fain, M.G.

McClinchy, William to Frances S. Ridley   14 Jan. 1850
    Sol. 20 Jan. 1850 at St. John's Rectory before witnesses
    E. H. Cressy, Rector, St. John's

McClure, Robert C. S. to Martha Goad   30 Oct. 1841
    Sol. 30 Oct. 1841, Tasewell S. Alderson, J.P.

McCollum, Isaac B. to Eliza T. Akin   30 Dec. 1848
    Sol. 2 Jan. 1849, B. F. Alexander, M.G.

McConnel, Harvey H. to Elizabeth L. Veatch   25 Nov. 1850
    Sol. 26 Nov. 1850, G. C. Stockard, M.G.

McConnell, John B. to Priscilla A. Gibson   14 Sept. 1848
    Sol. 17 Sept. 1848, Wade Barnett, Elder C. C.

McCord, Andrew J. to Eliza J. Smith   19 Dec. 1839
    Sol. 20 Dec. 1839, Robert Hardin, M.G.

McCormack, Archibald to Elizabeth Hill   17 Feb. 1840

McCrory, Samuel to Lucinda Woody   24 Jan. 1838
    Sol. 25 Jan. 1838, E. Hanks, M.G.

McDaniel, John to Miriam Hendley   15 Aug. 1843

McDonald, Alexander to Sarah M. Collier   1 Sept. 1845

McDonald, Allen to Caroline Casky   19 Sept. 1849
    Sol. 27 Sept. 1849, G. C. Stockard, M.G.

McDonald, Daniel H. to Elizabeth Jackson   23 Dec. 1840
    Sol. 24 Dec. 1840, G. C. Stockard, M.G.

McDonald, Hugh K. to Elizabeth A. Gill   9 Jan. 1840
    Sol. 9 Jan. 1840, Wade Barrett, Elder, C. Church

McDonald, William to Delia A. Green   2 Dec. 1850
    Sol. 3 Dec. 1850

McDonald, William H. to Rebecca Grimes   23 July 1840

McEwen, John A. to Selina J. Frierson   19 Oct. 1848
    Sol. 19 Oct. 1848, James M. Arnell, Pastor, Zion Church

McFadden, Carridge (?) to Anna Shires   17 Jan. 1844
    Sol. 17 Jan. 1844, J. C. Spinks, J.P.

McFaul, James to Nancy T. Cockrille   20 June 1846
    Sol. 21 June 1846, Andrew Scott, J.P.

McGaw, James C. to Margaret Harris   8 Oct. 1851
    Sol. 9 Oct. 1851, William Mack, M.G.

McGaw, John P. to Mary J. Bard (?)   17 Dec. 1845
    Sol. 17 Dec. 1845, A. T. Gray, J.P.

McGaw, Samuel P. to Eliza E. Cherry   9 Oct. 1850
    Sol. 10 Oct. 1850, J. B. Hamilton, Methodist Elder

McKay, Richard A. to Eliza J. Jennings   31 Jan. 1843
    Sol. 31 Jan. 1843, G. W. Mitchell, M.G.

McKee, George W. to Jane Taylor   29 June 1847
    Sol. 2 July 1847, M. Fitzgerald, J.P.

McKee, James H. to Mary L. Hilliard   16 Sept. 1851
    Sol. 17 Sept. 1851, John L. Hamilton, Elder, M.E. C.

McKee, John R. to Mahala J. McKee   29 Sept. 1838
    Sol. 4 Oct. 1838, Robert Campbell, J.P.

McKee, Nelson to Emily Rountree   29 Dec. 1841

McKee, Robert to Mary Rountree   14 Oct. 1839
    Sol. 14 Oct. 1839, Robert Campbell, J.P.

McKeel, James to Edney S. Galloway   20 Jan. 1847
    Sol. 21 Jan. 1847, G. Hanks, J.P.

McKeel, James L. to Mary E. Sparkman   4 Jan. 1849
    Sol. 4 Jan. 1849, A. T. Gray, J.P.

McKelvay, John to Jane McKibbon   12 Sept. 1844
    Sol. 12 Sept. 1844, Henry B. North, M.G.

McKennon, Daniel M. to Martha F. Wood   1 Feb. 1841
  Sol. 4 Feb. 1841, William W. Coleman, J.P.

McKennon, John H. to Elizabeth W. Wiley   29 Jan. 1844
  Sol. 30 Jan. 1844, J. W. Kilpatrick, J.P.

McKenzie, Garner F. to Elizabeth L. Henderson   1 July 1851
  Sol. 1 July 1851

McKinly, Dr. Samuel E. to Dilla E. Jaggers   6 Dec. 1849
  Sol. 6 Dec. 1849, J. B. Hamilton, E.M.E.C.

McKissack, James T. to Sylvania C. Roane   31 Jan. 1845
  Sol. 1 Feb. 1845, R. Garrison, V.D.M.

McKissack, John D. to Nancy E. Morrow   25 Jan. 1848
  Sol. 27 Jan. 1848, James Brownlow, M.G.

McKissack, William to Arabella White   12 Sept. 1843
  Sol. 13 Sept. 1843, Joseph Sherman

McKisseck, Spivey to Eliza Smiser   25 Oct. 1842
  Sol. 25 Oct. 1842, Joseph Sherman, M.G.

McKnight, George M. to Eliza A. McCafferty   30 Oct. 1849
  Sol. 31 Oct. 1849

McLean, Ephraim H. to Frances Porter   1 Mar. 1852
  Sol. 3 March 1852, G. H. Blair

McLean, Samuel to Sarah E. Rainey   2 Mar. 1841
  Sol. 4 March 1841, N. F. Moorall, M.G.

McLure, Samuel to Leacy Dark   21 Apr. 1838
  Sol. Laban Jordan, J.P.

McLurrey, Henry to M. J. Ashworth   8 Feb. 1844
  Sol. 8 Feb. 1844, Washington Oakley, J.P.

McMahon, Henderson to Eliza J. Blair   10 Apr. 1843
  Sol. 11 Apr. 1843, Berryman Hamblett, J.P.

McManus, Aaron to Mary A. McLean   13 Apr. 1841
  Sol. 14 Apr. 1841, Lewis G. Lanier, J.P.

McManus, Aaron to Mynan McClain   17 Jan. 1852
  Sol. 18 Jan. 1852, W. R. H. Mack, J.P.

McMaury, Joseph H. to Sarah E. Tate   6 Sept. 1847
  Sol. 8 Sept. 1847, W. H. Baldridge, M.G.

McMeen, Abdon A. to Amarintha F. O'Neal   21 May 1839
  Sol. 21 May 1839, H. H. Brown, E.M.E.C.

McMeen, James M. to Mary Jane Pauguss 22 Jan. 1845
 Sol. 22 Jan. 1845, E. Hanks, M.G.

McMeen, Joseph B. to Margaret E. Dodson 2 Dec. 1852
 Sol. 2 Dec. 1852, D. G. Moore, M.G.

McMeen, Joseph P. to Virginia C. Dodson 15 Dec. 1845
 Sol. 17 Dec. 1845, Benjamin F. Alexander, M.G.

McMeen, Thomas F. to Caroline Hadley 30 June 1852
 Sol. 1 July 1852, E. Hanks, M.G.

McMeen, William S. to Nancy McKay 7 Nov. 1838
 Sol. 8 Nov. 1838, Robert Hardin, M.G.

McMillan, Alexander W. to Mary Norman 3 Dec. 1839
 Sol. 4 Dec. 1839, Edward R. Freeman, J.P.

McMillan, Angus to Jane Glass 6 Dec. 1843
 Sol. 7 Dec. 1843, G. C. Stockard, M.G.

McMillan, J. A. to Mary J. Mayfield 17 Aug. 1852
 Sol. 17 Aug. 1852, Ezra Hardison, J.P.

McMurry, Samuel W. to Evelin P. Lipscomb 19 Dec. 1838
 Sol. 19 Dec. 1838, H. Shaw

McNabb, James to Elizabeth Powell 25 Feb. 1840
 Sol. 25 Feb. 1840, E. Hanks, M.G.

McNabb, John W. to Julia A. Cuthbertson 3 July 1844
 Sol. 3 July 1844, Aaron Vestal, J.P.

McNeelley, Eril to Sarah J. Gates 31 Sept. 1847
 Sol. 28 August 1847, R. A. Glenn, J.P.

McNeely, James to Margaret McCormack 2 Feb. 1846
 Sol. J. C. Spinks, J.P.

McNeese, Andrew General Jackson to Elizabeth Jones 13 Dec. 1841
 Sol. 14 Dec. 1841, Robert Thompson, M.G.

McNeese, Jacob to Caroline Allen 2 Dec. 1851
 Sol. 2 Dec. 1851, James M. White, J.P.

McNeill, William to Sarah P. Hardin 18 Dec. 1838
 Sol. 18 Dec. 1838, James M. Arnell, Pastor, Zion Church

McRady, E. W. to Margaret White 19 Nov. 1839
 Sol. 19 Nov. 1839, Thomas F. Scott, V.D.M.

McRae, Duncan to Sarah E. Rainy 24 March 1840

McWhirter, Moses to Mary Hunt 27 Oct. 1840
 Sol. 29 Oct. 1840, R. Stockard, J.P.

Meaders, Absalom A. to Julia A. McCafferty   19 Apr. 1838

Meadors, Absalom A. to Sarah A. Grigsby   15 May 1849
      Sol. 15 May 1849, Andrew Scott, J.P.

Meaders, Jason W. to Sarah Lesenby   7 Feb. 1839
      Sol. 14 Feb. 1839, Parke Street, J.P.

Medcalf, James to Elizabeth M. Waldrum   22 Dec. 1840

Meece, Richard to Susan S. Southall   28 June 1841

Meace, William C. to Hannah B. Fields   31 May 1838
      Sol. E. Hanks, M.G.

Meek, William H. to Nancy Stribling   20 Nov. 1838
      Sol. 20 Nov. 1838, T. E. Kirkpatrick, M.G.

Meredith, Washington to Mary T. Booker   18 Dec. 1850
      Sol. 18 Dec. 1850, William Mack, M.G.

Middleton, Hugh to Martha J. Collins   27 Nov. 1844
      Sol. 29 Nov. 1844, John T. Moss, M.G.

Miller, Eppa Milton to Nancy A. Brooks   13 Sept. 1843
      Sol. 14 Sept. 1843, A. T. Gray, J.P.

Miller, Frances A. to Mary J. Kinzer   8 Nov. 1849
      Sol. 8 Nov. 1849, A. B. Dickson, L.E., M.E.C.

Miller, Henry A. to Lydia E. Ridley   6 Sept. 1844
      Sol. 10 Sept. 1844, L. Brown

Miller, Jeremiah T. to Ruth L. Caughron   15 Dec. 1852
      Sol. 16 Dec. 1852, E. Hanks, M.G.

Miller, Martin C. to Martha J. Hill   1 Dec. 1849
      Sol. 2 Dec. 1849, Joseph F. Jordan, J.P.

Miller, William J. to Novalin R. Polk   6 Oct. 1849
      Sol. 6 Oct. 1849, William Mack, M.G.

Mills, Benjamin F. to Louisa Madden   14 Oct. 1851
      Sol. 14 Oct. 1851, E. Davis, J.P.

Mills, Jonathon to Elizabeth Bradley   1 Oct. 1846
      Sol. 11 Oct. 1846, Hugh C. Harrison, J.P.

Mills, John to Nancy Barker   22 Aug. 1844

Mills, John to Mary Alderson   9 March 1847
      Sol. 10 March 1847, G. Hanks, J.P.

Mills, Tilman to Mary Hutchinson   8 Nov. 1843

Mills, William A. to Nancy Williams   23 Sept. 1840
     Sol, 24 Sept. 1840, Samuel Wheatley, J.P.

Mills, William J. to Virginia Brown   22 Nov. 1851
     Sol. 23 Nov. 1851, Asa Hardison, M.G.

Minor, Benjamin B. to Virginia M. Otey   26 May 1842

Minor, James G. to Mary Dean   16 Jan. 1843
     Sol. 18 Jan. 1843, Samuel Wheatley, J.P.

Minor, Noah to Mary M. Street   22 Apr. 1848
     Sol. 23 Apr. 1848, R. A. Glenn, J.P.

Minor, Thomas G. to Amanda Dooley   13 Dec. 1845
     Sol. 14 Dec. 1845, D. Judd, L.E.

Minor, William W. to Elizabeth Dickerson   17 Jan. 1848
     Sol. 19 Jan. 1848, R. A. Glenn, J.P.

Mitchell, George W. to Sarah Bynum   30 May 1838

Mitchell, Giles to Martha J. McDonald   3 Jan. 1843
     Sol. 3 Jan. 1843, G. Hanks, J.P.

Mitchell, Jesse to Martha A. Latta   18 July 1846
     Sol. 19 July 1846, Berryman Hamlett, J.P.

Mitchell, Littleton to Isabella Brown   1 Oct. 1840
     Sol. 1 Oct. 1840, William Horsley

Mitchell, Richard D. to Adaline A. Parrish   7 Dec. 1848
     Sol. 7 Dec. 1848, William H. Wilkes, M.G.

Mitchell, Robert B. to Mary E. Martin   8 Nov. 1848
     Sol. 8 Nov. 1848, William Mack M.G.

Mitchell, Thomas to Joonna Whitfield   20 Aug. 1842
     Sol, 21 Aug. 1842, B. Gresham, J.P.

Mitchell, Thomas L. to Tabitha J. Hudson   17 July 1846
     Sol. 19 July 1846, J. T. Faris, J.P.

Montgomery, James H. to Mary F. Kerr   18 Nov. 1847
     Sol, 21 Nov. 1847, Joseph Brown

Moody, Francis T. to Ann W. Griffin   29 Jan. 1848
     Sol. 31 Jan. 1848, Rev. W. R. Candess (?)

Moore, Alexander to Margaret Matthews   27 Aug. 1845
     Sol, 30 Aug. 1845, J. K. Boyce, M.G.

Moore, Andrew to Sarah A. Hedge (Hodge)   13 Apr. 1852
     Sol. 13 Apr. 1852, W. D. Gilham, M. G.

Moore, David G. to Cynthia A. Ross   22 March 1842

Moore, Edward D. to Lucinda M. Dooley   5 Sept. 1838
     Sol. 5 Sept. 1838, H. H. Hill, M.G.

Moore, James C. to Margaret E. Walker   11 Nov. 1852
     Sol. 11 Nov. 1852, W. R. H. Mack, J.P.

Moore, James I. to Mary A. Bunch   31 Jan. 1848
     Sol. 1 Feb. 1848, R. C. Garrison

Moore, James T. to Mary A. Cooke   27 Aug. 1845
     Sol. 27 Aug. 1845, C. Cooke, J.P.

Moore, John C. to Elizabeth J. Passmore   14 May 1845
     Sol. 14 May 1845, W. H. Baldridge, M.G.

Moore, John L. to Angeline P. Oliphant   11 Oct. 1848
     Sol. 12 Oct. 1848, Thomas Witherspoon, J.P.

Moore, John S. to Mary Hyde   14 Nov. 1839
     Sol. 15 Nov. 1839, R. Stockard, J.P.

Moore, John W. to Levisa Cannon   16 Mar. 1839
     Sol. 16 Mar. 1839, Allen Richardson, M.G.

Moore, John W. to Malinda Williams   6 Jan. 1840

Moore, Joseph J. to Catherine T. Hicks   28 Feb. 1852
     Sol. 29 Feb. 1852, W. B. Gilham, M.G.

Moore, Thomas M. to Ann Jane Wilkins   19 Dec. 1839
     Sol. 19 Dec. 1839, H. H. Brown, E.M.E.C.

Moore, William E. to Martha J. Luker   9 Aug. 1848
     Sol. 10 Aug. 1848, M. H. Mays, J.P.

Moore, William F. to Nancy Boyd   3 Jan. 1848
     Sol. 4 Jan. 1848, W. H. Baldridge, M.G.

Moore, William H. to Dorcas J. Harberson   17 Dec. 1851
     Sol. 18 Dec. 1851, D. G. Moore, M.G.

Moore, William R. to Eliza Crutchfield   10 Mar. 1852
     Sol. 10 Mar. 1852, J. B. Hamilton, Methodist Minister

Moray, John L. to Elizabeth J. Wadkins   28 June 1841

Morgan, Alexander M. to Ann E. Hill   21 Apr. 1842
     Sol. 21 Apr. 1842, Joseph Sherman, M.G.

Morgan, David E. to Angeline Morris   29 June 1840
     Sol. 2 July 1840, Edward R. Freeman, J.P.

Morgan, James M. to Olivia E. Craig   20 July 1852
     Sol. 21 July 1852, M. W. Gray, M.G.

Morgan, John F. to Louisa J. Porter   29 June 1841
     Sol. 29 June 1841, Joseph Sherman, M.G.

Morgan, Joseph to Lucy Tylor   11 Dec. 1841
     Sol. 14 Dec. 1841, Thomas W. Randle, M.G.

Morris, Edmund to Malinda Driskill   28 Feb. 1841
     Sol. 3 March 1841, Absalom Bostick, M.G.

Morris, James H. to Marinda E. Dortch   16 July 1851
     Sol. 9 July 1851, James A. Moore, J.P.

Morris, John J. to Margaret A. Campbell   5 Sept. 1851
     Sol. 5 Sept. 1851, H. K. Shields, M.G.

Morgan, Joseph H. to Elizabeth O. Craig   22 Dec. 1852
     Sol. 23 Dec. 1852, W. J. Kirkpatrick

Morris, Reuben to Sarah Helton   10 July 1840

Morris, Samuel to Tabitha J. Goad   2 Feb. 1848
     Sol. 2 Feb. 1848, E. Hanks, M.G.

Morriss, William to Talitha Kincaid   16 March 1842
     Sol. 16 March 1842, C. Cooke, J.P.

Morrison, Amzi R. to Sarah J. Morgan   14 Jan. 1851
     Sol. 14 Jan. 1851, Asa Harrison, M.G.

Morrow, Alexander to Mary A. Hudson   5 Feb. 1840
     Sol. 6 Feb. 1840, James Calhoon

Morrow, Elijah to Elizabeth Gibson   6 Feb. 1844

Morrow, John D. to Mary N. Willcoxson   11 Sept. 1844
     Sol. 12 Sept. 1844, J. O. Griffith

Morrow, Joseph W. to Nancy C. Walters   1 Oct. 1849

Morrow, Noah R. to Cynthia K. Beasley   26 Sept. 1848

Mortin, Joseph to Julia A. Chaffin   14 Apr. 1851
     Sol. 15 Apr. 1851, William Mack, M.G.

Morton, Gabriel L. to Emily J. Hardeson   12 Dec. 1840
     Sol. 15 Dec. 1840, Joshua K. Speer, M.G.

Morton, Josiah to Comfort M. Guinn   5 Apr. 1843
     Sol. 6 Apr. 1843, G. W. Fly, Esquire

Moseley, George W. to Elizabeth Waters   31 Dec. 1838

Moseley, Hillery to Agnes F. Armstrong   23 Apr. 1839
     Sol. 23 Apr. 1839, James M. Arnell, Pastor, Zion Church

Moss, Daniel D. to Minerva M. Adkisson   28 May 1846
     Sol. 28 May 1846, G. C. Stockard, M.G.

Mullins, Green to Margaret Laimwood   1 Feb. 1841

Murphey, Nathaniel A. H. to Mary C. V. Mack   17 Dec. 1844

Murphey, Warren L. to Lucy Stacy   21 Dec. 1842
     Sol, 22 Dec. 1842, Hiram Anthony, J.P.

Myers, Bernard to Margaret A. Bradshaw   28 July 1840
     Sol. 28 July 1840, C. D. Elliott, M.G.

Myers, Leonard D. to Sarah H. Caruthers   7 Nov. 1848
     Sol. 7 Nov. 1848, William Mack, M.G.

N

Nance, Clement to Rachel Ann Owins   1 May 1838
     Sol. 1 May 1838, James Adkins, J.P.

Nance, James B. to Asenatt Lerinda Rickets   4 July 1842
     Sol. 20 July 1842, G. W. Mitchell, M.G.

Nance, Joseph to Elizabeth Pugh   26 Aug. 1840
     Sol. 26 Aug. 1840, John Hunter, M.G.

Nance, Joseph W. to Martha J. Hunt   2 Feb. 1846
     Sol, 3 Feb. 1846, Wade Barnett, Elder in C. Church

Nance, Philip W. to Manerva Browning   1 Apr. 1847

Nance, Robert to Eliza Church   20 Aug. 1838
     Sol. 20 Aug. 1838, James Adkins, J.P.

Nance, Thomas P. to Louisiana Holden   22 Nov. 1850
     Sol, 26 Nov. 1850, James N. Edmiston

Napier, Madison C. to Sarah C. Cofey   12 Nov. 1845
(She is listed in the index as Jassey.)

Napier, William C. to Rebecca B. Greenfield   4 July 1844
     Sol. 4 July 1844, J. H. Otey, Bishop of Tennessee

Nash, Peter to Martha Jones   11 Aug. 1848
     Sol. 11 Aug. 1848, Daniel Judd, M.E. Church

Neece, David S. to Julia Ann Brummet   16 Dec. 1843
     Sol. 16 Dec. 1843, J. C. Spinks, J.P.

Neely, Andrew E. to Juan F. Wilkins   1 Sept. 1851
     Sol. 2 Sept. 1851, John B. Hamilton, Methodist Minister

Neely, James C. to Rebecca Hines   23 Feb. 1842
    Sol. 3 Mar. 1842, R. C. Goodgion

Neely, James W. to Mary Fariss   22 Oct. 1838
    Sol. 25 Oct. 1838, S. Whiteside, J.P.

Neeley, John H. to Jennet A. Dobbin   6 Oct. 1842
    Sol. 6 Oct. 1842, William Hosley

Neely, John N. to Nancy E. Tate   15 Dec. 1849
    Sol. 18 Dec. 1849, W. H. Baldridge, M.G.

Neeley, Philip P. to Alice Towler   17 Nov. 1847
    Sol. 17 Nov. 1847, J. O. Church, Deacon, Methodist Church

Neeley, Thomas D. to Mary Ramsey   25 Feb. 1841
    Sol. 25 Feb. 1841, Robert Foster, J.P.

Nellums, William W. to Rhoda E. Lasley   16 May 1846
    Sol. 17 May 1846, Samuel W. Akin, J.P.

Nelms, George W. to Mary E. Reese   15 Jan. 1851
    Sol. 16 Jan. 1851, M. B. Molloy, M.G.

Nelson, Charles L. to Maria L. Smiser   1 Nov. 1847
    Sol. 5 Nov. 1847, F. G. Smith

Nelson, John D. to Mary Howard   13 Oct. 1840
    Sol. 14 Oct. 1840, Allen Hill

Nelson, Pleasant H. to Nancy A. Amis   8 Oct. 1849
    Sol. 11 Oct. 1849, G. C. Stockard, M.G.

Nelson, William P. to Lavina N. Kincaid   13 Oct. 1846
    Sol. 14 Oct. 1846, J. T. Moss, M.G.

Nevils, George B. to Lucilly Scott   20 May 1852
    Sol. 20 May 1852, E. Hanks, M.G.

Nevils, John T. to Eliza J. Davis   12 Feb. 1848
    Sol. 14 Feb. 1848, Hugh C. Harrison, J.P.

Nevils, John W. to Catherine J. Thompson   7 Feb. 1849
    Sol. 8 Feb. 1849, J. B. Hamilton, Methodist Elder

Nichols, Caleb G. R. to Frances J. Blakely   16 Feb. 1852
    Sol. 18 Feb. 1852

Nichols, John to Minerva Wooldridge   2 May 1840

Nichols, Willis to Eliza C. Smith   14 Mar. 1842

Nichols, Willis to Eliza L. Passmore   8 July 1846
    Sol. 8 July 1846, Benjamin F. Alexander, M.G.

Nicholson, James to Sarah D. Amis   12 Jan. 1848
    Sol. 13 Jan. 1848, Joshua K. Speer, M.G.

Nicholson, Lewis H. to Eliza H. Collins   25 Nov. 1848
    Sol. 30 Nov. 1848, Augustin W. Wortham, J.P.

Nicholson, Robert to Sarah Wilson   11 Jan. 1841

Nicholson, Young A. G. to Sarah E. Akin   14 Oct. 1841
    Sol. 14 Oct. 1841, Parke Street, J.P.

Nicks, Absalom O. to Margaret S. Blocker   14 June 1845
    Sol. 15 June 1845, A. T. Gray, J.P.

Nicks, Alfred H. to Flora M. Porter   21 May 1844

Nicks, Allen P. to Susan R. Blocker   20 Sept. 1841
    Sol. 21 Sept. 1841, George Gantt, M.G.

Nicks, Barton W. A. to Frances J. Blackburn   29 Nov. 1843
    Sol. 30 Nov. 1843, W. B. Harris

Nicks, William to Elizabeth A. Puckett   11 Apr. 1844
    Sol. 12 Apr. 1844, E. R. Osborne, E. C. C.

Niesler, David to Barbary Scott   13 Feb. 1839

Nix, Robert to Larica Cheek   13 Mar. 1844
    Sol. 15 Mar. 1844, Elder Church of Christ, Joseph McCord

Noble, John to Margaret Pedie   1 Aug. 1846
    Sol. 9 Aug. 1846, J. Landels, Presbyterian at
    St. Mark's Church, Williamsport, Tennessee

Nolen, Milton B. to Mary J. Bryant   26 Aug. 1843
    Sol. 28 Aug. 1843, Isaac N. Bills, J.P.

Nolen, Thomas A. to Mary M. Berry   24 July 1844

Nolen, Thomas A. to Margaret A. Grimes   25 Apr. 1849
    Sol. 25 Apr. 1849, George S. Arnold

Noles, Tiny (?) to Nancy C. Stockard   19 Nov. 1850
    Sol. 24 Nov. 1850, G. W. Mitchell, M.G.

Norman, Frances to Susan Jettun   1 July 1846
    Sol. 1 July 1846, George W. Johnston, J.P.

Norman, James H. to Lillis A. M. Matthews   28 March 1843

Norman, Joseph to Mary Law   14 May 1850
    Sol. 14 May 1850, J. T. Faris, J.P.

Norman, Samuel to Martha A. Epps   5 Jan. 1847
    Sol. 5 Jan. 1847, J. T. Faris, J.P.

Notgrass, William M. to Emaline P. Hughes   8 Dec. 1846
     Sol. 9 Dec. 1846, E. Hanks, M.G.

Nunalee, Timothy J. to Rachel H. Williams   21 Oct. 1850
     Sol. 22 Oct. 1850, John B. Hamilton, Methodist Minister

Nunnelly, William O. to Elenor D. Ketchum   25 Oct. 1839
     Sol. 25 Oct. 1839, C. B. Porter, M.G.

O

Oakes, William J. to Martha J. Zellner   31 Aug. 1843
     Sol. 31 Aug. 1843, Adam S. Riggs, M.G.

Oakley, Hardin J. to Eleanor Mays   8 Dec. 1842
     Sol. 8 Dec. 1842, Ishmael Stevens, J.P.

Oakley, Hardin P. to Lucinda H. Smith   2 Dec. 1845
     Sol. 4 Dec. 1845, Washington Oakley, J.P.

Oakley, James M. to Sarah A. Alexander   29 Mar. 1845
     Sol. 10 Apr. 1845, C. H. Baldridge, M.G.

Oakley, Washington to Elizabeth G. Harris   9 Dec. 1841
     Sol. Britain Garner

Oakley, William D. to Lemisa P. Harris   6 Jan. 1840
     Sol. Britain Garner

Oakley, William F. to Mary A. M. Younger   2 Jan. 1850
     Sol. 15 Jan. 1850, R. Baker, J.P.

Oatman, Leman to Martha A. Fleming   6 Apr. 1840
     Sol. 8 Apr. 1840, James M. Arnell, Pastor, Zion

O'Bryant, Willis to Jane W. Hagens   13 Mar. 1841
     Sol. 14 Mar. 1841, S. Whiteside, J.P.

Odil, David M. to Mary C. Dobbin   25 May 1843
     Sol. 31 May 1843, D. Brown, V. D. M.

Odil, Samuel A. to Elvira C. Smith   20 Mar. 1843

Ogilvie, Richard H. to Susan O. Akin   17 Oct. 1846
     Sol. P. P. Neeley

Ogilvie, William L. to Mary J. Stringfellow   9 Dec. 1844
     Sol. 12 Dec. 1844, James W. Edmiston

Old, Charles W. to Mary A. Jones   19 Feb. 1838
     Sol. 20 Feb. 1838, F. S. Ferguson, M.G.

Oliphant, John D. to Phebe C. M. Edwards   11 May 1846
     Sol. G. W. Fly, J.P.

Oliphant, William C. to Angeline P. McKee — 4 Dec. 1840

Oliver, George W. P. to Nancy J. Wiles — 27 Nov. 1848
    Sol. 30 Nov. 1848, Henry Harris, J.P.

Oliver, John A. to Sarah A. Dodson — 1 Apr. 1839
    Sol. 4 Apr. 1839, E. Hanks, M.G.

Oliver, Sandy to Mary J. Whitworth — 6 May 1848
    Sol. 9 May 1848, Henry Harris, J.P.

Ormes, John E. to Amanda J. Bolton — 28 Mar. 1851
    Sol. 28 Mar. 1851, J. B. Padgett, J.P.

Orr, Alexander to Loretto R. H. Kittrell — 13 Aug. 1845
    Sol. 14 Aug. 1845, M. W. Grey, Methodist Minister

Orr, John to Louisa A. Smith — 2 Mar. 1842
    Sol. 31 March 1842, D. Brown

Orr, John to Elmira L. Stockard — 3 July 1845

Orr, Joseph L. to Mary Alderson — 22 May 1850
    Sol. 23 May 1850, at residence of Lewis G. Lanier
    John B. Hamilton, Methodist Minister

Osborne, John F. to Mary M. Gregory — 29 Jan. 1841
    Sol. 3 Feb. 1841, Joseph Sherman, M.G.

Overstreet, Clayton to Margaret Cutberth — 12 Aug. 1848
    Sol. 13 Aug. 1848, J. T. Moss, M.G.

Overstreet, John H. to Matilda Renfro — 20 Jan. 1840

Overstreet, William to Sarah B. Bailey — 10 June 1848
    Sol. 11 June 1848, J. T. Moss, M.G.

Overton, James J. to Rebecca F. Lockridge — 24 Dec. 1851
    Sol. 25 Dec. 1851, M. B. Molloy, M.G.

Overton, John to Mary J. Jameson — 7 Oct. 1848
    Sol. 8 Oct. 1848, B. F. Alexander, M.G.

Owen, Frances M. to Elizabeth Stockard — 30 Oct. 1845
    Sol. 12 Nov. 1845, Joseph Foster, J.P.

Owen, John to Amanda Brown — 10 May 1843
    Sol. 10 May 1843, John B. Bond, J.P.

Owen, Obadiah to Nancy Brown — 16 Nov. 1841
    Sol. 16 Nov. 1841, Robert Foster, J.P.

Owen, Phillip A. to Barberry A. Rawsey — 12 Jan. 1852
    Sol. 13 Jan. 1852, Joseph Brown

Owens, David to Mary Ann Randall   16 May 1838
     Sol. 16 May 1838, Ishmael Stevens, J.P.

Owens, John to Lucinda Husbands   9 March 1842
     Sol. 9 March 1842, S. Whiteside, J.P.

Owens, John A. to Rachel A. Morrow   31 Mar. 1852
     Sol. 1 Apr. 1852, D. G. Moore, M.G.

Owens, Noah B. to Martha J. Lockhart   12 Apr. 1842

Owens, Thomas to Elizabeth Latta   2 Sept. 1846

P

Pack, John J. to Atmayer E. Oliver   17 Sept. 1839
     Sol. 18 Sept. 1839, B. Gresham, J.P.

Painter, Samuel A. to Cynthia R. Holden   17 Mar. 1851
     Sol. 18 Mar. 1851

Pardue, Pleasant to Ann Roberts   8 Jan. 1839
     Sol. 10 Jan. 1839, Lewis G. Lanier, J.P.

Parham, Bryant to Ann E. Speed   3 Nov. 1846
     Sol. 3 Nov. 1846, A. Clark, J.P.

Parham, William T. to Mary E. Hackny   27 Sept. 1849

Park, John J. A. to Winniford E. Steele   29 Sept. 1849
     Sol. 2 Oct. 1849, Edward R. Puckett, J.P.

Parker, Francis to Emeline Grimes   23 Apr. 1845
     Sol. 24 Apr. 1845, Park Street, J.P.

Parker, William J. to Eliza A. Beasley   5 Nov. 1851
     Sol. 9 Nov. 1851, Thomas W. Rasco, M.G.

Parr, James M. to Jane Lewis   2 Feb. 1841

Parr, John C. to Elmira P. Crafford   23 Jan. 1843
     Sol. 24 Jan. 1843, George C. Stockard, M.G.

Partin, John H. to Lydia Mays   31 May 1848
     Sol. 31 May 1848, A. T. Gray, J.P.

Passmore, James H. to Mary A. Alexander   9 June 1842
     Sol. 10 June 1842, R. H. Timmons, J.P.

Pate, John B. to Sarah Lesley   16 Dec. 1843
     Sol. 18 Dec. 1843, J. G. Harris, J.P.

Patterson, James A. to Susan Stubbins   1 July 1840

Patterson, Jared E. to Agenes S. Matthews   3 Sept. 1840
     Sol. 3 Sept. 1840, H. Shaw

Patton, Andrew J. to Elizabeth Kerr   6 Mar. 1841
     Sol. 11 Mar. 1841, Absalom Bostick, M.G.

Paul, James L. to Nancy E. Bates   14 Nov. 1848
     Sol. 14 Nov. 1848, William Horsley, M.G.

Payne, George to Thursa Litton   19 Apr. 1842

Payne, James B. to Sarah E. Cooper   9 Nov. 1850
     Sol. 14 Nov. 1850

Payne, James M. to Caroline Wright   23 May 1848
     Sol. 23 May 1848, A. G. Kelly, M.G.

Payton, Joseph to Manerva Akin   10 Oct. 1843
     Sol. 12 Oct. 1843, R. W. Fain

Peery, Charles B. to Mary A. Lusk   2 Dec. 1852

Peerey, William H. to Florah A. Harbison   16 Nov. 1841
     Sol. 18 Nov. 1841, W. H. Baldridge

Pennington, Leroy to Mary A. Garton   18 June 1852
     Sol. 20 June 1852, R. M. King, J.P.

Pennington, William H. to Nancy P. Bailey   27 Sept. 1842
     Sol. 29 Sept. 1842, R. Stockard, J.P.

Pentecost, William to Margaret E. Woody   13 Jan. 1848
     Sol. 13 Jan. 1848, John G. Williams, J.P.

Peoples, Thomas to Sarah Oven   7 Aug. 1848
     Sol. 8 Aug. 1848, William R. Sharp, J.P.

Perkins, Samuel to Catherine Mabrey   8 July 1842
     Sol. 8 July 1842, John B. Bond, J.P.

Perry, Burkly to Elizabeth L. Taylor   26 Nov. 1849
     Sol. 27 Nov. 1849, Jonathan S. Hunt, J.P.

Perry, Francis A. to Ann E. Wortham   20 Dec. 1849
     Sol. 20 Dec. 1849, E. N. Hatcher, M.G.

Perry, Henry to Mahala Campbell   12 Nov. 1839
     Sol. 14 Nov. 1839, Jonathan S. Hunt, J.P.

Perry, Jeremiah to Malinda Jones   6 May 1850

Perry, Jeremiah to Mary M. Jones   7 Nov. 1851
     Sol. 7 Nov. 1851, Joseph A. Wright, J.P.

Perry, John A. to Eliza D. Witherspoon   19 Aug. 1841
     Sol. 19 Aug. 1841, G. W. Sneed, M.G.

Perry, John S. to Mary E. Jones   7 Jan. 1846
     Sol. 7 Jan. 1846, P. F. Neely, M.G.

Perry, Nathan to Mary J. Amis   15 Oct. 1849
     Sol. 15 Oct. 1849, G. C. Stockard, M.G.

Perry, Robert T. to Sarah C. Wade   9 Sept. 1841
     Sol. 9 Sept. 1841, J. B. Walker, M.G., M.E. Church

Perry, William to Mary Williams   25 Apr. 1839
     Sol. 28 Apr. 1840, Wade Barrett, W. in C. Church

Perry, William, Jr. to Martha Ann Wortham   15 May 1838
     Sol. 16 May 1838, H. H. Brown, E.M.E.C.

Perry or Berry, William R. to Mahala C. Mays   29 Oct. 1839

Perry, Willis to Frances E. Flanigan   22 Dec. 1848
     Sol. 24 Dec. 1848, F. A. Burke, J.P.

Petty, Gideon to Elizabeth Church   16 Jan. 1839
     Sol. 16 Jan. 1839, Ishmael Stevens, J.P.

Petty, James to Mahala C. Wrenn   19 Apr. 1842
     Sol. 20 Apr. 1842, Ishmael Stevens, J.P.

Petty, Jesse B. to Sarah Church   18 Nov. 1846
     Sol. 20 Nov. 1846, Ishmael Stevens, J.P.

Petty, William T. to Louisiana Gray   16 Mar. 1843
     Sol. 17 Mar. 1843, G. W. Fly, Esquire

Phillips, Andrew B. to Cloe G. Hardison   28 Dec. 1847
     Sol. 4 Jan. 1848, Asa Hardison, M.G.

Phillips, Joel to Mildred R. Webb   1 Jan. 1838

Phillips, Leroy to Rebecca Fitzgerald   27 Nov. 1850
     Sol. 28 Nov. 1850

Pickard, Isaac S. to Sarah Barnes   20 Apr. 1840
     Sol. 23 Apr. 1840, G. W. Mitchell, M.G.

Pickard, Jesse to Rachel Hardin   18 Jan. 1851
     Sol. 19 Jan. 1851, W. B. Gillham, M.G.

Pickens, Thomas J. to Elizabeth N. Baily   30 Oct. 1849
     Sol. 31 Oct. 1849

Pickett, William S. to Mary Eliza Walker   11 July 1842

Pierce, Zadock to Eliza J. Garrigus   30 Sept. 1844
     Sol. 3 Oct. 1844, George W. Johnston, J.P.

Pigg, Daniel J. to Elizabeth P. Sparkman   22 Sept. 1840

Pigg, George W. to Parthena Fitzgerald   5 Aug. 1840
     Sol. 5 Sept. 1840, Ishmael Stevens, J.P.

Pigg, Thomas to Mararil Latta   15 Jan. 1851
    Sol. 16 Jan. 1851

Pilkinton, Minor C. to Elizabeth J. Mangrum   11 Sept. 1844

Pillow, Anthony L. to Mary F. Young   14 Jan. 1847
    Sol. 14 Jan. 1847, Philip P. Neely, M.G.

Pillow, Claiborne to Emily Ginger   27 Jan. 1848

Pillow, William R. to Narcissa Terry   16 May 1842
    Sol. 16 May 1842, Samuel W. Akin, J.P.

Pinkston, Peter R. to Elizabeth Cooper   5 Feb. 1849
    Sol. 9 Feb. 1849, Edward Puckett, J.P.

Pinkston, William W. to Mary S. Watson   25 June 1840

Pinnel, Stokes to Polly Pinnel   29 Aug. 1845
    Sol. 31 Aug. 1845, J. G. Harris, J.P.

Piper, Ira A. to Ann A. McCloud   22 Sept. 1852
    Sol. 22 Sept. 1852, Henry A. Miller, J.P.

Pipkin, Enos D. to Eliza P. Jaggers   5 Mar. 1838
    Sol. 6 Mar. 1838, Thomas Kelsey, J.P.

Pipkin, Greiss E. to Dicy Sargent   30 Apr. 1840
    Sol. 30 Apr. 1840, Thomas Kelsey, J.P.

Pipkin, John P. to Elizabeth J. Stallings   2 Sept. 1851
    Sol. 2 Sept. 1851, A. T. Gray, J.P.

Pipkin, Noah E. to Martha White   24 Oct. 1850
    Sol. 26 Oct. 1850, A. T. Gray, J.P.

Pipkin, Thomas P. to Martha Johnson   17 Jan. 1850
    Sol. 17 Jan. 1850, A. T. Gray, J.P.

Pittis, William D. to Elizabeth N. Frierson   5 Jan. 1848

Pleasants, Daniel B. to Julia A. Kusu   5 Nov. 1839
    Sol. 5 Nov. 1839, Thomas F. Scott, V.D.M.

Plummer, Emsley to Malissa Dickson   25 Mar. 1839
    Sol. 27 Mar. 1839, G. W. Mitchell, M.G.

Pogue, Anderson to Minda Long   8 Oct. 1840
    Sol. 11 Oct. 1840, Samuel Whiteside, J.P.

Pogue, Eli to Mary Whiteside   2 Oct. 1839
    Sol. 3 Oct. 1839, Richard Anderson, J.P.

Pogue, Isaac to Judith Mattox   28 July 1841
    Sol. 28 July 1841, Ishmael Stevens, J.P.

Pogue, James M. to Sarah C. Graham   3 Sept. 1852
     Sol. 5 Sept. 1852, Andrew Akin, J.P.

Pointer, Henry P. to Martha J. Caldwell   19 July 1852

Polk, John A. to Frances A. Taylor (?)   22 Dec. 1851
     Sol. 24 Dec. 1851, R. M. Ring, J.P.

Polk, Joseph L. to Charity B. Wood   17 Feb. 1838
     Sol. 22 Feb. 1838, Thomas E. Kirkpatrick, M.G.

Polk, William to Susan J. Bridgeforth   7 Nov. 1848
     Sol. 9 Nov. 1848, A. T. Gray, J.P.

Pope, John A. to Sarah E. Haley   8 May 1849
     Sol. 8 May 1849, William B. Gillham

Pope, McCajah to Rachel Clendenin   22 Jan. 1852
     Sol. 25 Jan. 1852, G. W. Mitchell, M.G.

Pope, William L. to Sarah C. M. Faris   19 Oct. 1848
     Sol. 19 Oct. 1848, William Mack, M.G.

Porter, James to Mary Walton   29 May 1843
     Sol. 30 May 1843, James H. Otey, Bishop of Protestant
     Episcopal Church in Tennessee

Porter, John J. to Mary C. Hill   23 Oct. 1843
     Sol. 23 Oct. 1843, J. W. Kilpatrick, J.P.

Porter, John N. to Emily F. Freeman   28 Dec. 1841

Porter, Thomas N. to Mary F. E. Hardin   20 Jan. 1845

Porter, William B. to Sarah D. Todd   15 Sept. 1840
     Sol. 15 Sept. 1840, Joseph Sherman, M.G.

Porter, William R. to Sarah E. Leftwich   5 Aug. 1845
     Sol. 5 Aug. 1845, Philip P. Neely, M.G.

Potter, James C. to Eliza C. Dodson   3 Dec. 1845
     Sol. 3 Dec. 1845, James B. Porter, M.G.

Potts, Anderson to Mary Woods   4 Jan. 1840
     Sol. 7 Jan. 1840, Robert Wilson, J.P.

Potts, Calvin to Lucy Lavender   24 Nov. 1852
     Sol. 25 Nov. 1852, R. Baker, J.P.

Potts, James P. to Nancy S. Goodgion   10 May 1842
     Sol. 11 May 1842, G. G. Arnold, M.G., M.E.C.

Potts, Jonathon H. to Mary E. Statlings   8 Nov. 1841
     Sol. 9 Nov. 1841, John E. Williams, J.P.

Powell, Charles to Permelia Grimes   28 Nov. 1842

Powell, Eli A. to Lucinda Tucker   20 July 1852
    Sol. J. N. Edmiston, M.G.

Powell, Isaac M. to Elmira N. Wilson   28 Sept. 1843
    Sol. 28 Sept. 1843, Adam S. Riggs, M.G.

Powell, James F. to Lucinda A. Priest   1 Nov. 1851
    Sol. 2 Nov. 1851, M. B. Molloy, M.G.

Pressgrove, Riley to Mary A. C. Roan   3 July 1845
    Sol. 3 July 1845, Hugh C. Harrison, J.P.

Preston, Thomas W. to Susan B. Maguire   21 Sept. 1852
    Sol. William Mack, M.G.

Prewett, Clovis L. to Amanda E. Fitzpatrick   21 Oct. 1850
    Sol. 23 Oct. 1850, W. H. Baldridge, M.G.

Price, Frances to Lavonia C. Ridley   19 Oct. 1841
    Sol. 20 Oct. 1841, G. W. Mitchell, M.G.

Price, William to Sally Maberry   3 Sept. 1839
    Sol. 3 Sept. 1839, Richard Stockard, J.P.

Priest, William to Manerva Priest   27 Nov. 1839
    Sol. 28 Nov. 1839, Robert Campbell, J.P.

Priest, William S. to Mary J. Powell   29 Oct. 1851
    Sol. 29 Oct. 1851, A. T. Gray, J.P.

Primm, Thomas to Elizabeth Jackson   23 May 1850
    Sol. 23 May 1850, William R. Sharp, J.P.

Pritchett, Thomas B. to Mary F. Harrison   19 Aug. 1844
    Sol. 19 Aug. 1844, James H. Otey

Pruett, John B. to Susan M. Love   22 June 1843
    Sol. 22 June 1843, Joseph Brown, M.G.

Puckett, Hartwell to Mary P. Westmoreland   17 July 1838
    Sol. 19 July 1838, Andrew Smith, M.G.

Puckett, Hartwell to Margaret Westmoreland   6 Dec. 1842
    Sol. 6 Dec. 1842, B. Gresham, J.P.

Puckett, Hiram W. to Caroline C. True   18 Dec. 1848
    Sol. 18 Dec. 1848, Thomas Hanks, M.G.

Puckett, James W. to Eliza J. True   10 Dec. 1842
    Sol. 11 Dec. 1842, Powhatan Gordon, J.P.

Puckett, Wiley F. to Sophrona G. Moore   27 May 1852

Pugh, Joseph to Mary Osteen   29 Jan. 1838
    Sol. James W. Grimes

Pugh, William P. to Eleanor Mabry   30 Dec. 1846
    Sol. 30 Dec. 1846, R. Stockard, J.P.

Pullen, Elisha to Nancy E. Scott   20 March 1848
    Sol. 22 March 1848, Joseph Brown

Pulliam, James to Jane M. Wortham   28 Apr. 1841
    Sol. 4 May 1841, G. W. Mitchell, M.G.

Purdue, Pleasant to Grishen Bishop   11 May 1852
    Sol. 12 May 1852, J. F. Holt, J.P.

Putnam, A. Waldo to Mary O. Edwards   18 July 1848
    Sol. 19 July 1848, James M. Arnell, Zion Pastor

R

Ragan, John to Amanda Derryberry   9 May 1850
    Sol. 9 May 1850, L. W. Hardison, J.P.

Rail, James to Harriet Swinney   12 June 1845
    Sol. 13 June 1845, G. W. Fly, J.P.

Rail, James to Nancy Victory   22 March 1849

Rainey, Robert R. to Mary J. Archer   2 Nov. 1848
    Sol. 2 Nov. 1848, William Mack, M.G.

Rainey, Winfred to Mary T. Minter   12 Aug. 1841
    Sol. 12 Aug. 1841, Joseph Sherman, M.G.

Ralston, David to Elizabeth Strayhorn   29 June 1841
    Sol. 9 July 1841, Samuel S. Ralston, M.G.

Ralston, Samuel S. to Mary A. Hill   5 June 1838
    Sol. 5 June 1838, R. M. Galloway

Ramsey, Andrew C. to Mary J. Kerr   12 Aug. 1851
    Sol. 21 Aug. 1851, G. C. Stockard, M.G.

Ramsey, David to Eliza Malone   22 Aug. 1842
    Sol. 23 Aug. 1842, George Ninon, J.P.

Ramsey, James to Ann Curry   30 Jan. 1840
    Sol. 30 Jan. 1840, Robert Foster, J.P.

Ramsey, John G. to Nancy Nisbet   3 Oct. 1844
    Sol. 3 Oct. 1844, Hiram Anthony, J.P.

Ramsey, Robert G. to Maria M. Hill   19 Nov. 1849
    Sol. 20 Nov. 1849, W. H. Wilkes, M.G.

Ramsey, William H. to Elizabeth A. Kerr   16 Feb. 1842
    Sol. 17 Feb. 1842, Hugh Shaw

Rankin, Joseph F. to Sarah A. Frierson   23 Oct. 1848
  Sol. 24 Oct. 1848, James M. Arnell, Zion Pastor

Randle, Thomas W. to Eleanor J. Plummer   11 May 1842
  Sol. 11 May 1842, A. L. P. Green, M.G.

Rason, E. H. to Catherine Forgey   27 Sept. 1847
  Sol. 28 Sept. 1847, John F. Hughes

Ray, Benjamin F. to Emily Morris   25 Mar. 1845

Ray, Stanford to Mary Ferrell   12 Apr. 1841
  Sol. 12 Apr. 1841, Thomas Kelsey, J.P.

Reading, Samuel R. to Laura C. Long   8 May 1852
  Sol. 12 May 1852, Edward C. Slater, M.G.

Reaves, Middleton to Laurena Christopher   17 Sept. 1840
  Sol. 17 Sept. 1840, Parke Street, J.P.

Reavis, William F. to Dorothy S. Myrick   30 Jan. 1849
  Sol. 31 Jan. 1849, R. A. Glenn, J.P.

Redding, Armsted W. to Betsy J. Tomlinson   20 July 1850
  Sol. 21 July 1850, F. A. Burke, J.P.

Redding, Isaac to Naomi Davis   25 July 1850
  Sol. 25 July 1850, F. A. Burk, J.P.

Redick, William H. to Sarah E. Dew   25 Sept. 1846

Reed, Marion to Clara W. Crosby   11 Sept. 1845
  Sol. 13 Sept. 1845, J. A. Otey

Reed, Robert to Hannah A. Edgin   3 July 1852
  Sol. 4 July 1852, William R. Sharp, J.P.

Renfro, Alfred F. to Nancy R. Evans   23 Dec. 1847
  Sol. 23 Dec. 1847, Hugh C. Harrison, J.P.

Renfrow, Green to Nancy Stringfellow   27 Apr. 1842
  Sol. 27 Apr. 1842, James Smith, J.P.

Renfro, James S. to Delia R. Bryant   21 Nov. 1848
  Sol. 21 Nov. 1848, F. A. Burke, J.P.

Renfro, Jesse to Terrecy Loftin   2 June 1845
  Sol. 3 June 1845, Hugh C. Harrison, J.P.

Renfrow, John to Susan Daimwood   6 Mar. 1838

Renfro, Rufus R. to Mary E. Johnson   2 Oct. 1852
  Sol. 3 Oct. 1852, J. F. Holt, J.P.

Reynolds, Isom to Mary A. Grigg   21 Feb. 1852
     Sol. 22 Feb. 1852, Joseph Brown, M.G.

Reynolds, Seymour to Caroline J. B. Wilson   9 Feb. 1838
     Sol. 9 Feb. 1838, Thomas Fielding Scott, V.D.M.

Richardson, Amos to Elizabeth Lindsey   28 Dec. 1842
     Sol. 29 Dec. 1842, C. Y. Hudson, J.P.

Richardson, John W. to Lucy Vincent   4 Dec. 1841
     Sol. 9 Dec. 1841, Alexander Johnson, J.P.

Richardson, Oran A. to Sarah L. Smith   7 Apr. 1842
     Sol. 7 Apr. 1843, Loyd Richardson, M. G., M.E.C.

Richardson, William B. to Sarilda Kennedy   27 Apr. 1848
     Sol. 27 Apr. 1848, W. D. F. Saurie, M.G.

Richardson, William C. to Mary A. Hunt   10 Mar. 1852
     Sol. 11 Mar. 1852, Joseph Brown, M.G.

Richardson, Willis J. to Mary Ann Stokes   11 Jan. 1840
     Sol. 14 Jan. 1840, P. Ball, M.G.

Richmond, James W. to Elizabeth A. Wood   29 June 1842
     Sol. 30 June 1842, W. Oakley, J.P.

Ricketts, Robert D. to Mary A. Smith   3 Oct. 1843
     Sol. 5 Oct. 1843, R. Stockard, J.P.

Rickets, William to Nancy H. Johnston   21 Sept. 1847
     Sol. 21 Sept. 1847, J. M. Gordon, J.P.

Ridley, Rufus R. to Catherine M. Leach   11 Sept. 1838
     Sol. 12 Sept. 1838, G. W. Mitchell, M.G.

Rieves, Joel S. to Eliza Johnson   18 Nov. 1845
     Sol. 18 Nov. 1845, D. Judd

Rieves, William J. to Haskey Maddox   29 May 1849
     Sol. 29 May 1849, Henry Harris, J.P.

Riggins, Joel to Sarah Robinson   11 Mar. 1851
     Sol. 11 Mar. 1851, R. A. Glenn, J.P.

Riggins, John to Louisa Turbefield   12 Dec. 1839
     Sol. 15 Dec. 1839, H. W. Derryberry

Riggins, Lewis L. to Lucinda L. Driskill   19 Sept. 1844
     Sol. 19 Sept. 1844, C. Cooke, J.P.

Riggins, William C. to Bathena Kincaid   28 Oct. 1848
     Sol. 29 Oct. 1848, John Glenn, J.P.

Riggs, Adam L. to Sarah M. Hurt   4 Mar. 1845
     Sol. 5 Mar. 1845, R. G. Irvins, M.G.

Rine, Christopher to Cynthia Hesket   12 May 1841
    Sol. 13 May 1841, William Davis, M.G.

Ring, Aaron to Margaret J. McClain   16 Oct. 1851
    Sol. 18 Oct. 1851, W. R. H. Mack, J.P.

Ring, James H. to Malissa Bell   25 Aug. 1847
    Sol. 26 Aug. 1847, James O. Griffith, J.P.

Ritchie, Gillian to Sarah Smith   11 Jan. 1841
    Sol. 18 Jan. 1841, Jonathan S. Hunt, J.P.

Rittenberry, Ransom N. L. to Lucy A. E. Sammons   15 July 1846
    Sol. 17 July 1846, James N. Edmiston, M.G.

Rittenberry, Thomas J. to Naomi N. Sealy   8 Jan. 1849
    Sol. 11 Jan. 1849

Roach, James F. to Margaret Harris   25 Feb. 1846
    Sol. 26 Feb. 1846, George R. Hoge, M.G.

Roach, John L. to Louisa Oakley   5 Nov. 1839
    Sol. Britain Garner, Primitive Baptist

Roach, John L. to Sarah Foster   13 Nov. 1852

Roach, William to Dolly Pierce   4 July 1840
    Sol. 5 July 1840, William W. Grimes, M.G.

Roan, Calvin to Elizabeth A. Meaders   13 Aug. 1840
    Sol. 16 Aug. 1840, William Harris, M.G.

Roan, Carter to Rosannah M. Burruss   3 Nov. 1840

Roan, Chesley to Emily Ferguson   1 July 1840
    Sol. 1 July 1840, Thomas Kelsey, J.P.

Roan, James to Sarah Chandler   23 Oct. 1839

Roan, Jesse to Mary Chumbley   23 Jan. 1840

Roane, Levi to Martha J. Lancaster   20 Mar. 1845
    Sol. 20 March 1845, J. G. Harris, J.P.

Robard, Francis S. to Martha A. Kincaid   20 Feb. 1850
    Sol. 20 Feb. 1850

Robards, Nathaniel to Susan B. Chadduck   18 May 1842
    Sol. 19 May 1842, Justice Williams, M.G.

Robards, Williams A. to Mary A. Mills   29 Jan. 1844
    Sol. 31 Jan. 1844, Berryman Hamlett, J.P.

Roberson, James to Ann L. Dale   6 Oct. 1845
    Sol. 8 Oct. 1845, P. P. Neely, M.G.

Roberson, William H. to Malvina L. Matthews   15 June 1843
    Sol, 15 June 1843, James O. Griffith, Esquire

Roberts, John A. to Malvina Wallis   10 Sept. 1852
    Sol. 12 Sept. 1852, J. Stephens, M.G.

Roberts, John W. to Mary J. McKnight   14 Oct. 1851
    Sol. 16 Oct. 1851

Roberts, Joseph to Margaret McKnoll   27 Mar. 1844
    Sol. 27 Mar. 1844, Aaron Vestal, J.P.

Roberts, Robert R. to Lydia V. McKnight   27 Aug. 1851
    Sol, 28 Aug. 1851

Roberts, Samuel J. to Angeline R. Wisener   14 Oct. 1852
    Sol. 15 Oct. 1852, R. C. Irwin, M.G.

Roberts, William A. to Hannah Kincaid   20 July 1850
    Sol. 22 July 1850, Joseph F. Jordan, J.P.

Robertson, James to Elizabeth Jeffreys   27 Mar. 1845

Robertson, Maison to Elizabeth Pearce   3 Jan. 1844

Robinson, Henry C. to Nancy J. Hassell   8 Apr. 1851
    Sol, 8 Apr. 1851, M. D. Molloy, M. G.

Robison, William C. to Lucy A. Chumbley   19 Aug. 1847
    Sol. 22 Aug. 1847, L. W. Hardeson, J.P.

Rogers, John F. to Mary S. Craig   21 July 1848
    Sol. 23 July 1848, Coleman Goad, J.P.

Rogers, John H. to Nancy C. Miller   22 Apr. 1840

Rogers, Robert M. to Sarah A. Ashworth   6 Jan. 1851

Rogers, William to Jane Craig   31 Dec. 1845

Rolen, Michail C. to Nancy C. Coffey   12 Feb. 1852
    Sol. 12 Feb. 1852, F. A. Burke, J.P.

Rolen, Wiley to Sarah M. Partin   1 Sept. 1852
    Sol. 1 Sept. 1852, William Mack, M.G.

Rook, Samuel P. to Margaret E. Craig   16 Jan. 1850
    Sol. 16 Jan. 1850, J. W. Westmoreland, J.P.

Roop, Washington to Martha H. Allen   9 May 1849
    Sol. 14 May 1849, F. S. Petway

Rope, Andrew F. to Irene W. Wortham   23 Mar. 1840
    Sol. 26 Mar. 1844, G. W. Mitchell, M.G.

Ross, Morgan H. to Lucinda Coffey   3 Jan. 1838
    Sol. 3 Jan. 1838, F. S. Perry

Rountree, Cicero to Martha A. Priest   24 May 1845

Rountree, John to Mary McKee   26 Oct. 1852
     Sol. 28 Oct. 1852, B. F. Alexander, M.G.

Rountree, John J. to Margaret McKee   19 Mar. 1838
     Sol. 21 Mar. 1838, Robert Campbell, J.P.

Rountree, Joseph to Orpha Griffin   10 Oct. 1838
     Sol. 11 Oct. 1838, Robert Campbell, J.P.

Rucker, Thomas W. to Lavinia Dixon   6 Feb. 1849
     Sol. 6 Feb. 1849, F. A. Burn, J.P.

Rumbo, Elias to Mary Priest   27 Feb. 1839
     Sol. 28 Feb. 1839, R. W. Morris, E. M. P. Church

Rummage, John to Caroline Huey   Oct. 4, 1847
     Sol. 4 Oct. 1847, John Brown, J.P.

Rushton, George W. to Sarah H. S. Fitzgerald   1 Jan. 1852
     Sol. 2 Jan. 1852, B. R. Gant, M.G.

Rushton, Jesse G. to Sarah W. Dawson   13 Dec. 1845
     Sol. 14 Dec. 1845, E. Hanks, M.G.

Rushton, William W. to Cynthia Morris   30 July 1849
     Sol. 31 July 1849, R. G. Irvine, M.G.

Russell, Edward A. to Jemima Owens   19 Nov. 1851
     Sol. 19 Nov. 1851, D. Moore, M.G.

Russell, Haley W. to Milly Hare   10 June 1842

Russell, Jordan to Susan J. Russell   19 Dec. 1846

Russell, Madison M. to Rachel A. Jones   21 Oct. 1841
     Sol. 22 Oct. 1841, E. Hanks, M.G.

Russell, Washington B. to Charity M. Jones   26 Dec. 1838
     Sol. 27 Dec. 1838, William W. Coleman, J.P.

Ruston, William W. to Mary M. Wrenn   28 Aug. 1852
     Sol. 29 Aug. 1852, D. G. Moore, M.G.

Rutledge, Edward A. to Mary F. Young   11 Apr. 1843

Rutledge, Samuel J. to Emaline Hogan   23 Sept. 1843
     Sol. 24 Sept. 1843, James M. Richardson, J.P.

Rye, Joseph C. to Martha W. Keeble   12 June, 1850
     Sol. 12 June 1850, William Mack, M.G.

Sanders, Overton to Mary N. Douglas   19 Sept. 1838
     Sol. 20 Sept. 1838, Robert Hill, J.P.

Sandford, R. J. to Maria W. Yancy   4 Mar. 1850
     Sol. 4 Mar. 1850, R. C. Garrison

Sandford, William to Rebecca A. Mackey   4 Oct. 1848
     Sol. 5 Oct. 1848, W. H. Baldridge, M.G.

Sandford, William A. to Eliza B. Garland   11 June 1845
     Sol. 20 June 1845, Joseph Sherman, M.G.

Sandsberry, John S. to Sarah E. Lindsey   15 Nov. 1848

Sansom, Richard to Mary A. Cooper   29 July 1847
     Sol. 29 July 1847, James M. Arnell, Zion Pastor

Sarrie, Benjamin to Frances Hite   3 Mar. 1840
     Sol. 3 Mar. 1840, Ishmael Stevens, J.P.

Satterfield, Addison to Sarah P. Leetch   1 Sept. 1852
     Sol. 1 Sept. 1852, G. C. Stockard, M.G.

Satterfield, Alvis to Matilda G. Alexander   19 Dec. 1848
     Sol. 20 Dec. 1848, B. F. Alexander, M.G.

Satterfield, Joseph to Martha J. Jacobs   30 Jan. 1850
     Sol. 31 Jan. 1850

Saunders, Allen W. to Martha J. Davis   29 June 1843
     Sol. 30 June 1843, George R. Hoge, M.G.

Scantlin, Jenkins D. to Mary F. A. Davis   3 Feb. 1841
     Sol. 4 Feb. 1841, B. D. Neal

Scott, Fountain to Leoticy Griffin   25 Aug. 1852
     Sol. 26 Aug. 1852, E. W. Benson, M.G.

Scott, James M. to Sarah J. Carter   26 Sept. 1842
     Sol. 27 Sept. 1842, E. Hanks, M.G.

Scott, John M. to Eliza L. Coleburn   25 July 1850
     Sol. 25 July 1850, J. T. Moss, M.G.

Scott, Milton to Mary A. Christopher   19 Aug. 1847
     Sol. 19 Aug. 1847, Parke Street, J.P.

Scott, Newton to Nancy I. Bryant   18 Nov. 1847
     Sol. 18 Nov. 1847, Park Street, J.P.

Scott, Robert M. to Sarah M. Walker   24 June 1847
     Sol. 26 June 1847, J. K. Boyce, M.G.

Scott, Samuel C. to Frances M. Bacheler   3 Feb. 1840

Scott, Samuel C. to Frances Cooper   2 Dec. 1850
     Sol. 5 Dec. 1850, J. W. Westmoreland, J.P.

Scott, Samuel W. to Nancy L. Boyd   8 Dec. 1841
    Sol. 9 Dec. 1841, Hugh Shaw

Scott, Wiley to Margaret C. Owens   13 Mar. 1838
    Sol. 15 Mar. 1838, Robert Foster, J.P.

Scott, William N. to Mary Reaves   1 Feb. 1840
    Sol. 2 Feb. 1840, Park Street, J.P.

Scott, William P. to Mildred A. E. Carter   6 Oct. 1841
    Sol. 22 Oct. 1841, Thomas E. Kirkpatrick, M.G.

Scott, William S. to Sarah Liffle   24 Sept. 1839

Scott, William S. to Holey Vincent   14 June 1842
    Sol. 15 June 1842, James W. Richardson

Scribner, John to Rebecca A. Aydelott   2 Jan. 1846
    Sol. 2 Jan. 1846, Hiram Anthony, J.P.

Scribner, John A. T. to Hulda G. Garrett   31 July 1851
    Sol. 31 July 1851, F. A. Burke, J.P.

Sealey, Samuel D. to Sarah F. Strange   5 Jan. 1841
    Sol. 5 Jan. 1841, Thomas Kelsey, J.P.

Sedberry, Benjamin C. to Sarah A. V. Cappell   23 Sept. 1851
    Sol. 25 Sept. 1851, E. R. Grant, M.G.

Sedberry, George F. to Rebecca A. Williams   11 Sept. 1850
    Sol. 12 Sept. 1850, R. G. Irvine, M.G.

Sedberry, John L. to Margaret B. Alexander   10 Dec. 1851
    Sol. 11 Dec. 1851, R. G. Irvine, M.G.

Sedberry, William R. to Caroline H. Alexander   23 Jan. 1843
    Sol. 26 Jan. 1843, F. G. Ferguson, M.G.

Seely, Samuel W. to Sarah Kerr   21 Dec. 1842
    Sol. 22 Dec. 1842, G. Hanks, J.P.

Sellers, Anderson to Nancy Latta   15 Sept. 1849
    Sol. 16 Sept. 1849, R. G. Irvine, M.G.

Sellers, Eli B. to Sarah Donaldson   11 Dec. 1850
    Sol. 12 Dec. 1850, E. Hanks, M.G.

Sellers, Isaac to Sarah J. West   22 Feb. 1847
    Sol. 23 Feb. 1847, Berryman Hamlett

Sellers, Isom to Elizabeth Douglas   26 Feb. 1846
    Sol. 26 Feb. 1846, A. T. Gray, J.P.

Sellers, James L. to Eliza Garner   3 May 1852
    Sol. 5 May 1852, William W. Coleman, J.P.

Sellers, William B. to Mahala J. Estes   23 May 1839
     Sol. 23 May 1839, Berryman Hamlett, J.P.

Sewell, Robert to Sarah J. Wrenn   18 July 1842
     Sol. 20 July 1842, Ishmael Stevens, J.P.

Shannon, David to Lucretia T. Chaffin   7 Aug. 1848
     Sol. 8 Aug. 1848, James Edmiston, M.G.

Sharber, Joseph W. to Mary J. Porter (he, a doctor)   23 Oct. 1846
     Sol. 23 Oct. 1846, W. H. Baldridge, M.G.

Sharp, Isaac H. to Leonna Kelley   10 Aug. 1843
     Sol. 10 Aug. 1843, Thomas Dotson, M.G.

Sharp, William to Minerva Mayfield   20 Feb. 1839

Shaw, James G. to Martha Lasley   27 Jan. 1838
     Sol. 28 Jan. 1838, Alexander Dickson, T. Elder

Shaw, Samuel to Susannah Maddox   6 May 1844
     Sol. 7 May 1844, E. Blocker, J.P.

Sheham, Robert F. to Emily Hull   22 Dec. 1846
     Sol. 31 Jan. 1847, Alvis Williams, J.P.

Sheppard, James M. to Emma C. Harrison   17 Nov. 1849
     Sol. 19 Nov. 1849, G. W. Mitchell, M.G.

Sheppherd, John R. to Amelia A. Bain   6 June 1850
     Sol. 6 June 1850, Asa Hardison, M.G.

Sheppard, William C. to Parthena Moore   14 Jan. 1845

Sherman (or Shannon) Daniel J. to Amanda Noles   28 Oct. 1847
     Sol. 28 Oct. 1847, John Mack, J.P.

Sherrod, Arthur P. to Maria Mays   23 Feb. 1846
     Sol. 24 Feb. 1846, Ishmael Stevens, J.P.

Shettlesworth, Elijah M. to Mary E. Barnes   18 Nov. 1848
     Sol. 20 Nov. 1848, William J. Strayhorn, J.P.

Shires, David to Myra L. Tigner   20 June 1851
     Sol. 20 June 1851, Asa Hardison, M.G.

Shires, Joel to Sarah Chun   13 June 1840

Shires, Solomon to Martha Harris   21 Nov. 1843
     Sol. 22 Nov. 1843, R. A. Glenn, J.P.

Shoemaker, William to Harriet Pretty   16 Dec. 1845
     Sol. 19 Dec. 1845, Washington Oakley, J.P.

Short, Major to Mary Trulove   8 March 1842
     Sol. 8 March 1842, William Davis, M.G.

Simpson, Thomas to Catherine Pursell   13 Apr. 1848
    Sol. 13 Apr. 1848, J. M. White, J.P.

Simons, John W. to Mary C. Moore   2 Mar. 1844
    Sol. 3 Mar. 1844, I. N. Bills, J.P.

Simons, Samuel C. to Elizabeth Lawrence   27 Jan. 1844
    Sol. 29 Jan. 1844, James M. Richardson, J.P.

Sims, Alfred A. to Martha Finch   23 Aug. 1842
    Sol. 23 Aug. 1842, Powhatan Gordon, J.P.

Sims, Augustus to Evaline L. Morgan   27 Apr. 1840
    Sol. 8 June 1840, Joseph E. Douglas, Elder, M.E. Church

Sims, John to Jemima Vincent   6 June 1843
    Sol. 6 June 1843, Thomas Dotson, M.G.

Sims, Parris L. to Margaret Turnbo   14 Dec. 1840

Skelly, Ruse F. to Mary A. Capoot   1 Feb. 1840
    Sol. 4 Feb. 1840, William W. Coleman, J.P.

Skinner, George W. to Mary L. Chappell   14 Feb. 1844
    Sol. 14 Feb. 1844, Finch P. Scruggs, M.G.

Skinner, George W. to Laura C. Porter   26 Aug. 1846
    Sol. P. P. Neeley

Skipper, William to Mary A. M. Goodjion   1 March 1842
    Sol. 1 March 1842, G. G. Arnold, M.G., M.E.C.

Slayden, Elial to Martha Bullock   10 Jan. 1838
    Sol. 11 Jan. 1838, William W. Coleman, J.P.

Slayden, Joseph E. to Martha A. Johnson   19 Sept. 1839
    Sol. 19 Sept. 1839, T. G. Hunter, J.P.

Small, M. D. to Martha G. Arington   27 Mar. 1849
    Sol. 27 Mar. 1849, J. J. Trott, M.G.

Small, William M. to Mary J. Wood   15 May 1851
    Sol. 15 May 1851, Edward C. Slater, M.G.

Smiser, James to Charlotte P. Booker   26 Oct. 1847
    Sol. 27 Oct. 1847, Joseph Sherman, M.G.

Smith, Andrew D. to Mary E. Moore   15 July 1852
    Sol. 15 July 1852, at Richard E. Moore's by William P. Martin
    of 8th district

Smith, Beauford J. to Eliza J. Wingfield   3 Nov. 1840
    Sol. 3 Nov. 1840, Joseph Sherman, M.G.

Smith, Benjamin D. to Mary Robason   9 Feb. 1838
    Sol. 13 Feb. 1838, Joshua K. Speer, M.G.

Smith, Benjamin F. to Elizabeth K. W. Daniel   24 Aug. 1840

Smith, Benjamin F. to Margaret E. Hill   27 Mar. 1845
    Sol. 27 Mar. 1845, R. C. Garrison, V.L.M.

Smith, Clem to Nancy Turner   7 May 1839

Smith, David W. to Nancy M. Brown   18 July 1851
    Sol. 20 July 1851, J. E. McCherd, M.G.

Smith, Edward E. to Rebecca A. Shull   27 Apr. 1852
    Sol. 28 Apr. 1852, John L. Faris, J.P.

Smith, Enoch K. to Elizabeth R. Sowell   29 June 1847
    Sol. 1 July 1847, Powhatan Gordon, J.P.

Smith, Erastus C. to Louisa Bryan   30 Sept. 1845
    Sol. 2 Oct. 1845, M. W. Gray, M.G.

Smith, Francis J. to Evaline F. Blakely   26 Sept. 1842
    Sol. 27 Sept. 1842, James M. Arnell, Zion Pastor

Smith, George W. to Mary Hawks   9 Nov. 1850
    Sol. 12 Nov. 1850, James Calhoun

Smith, Gideon W. to Martha A. Chalk   2 Apr. 1839
    Sol. 4 Apr. 1839, H. A. McMackin, J.P.

Smith, Israel L. to Olly G. Roberson   13 Dec. 1843
    Sol. 14 Dec. 1843, George W. Fly, J.P.

Smith, James to Sarah J. Nicholson   14 Dec. 1842
    Sol. 15 Dec. 1842, Samuel Wheatley, J.P.

Smith, James A. to Lucinda Loftin   25 Aug. 1845
    Sol. 26 Aug. 1845, Park Street, J.P.

Smith, James F. to Martha J. Wilkes   29 May 1848
    Sol. 30 May 1848, Joseph Brown, M.G.

Smith, James H. to Matilda Perry   5 Nov. 1845
    Sol. 6 Nov. 1845, D. Brown, V. D. M.

Smith, James W. to Martha Bailey   14 Oct. 1839
    Sol. 15 Oct. 1839, William W. Grimes, M.G.

Smith, Jared E. to Sarah R. Mack   16 Dec. 1846
    Sol. 16 Dec. 1846, James N. Edmiston, M.G.

Smith, John L. to Matilda A. Craig   11 Feb. 1851
    Sol. 11 Feb. 1851, J. W. Westmoreland, J.P.

Smith, Leonard L. to Elizabeth Erwin   2 Dec. 1840
    Sol. 3 Dec. 1840, William W. Coleman, J.P.

Smith, Philip to Lettatitia Davis   17 July 1838
     Sol. 18 July 1838, Andrew Smith, M.G.

Smith, Preston to Mary A. Crofford   8 Oct. 1846
     Sol. 8 Oct. 1846, William Mack, M.G.

Smith, Robert to Ursula Dew   6 Aug. 1851
     Sol. 7 Aug. 1851, James N. Edmiston, M.G.

Smith, Samuel F. to Lucy L. Reynolds   7 Sept. 1844
     Sol. 8 Sept. 1844, R. A. Glenn, J.P.

Smith, Thomas S. to Caroline M. Bond   16 Nov. 1840
     Sol. 17 Nov. 1840, G. W. Mitchell, M.G.

Smith, William to Mary Brown   23 Nov. 1840

Smith, William B. to Elizabeth M. A. Brown   30 Dec. 1848
     Sol. 31 Dec. 1848, D. F. A. Burke, J.P.

Smith, William H. to Martha A. Anderson   23 Nov. 1848
     Sol. 23 Nov. 1848, William H. Wilkes, M.G.

Smith, William L. to Portia Logue   11 July 1839
     Sol. 11 July 1839, G. C. Stockard, M.G.

Smithson, Henry C. to Mary Brooks   30 June 1849
     Sol. 1 July 1849, Coleman Goad, J.P.

Smithson, John L. to Caroline Philips   31 Mar. 1851
     Sol. 3 Apr. 1851, Thomas Hudspeth, M.G.

Smithson, Peyton C. to Perlina Brooks   27 May 1846

Smithson, Sylvanus W. to Myra Hadden   27 Nov. 1851
     Sol. 27 Nov. 1851, Edward C. Slater, M.G.

Smithson, William Q. A. to Nancy A. Trotter   8 May 1847

Smithwick, A. A. to Mary L. Love   12 Oct. 1846
     Sol. 14 Oct. 1846, William Mack, M.G

Southall, William A. to Sarah A. N. Scott   19 Dec. 1844

Southern, Asa to Tempe Williams   15 Jan. 1838
     Sol. 15 Jan. 1838, Elijah Hanks, M.G.

Southern, Isaiah to Stacy Gaskill   19 May 1847
     Sol. 19 May 1847, Ishmael Stevens, J.P.

Southern, John K. to Mary E. True   18 Aug. 1848
     Sol. 20 Aug. 1848, M. B. Molloy, M.G.

Southworth, A. W. to Frances O. Mitchell   11 Apr. 1848

Sowell, Augustus to Dorothy C. Webber   16 Oct. 1841
    Sol. 17 Oct. 1841, William Thomas Leacock

Sowell, David R. to Mary M. Bingham   16 Jan. 1838
    Sol. 18 Jan. 1838, Thomas Kelsey, J.P.

Sowell, Henry C. to Jane C. King   22 Nov. 1849
    Sol. 23 Nov. 1849, R. G. Irvine, M.G.

Sowell, James H. to Mahala Ashworth   31 July 1844
    Sol. 31 July 1844, Ishmael Stevens, J.P.

Sowell, James M. to Sarah C. Walker   25 Aug. 1846
    Sol. 25 Aug. 1846, Powhatan Gordon, J.P.

Sowell, James W. to Minerva M. Fitzgerald   12 Jan. 1850
    Sol. 13 Jan. 1850, John B. Hamilton, Elder, M.E.C.

Sowell, Jethro to Sarah C. P. Morrow   13 Feb. 1843

Sowell, Joseph M. to Mary A. Blakely   24 Dec. 1851
    Sol. 24 Dec. 1851

Sowell, Nathaniel to Susan Simmons   9 Oct. 1847
    Sol. 10 Oct. 1847, L. W. Hardeson, J.P.

Sowell, Thomas to Sarah A. Tatum   5 June 1852
    Sol. 6 June 1852, Joseph Foster, J.P.

Sowell, William J. to Emily J. Hardison   8 May 1850
    Sol. 8 May 1850, Ezra Hardison, J.P.

Spain, Nevil G. to Sarah L. Benderman   9 Oct. 1848
    Sol. 10 Oct. 1848, J. K. Boyce, G. M.

Sparkman, Calvin P. to Amanda H. Wollard   18 Dec. 1850
    Sol. 19 Dec. 1850

Sparkman, Jesse Y. to Rosannah Sparkman   5 Feb. 1840
    Sol. 5 Feb. 1840, E. R. Osborne, E. C. C.

Sparkman, Thomas W. to Delila P. Fitzgerald   22 Sept. 1840
    Sol. 24 Sept. 1840, R. W. Morris, E. M. E. Church

Sparkman, Thomas W. to Milley A. White   16 Mar. 1843
    Sol. 16 Mar. 1843, A. T. Gray, J.P.

Sparkman, William D. to Jane C. Raney   22 Dec. 1847
    Sol. 22 Dec. 1847, A. T. Gray, J.P.

Sparkman, William S. to Mary A. Moore   4 Jan. 1845
    Sol. 5 Jan. 1845, Peter Wrenn, J.P.

Sparkman, William W. to Elizabeth J. Fitzgerald   21 Nov. 1840

Spence, William H. to Mahala Goldman   30 Aug. 1841
     Sol. G. C. Stockard, M.G.

Spencer, Hiram to Jane Powell   27 Dec. 1843

Spencer, John to Evaline Holt   9 July 1841

Spindle, John P. to Ann S. Johnson   17 July 1845
     Sol. 17 July 1845, Joseph Sherman, M.G.

Sprinkles, Moses to Martha J. Thomason   26 Feb. 1850
     Sol. 27 Feb. 1850, J. F. Holt, J.P.

Sprinkle, William to Susan Sprinkle   8 July 1852
     Sol. 8 July 1852, Thomas B. Stone

Stacy, Eli R. to Harriet C. Hand   6 Aug. 1840
     Sol. 6 Aug. 1840, W. W. Cockran, M.G.

Stacy, Jesse to Caroline Leonard   2 Dec. 1848

Stallings, William to Louisa Morrow   29 Aug. 1848
     Sol. 31 Aug. 1848, Joseph Foster, J.P.

Stallings, Zachariah to Prudy Anderson   6 July 1839
     Sol. 6 July 1839, Joseph Henson (?), J.P.

Stamps, William E. to Sarah Everett   4 Feb. 1846
     Sol. 5 Feb. 1846, Hugh C. Harrison, J.P.

Stanfield, McCoy to Mary Ring   26 Aug. 1844
     Sol. 26 Aug. 1844, Thomas Kelsey, J.P.

Stanfill, Joseph E. to Mary C. Young   19 Jan. 1840
     Sol. 22 Jan. 1840, Thomas E. Kirkpatrick, M.G.

Stanley, Austin C. to Rhoda C. McConnico   24 Nov. 1841
     Sol. 25 Nov. 1841, W. H. Baldridge, M.G.

Starkes, Rhesa L. to Malinda E. Hunter   29 May 1840
     Sol. 4 June 1840, G. W. Mitchell, M.G.

Starkey, James M. to Elizabeth Y. Ridley   14 Mar. 1843
     Sol. 3 April 1843, James Daly, J.P.

Steele, Nathaniel H. to Elizabeth L. Griffin   6 Sept. 1851
     Sol. 7 Sept. 1851, Edward R. Puckett

Steele, Robert M. to Jane E. McKelvey   3 Feb. 1851
     Sol. 3 Feb. 1851, F. A. Burke, J.P.

Stephens, Alexander to Eliza Green   4 Nov. 1851
     Sol. 4 Nov. 1851, Henry A. Miller, J.P.

Stephens, Anderson P. to Margaret Brown   20 Oct. 1846

Stephens, David H. to Martha C. Scott   26 Aug. 1841

Stephenson, John G. to Lucinda Rogers   24 Mar. 1849
    Sol. 25 Mar. 1849, W. R. Sharp, J.P.

Stephenson, William C. to Martha A. Isbell   17 Jan. 1849
    Sol. 18 Jan. 1849, J. Crafton, J.P.

Stewart, John W. to Amanda C. Payton   5 July 1849
    Sol. 6 July 1849, L. A. Nichols, E. C. C.

Stewart, Pleasant to Sarah Smith   18 Aug. 1844
    Sol. 18 Aug. 1844, H. Harrison, J.P.

Stewart, William to Ruth Smith   2 Oct. 1845
    Sol. 2 Oct. 1845, Richard Stockard, J.P.

Stewart, William A. to Susan Mitchell   3 Jan. 1849
    Sol. 4 Jan. 1849, R. G. Irvine, M.G.

Stewart, William A. to Mahala Powell   no date

Stewart, William P. to Mary Gordon   11 Jan. 1845
    Sol. 12 Jan. 1845, J. N. Gordon, J.P.

Stiles, Guilford to Mary N. Passmore   9 Aug. 1843
    Sol. 9 Aug. 1843, C. H. Baldridge, M.G.

Stockard, George C. to Esther E. Thompson   24 Jan. 1838
    Sol. 30 Jan. 1838, C. B. Porter, G. M.

Stockard, James W. to Mary L. Jennings   21 Nov. 1844
    Sol. 26 Nov. 1844, G. W. Mitchell, M.G.

Stockard, John to Eliza J. Lusk   15 June 1841
    Sol. 17 June 1841, G. W. Mitchell, M.G.

Stockard, Joseph C. to Susan E. Gibbs   17 Apr. 1848

Stockard, Martin L. to Camilla A. Griffin   19 July 1848
    Sol. 19 July 1848, G. W. Mitchell, M.G.

Stockard, Samuel J. to Lorey J. Howard   7 Jan. 1843
    Sol. 8 Jan. 1843, G. C. Stockard, M. G.

Stockard, William P. to Margaret A. Jones   20 Apr. 1843
    Sol. 21 Apr. 1843, John B. Bond, J.P.

Stockton, L. D. to Margaret C. Alexander   23 Nov. 1848
    Sol. 23 Nov. 1848, R. C. Garrison, M.G.

Stoddart, Felix to Mary A. C. Porter   20 July 1841
    Sol. 20 July 1841, Joseph E. Walker, M.G., M.E. Church

Stone, Elijah F. to Caroline Carothers   13 Sept. 1849
    Sol. 13 Sept. 1849, James H. Burns, M.G.

Stone, George W. to Elizabeth Akin
     Sol. 9 Dec. 1840, Willie Ledbetter, L.E., M.E.C.
8 Dec. 1840

Stone, Thomas J. to Ann E. Wilks
     Sol. 27 June 1850, William Mack, M.G.
27 June 1850

Stone, William A. to Mary J. Johnson
     Sol. 7 Apr. 1840, Thomas E. Kirkpatrick, M.G.
3 Mar. 1840

Stone, William F. to Mildred H. Dowdy
     Sol. 13 Oct. 1841, G. C. Stockard, M.G.
12 Oct. 1841

Stone, (or Starns), William R. to Eliza Stone
9 Jan. 1850

Story, William C. to Frances Runyan
     Sol. 11 Aug. 1842, William Chalk, J.P.
10 Aug. 1842

Stout, Isaiah to Mary E. Kinnard
     Sol. 3 July 1850, T. N. McKee, M.G.
3 July 1850

Strange, Thomas to Nancy Sealey
     Sol. 15 Jan. 1841, William W. Coleman, J.P.
15 Jan. 1841

Strayhorn, Joseph H. to Mary C. Akin
     Sol. 5 Jan. 1843, Willie Ledbetter, L.E.,M.E.C.
4 Jan. 1843

Strayhorn, Josiah K. to Emaline E. Kinzer
     Sol. 8 Dec. 1841, Justice Williams, M.G.
4 Dec. 1841

Strayhorn, Samuel J. to Hannah Foster
13 Sept. 1841

Stricklin, Francis to Duritha T. Nicks
     Sol. 14 June 1840, William W. Coleman, J.P.
12 June 1840

Strozzi, William A. to Nancy Blair
     Sol. 17 Aug. 1848, W. D. F. Saurie, M.G.
15 Aug. 1848

Studdurt, Joseph B. to Narcissa C. Wooldridge
     Sol. 6 Dec. 1848, T. Witherspoon, M.G.
6 Dec. 1848

Studdurt, William J. to Mary K. Wooldridge
     Sol. 1 Oct. 1848, R. G. Irvine, M.G.
1 Oct. 1848

Studivan, Sylvanus to Lucy Forsythe
     Sol. 18 Mar. 1847, Andrew Scott, J.P.
18 Mar. 1847

Sullivan, William M. to Elizabeth E. M. Bostick
     Sol. 18 Jan. 1843, Parke Street, J.P.
16 Jan. 1843

Surrenkross, Edward A. to Isabella Ann Smith
     Sol. 14 Mar. 1851 at St. John's Church by Rector E. H. Cressy
12 Mar. 1851

Sutton, James R. to Elizabeth J. Derryberry
     Sol. 31 Jan. 1843, Joshua K. Speer, M.G.
23 Jan. 1843

Sutton, Samuel J. to Jane A. Q. Williams   19 Apr. 1848
     Sol, 20 Apr. 1848, W. D. F. Saurie, M.G.

Swanson, James to Minerva B. Theobald   27 Oct. 1847
     Sol. 27 Oct. 1847, Philip P. Neely, M.G.

Swanson, Svante (?) M. to Susan H. McRady   27 Sept. 1851
     Sol. 29 Sept. 1851, William Mack, M.G.

Sweet, Moses to Nancy Smith   21 June 1838
     Sol. 21 June 1838, James Adkins, J.P.

Sweet, William to Caroline Bunch   31 Dec. 1850
     Sol, 31 Dec. 1850, John Glenn, J.P.

Sykes, William J. to Susan J. Caruthers   27 Sept. 1843
     Sol, 27 Sept. 1843, W. D. F. Sowell, M.G.

T

Tally, Benjamin F. to Matilda Hudson   5 Nov. 1845
     Sol. 5 Nov. 1845, J. T. Faris, J.P.

Talley, James A. to Catherine A. Tranum   26 Feb. 1842

Talley, Richard to Catherine J. Fortner   25 Nov. 1840

Tanner, David to Eliza Haley   14 Oct. 1841
     Sol. 15 Oct. 1841, Benony Gresham

Tanner, William J. to Martha G. Smith   25 June 1850
     Sol. 25 June 1850, J. W. Westmoreland, J.P.

Tarkington, William W. to Ruth Brooks   4 Jan. 1844
     Sol. 4 Jan. 1844, Berryman Hamblett

Tate, Alexander J. to Sarah J. Bryon   7 Dec. 1842
     Sol, 8 Dec. 1842, C. H. Baldridge, M.G.

Tate, John H. to Lucy A. McGowen   15 Nov. 1849
     Sol. 15 Nov. 1849

Tate, Joseph P. to Nancy C. Alderson   24 Sept. 1846
     Sol. 24 Sept. 1846, James N. Edmiston, M.G.

Tatum, Alfred to Margaret Duncan   11 Aug. 1851
     Sol. 11 Aug. 1851, R. A. Glenn, J.P.

Tatum, Jesse B. to Harriet E. Reese   30 July 1847
     Sol. 30 July 1847, D. K. Hood, J.P.

Taylor, Claborne to Elizabeth Foster   19 Dec. 1840
     Sol. 24 Dec. 1840, Jonathan S. Hunt, J.P.

Taylor, Henry to Sarah A. N. Killingsworth   26 Apr. 1849
     Sol, 26 Apr. 1849, Jonathan S. Hunt, J.P.

Taylor, James to Adaline Watson   19 Dec. 1850
       Sol. 19 Dec. 1850, Samuel W. Akin, J.P.

Taylor, John to Mildred Baty   18 June 1846
       (did not marry)

Taylor, Lewis to Elizabeth Barbour   10 Oct. 1838

Taylor, William to Nancy Hammond   12 Nov. 1845

Taylor, William H. to Martha C. Oakley   30 Aug. 1851
       Sol. 31 Aug. 1851

Taylor, William P. to Nancy D. Scott   5 Mar. 1849

Temple, Jeremiah to Julia Ann Pillow   19 Feb. 1865
       Sol. 19 Feb. 1865, Andrew T. Gray, J.P.

Terass, John W. to Mary E. Hoge   15 Nov. 1852

Terry, Alexander J. to Martha F. G. Thomas   10 Oct. 1848
       Sol. 11 Oct. 1848, John F. Hughes

Tharpe, Thomas E. to Mary E. Gill   3 Sept. 1849
       Sol. 11 Sept. 1849, John B. Hamilton, Elder in M.E.C.S.

Thomas, A. W. to Lucy A. Smith   3 Dec. 1842
       Sol. 4 Dec. 1842, J. L. Brown, M.G.

Thomas, David to Fanny D. Sprowl   29 May 1850
       Sol. 30 May 1850, John B. Hamilton, Methodist Minister

Thomas, David to Sarah A. Witham   19 Oct. 1852
       Sol. 20 Oct. 1852, E. C. Slater, M.G.

Thomas, John W. to Nancy J. Priest   15 Dec. 1841
       Sol. 16 Dec. 1841, R. W. Morris, M.G.

Thomas, Madison W. to Elizabeth N. Foster   4 Dec. 1848
       Sol. 4 Dec. 1848, Daniel Judd of M.E.C.

Thomason, James to Mary Thomason   23 Sept. 1840

Thomason, John to Nancy J. Green   7 Dec. 1842

Thomason, Micajah to Mary McManus   31 July 1841

Thomason, William to Mary Bennett   2 Mar. 1839
       Sol. 4 Mar. 1839, Lewis G. Lanier, J.P.

Thompson, Elijah to Sarah A. Reilly (Mary written in) 4 Oct. 1841
       Sol. 7 Oct. 1841, Robert C. Garrison

Thompson, Frederick A. to Sarah M. Holland   11 Mar. 1846
       Sol. 12 Mar. 1846, William Mack, M.G.

Thompson, James M. to Mary Mangrum   9 Nov. 1840
    Sol. 9 Nov. 1840, W. W. Cockran, M.G.

Thompson, Jesse G. to Mary Lindsey   20 Feb. 1838
    Sol. 14 Mar. 1838, Richard Stockard, J.P.

Thompson, John A. to Mary Ann Wiern (Wiser?)   7 Aug. 1852
    Sol. 10 Aug. 1852, S. S. Yarbrough, M.G.

Thompson, John W. to Martha J. Smithson   26 Jan. 1850
    Sol. 27 Jan. 1850, James A. Moore, J.P.

Thompson, John W. to L. E. Harris   3 June 1851
    Sol. 3 June 1851

Thompson, Samuel S. to Julia A. Jones   16 Dec. 1840
    Sol. 16 Dec. 1840, William Watkins, J.P.

Thompson, Silas D. to Susan S. Brown   13 July 1843
    Sol. 13 July 1843, Adam A. Riggs, M.G.

Thompson, Solomon K. to Sally Adcock   20 Oct. 1845
    Sol. 20 Oct. 1845, R. H. Simmons, J.P.

Thompson, Sterling B. to Rebecca Terry   4 Feb. 1842

Thompson, Thomas N. to Nancy E. Hiett   25 July 1850
    Sol. 25 July 1850, Andrew Scott, J.P.

Thompson, William to Mary Gilbreath   4 Oct. 1843
    Sol. 4 Oct. 1843, D. Gresham, J.P.

Thomson, Alexander to Lucy P. Jeffreys   13 Apr. 1839
    Sol. 16 Apr. 1839, Robert Hardin, M.G.

Thornton, Harden N. to Lackey A. Dallas   24 Jan. 1840
    Sol. 27 Jan. 1840, P. Hall, M.G.

Thorp, William to Mary C. Johnston   2 Dec. 1839
    Sol. 5 Dec. 1839, Wilie Ledbetter, L.E.M.E.C.

Thoumbs, William W. to Mary Perry   20 Sept. 1845

Thurmond, Adison S. to Sarah J. Fitzgerald   25 Jan. 1849
    Sol. 25 Jan. 1849, B. D. Wall, J.P.

Thurmond, Alphus to Elizabeth Dodson   21 Sept. 1843
    Sol. 21 Sept. 1843, E. Hanks, M.G.

Thurmond, Benjamin J. to Martha Crowder   5 June 1847
    Sol. 10 June 1847, Thomas Hudspeth, M.G.

Thurmon, Holland to Lucinda Johnson   12 Dec. 1845
    Sol. 12 Dec. 1845, G. W. Johnston, J.P.

Thurmond, James H. to Julia Ann Bridgeforth   7 Feb. 1843
     Sol. 10 Feb. 1843, E. Hanks, M.G.

Thurman, Naett to Mary Carter   27 July 1850
     Sol. 29 July 1850, Andrew Scott, J.P.

Thurmond, Norvell T. to Mary Slayden   1 Aug. 1849

Thurmond, Thomas J. to Nancy Fitzgerald   14 May 1840
     Sol. 14 May 1840, James Caughran, J.P.

Tibbs, William A. to Celia C. Bates   30 Mar. 1849
     Sol. 1 Apr. 1849, A. T. Gray, J.P.

Tidwell, Greenberry to Sarah Pilkinton   22 July 1850
     Sol. 23 July 1850, William Doss, Minister

Tidwell, Joseph to Nancy Tidwell   29 Nov. 1852

Tillman, Josiah to Barbary E. Tillman   8 Feb. 1842
     Sol. 8 Feb. 1842, William Davis, M.G.

Timmons, Squire H. to Malinda J. Sellers   17 July 1838
     Sol. 18 July 1838, Berryman Hamlett, J.P.

Tindall, Clark to Alice W. Gee   23 July 1850
     Sol. 25 July 1850, John B. Hamilton, Methodist Minister

Titcomb, Samuel H. to Sarah M. N. Terrell   15 Jan. 1849
     Sol. 18 Jan. 1849, Robert A. Young

Todd, Hugh S. to Susan A. Stockard   3 Dec. 1846
     Sol. 3 Dec. 1846, G. C. Stockard

Todd, Joel J. to Mary J. Fogg   27 Oct. 1838

Todd, John to Amanda M. Flanegan   15 Sept. 1852
     Sol. 15 Sept. 1852, Jonathan S. Hunt, J.P.

Tombs, John H. to Elizabeth P. Hill   6 May 1844
     Sol. 6 May 1844, Hiram Anthony, J.P.

Tomes, Charles to Henrietta C. Otey   24 Nov. 1846

Tomlinson, Charles A. to Sarah Foster   5 Dec. 1838
     Sol. 7 Dec. 1838, Jonathan S. Hunt, J.P.

Tomlinson, Elijah B. to Mary Redding   13 Dec. 1844
     Sol. 14 Dec. 1844, E. Hanks, M.G.

Towler, Joseph M. to Catherine C. Voorhies   15 Mar. 1847
     Sol. 16 Mar. 1847, Joseph Sherman, M.G

Towns, John to Eleanor Reaves   5 Feb. 1839
     Sol. 6 Feb. 1839, Parke Street, J.P.

Trainum, Pleasant to Martha E. Carter   23 Oct. 1851
     Sol. 23 Oct. 1851, James M. White, J.P.

Tranum, Cornelius W. to Sarah T. Fortner   13 Oct. 1841

Tredway, Thomas to Sarah J. Gale   16 Jan. 1838
     Sol. 18 Jan. 1838, D. Brown, V.D.M.

Trotter, John to Eliza C. Slayden   5 Dec. 1846
     Sol. 6 Dec. 1846, E. Hanks, M.G.

Trotter, Joseph to Sarah Maria Rivers   18 June 1843

Trousdale, James W. to Martha A. Kinzer   11 Nov. 1847
     Sol. 16 Nov. 1847, Thomas Kelsey, J.P.

Truett, Levi to Rhoda Aydelott   27 Aug. 1839
     Sol. 27 Aug. 1839, Jonathan S. Hunt, J.P.

Trulove, James C. to Frances J. Bouman   20 Oct. 1843
     Sol. 20 Oct. 1843, John H. Wooldridge, J.P.

Trulove, Jesse R. to Eliza Adkerson   14 Oct. 1848
     Sol. 14 Oct. 1848, William R. Sharp, J.P.

Trulove, John C. to Frances J. Bouman   20 Oct. 1844

Tucker, H. G. to Adah Leigh   26 Oct. 1847
     Sol. 27 Oct. 1847, A. H. Reaves, M.G.

Tucker, Jesse O. to Elizabeth D. Warren   7 Dec. 1840
     Sol. 10 Dec. 1840, Absalom Bostick, M.G.

Tucker, John A. to Eugenia H. Wilson   6 Oct. 1842
     Sol. 5 Oct. 1842, Thomas W. Randle, M.G.

Tucker, Joseph F. to Mary J. Faris   4 Feb. 1847
     Sol. 4 Feb. 1847, P. P. Neely

Tucker, Wilson to Mary F. Kilcrease   5 June 1839

Tuckins, Thomas J. to Sarah E. Hilliard   14 Nov. 1840
     Sol. 15 Nov. 1840, Joseph B. Walker, M.G.

Tullass (or Tullap), John E. to Sarah A. Scott   11 Apr. 1840
     Sol. 14 Apr. 1840, D. D. Neal

Tune, Kister L. to Mary A. Grimes   17 Dec. 1838
     Sol. 18 Dec. 1838, R. Stockard, J.P.

Turnbow, Andrew H. to Elizabeth Turnbow   6 Feb. 1845
     Sol. 9 Feb. 1845, James Brownlow, M.G.

Turnbow, Andrew J. to Sarah A. Spain   17 April 1848
     Sol. 18 April 1848, J. T. Moss, M.G.

Turnbow, William C. to Sarah J. Matthews   29 Apr. 1851
    Sol. 1 May 1851, G. C. Stockard, M.G.

Turner, Joshua C. to Cynthia A. Flanigan   15 Aug. 1849
    Sol. 21 Aug. 1849, Edward R. Puckett, J.P.

Turner, William to Mary V. Jones   21 May 1845

Tyler, John to Pernecy White   5 Apr. 1850
    Sol. 7 Apr. 1850, John Bell Hamilton, M.G., Methodist

Tyler, Seaborn to Lucretia J. Braden   16 Aug. 1845
    Sol. 21 Aug. 1845, James M. Richardson, J.P.

U

Underwood, Anderson to Nancy Bowman   24 Dec. 1840
    Sol. 24 Dec. 1840, C. Cooke, J.P.

Ussery, Joseph C. to Susan M. Gilbreath   12 Dec. 1851
    Sol. 14 Dec. 1851, James Brownlow, M.G.

V

Vaughan, Francis M. to Mary F. Barker   24 Sept. 1850
    Sol. 25 Sept. 1850, E. Hanks, M.G.

Vaughn, Henry to Frances Davis   17 July 1838
    Sol. 18 July 1838, Andrew Smith, M.G.

Vaughn, Joseph to Rachel Ashton   20 Feb. 1838
    Sol. 20 Feb. 1838, R. F. Denham, J.P.

Vaughan, Peterson to Mary W. Westmoreland   7 Nov. 1842
    Sol. 10 Nov. 1842, Hiram Anthony, J.P.

Veach, Ethelbert to Nancy H. W. L. Mack   31 May 1848
    Sol. 31 May 1848, James Edmiston, M.G.

Venable, John to Laura Gantt   11 Mar. 1850
    Sol. 12 Mar. 1850

Vestal, Charles W. to Sarah Y. Caldwell   23 July 1840
    Sol. 23 July 1840, Ishmael Stevens, J.P.

Vestal, James M. to Virginia W. Pickard   2 Jan. 1850
    Sol. 3 Jan. 1850, E. Hanks, M.G.

Vestal, James M. to Rachel E. Younger   10 Nov. 1852
    Sol. 11 Nov. 1852, E. Hanks, M.G.

Vestal, John T. to Catherine M. Tate   29 Oct. 1840
    Sol. 29 Oct. 1840, T. E. Kirkpatrick, M.G.

Vestal, William J. to Rebecca A. Fitzgerald 17 Dec. 1844
    Sol. 18 Dec. 1844, G. Hanks, J.P.

Victory, Warren P. to Cynthia J. H. Scott   5 June 1843
       Sol. 6 June 1843, F. Zollicoffer, J.P.

Vincent, Jones to Elizabeth Sharp   6 June 1843
       Sol. 6 June 1843, Thomas Dotson, M.G.

Viser, James H. to Almelia F. Black   28 July 1841
       Sol. 29 July 1841, Joseph Sherman, M.G.

Voorhies, Isaac G. to Nancy E. Walker   2 Feb. 1848
       Sol. 2 Feb. 1848, R. G. Irvine, M.G.

Voorhies, James G. to Susan D. Chappell   19 July 1843
       Sol. 20 July 1843, Adam A. Riggs, M.G.

W

Wade, Josiah A. To Emily Forguson   8 Feb. 1851
       Sol. 9 Feb. 1851

Wade, Marnia D. to Ruth R. Thompson   25 Jan. 1848
       Sol. 25 Jan. 1848, James G. Harris, J.P.

Wade, Pleasant C. to Mary A. H. Robison   1 Jan. 1845
       Sol. 2 Jan. 1845, Joseph Foster, J.P.

Wade, Samuel to Nancy K. Speer   24 June 1847
       Sol. 4 July 1847, Joshua K. Speer, M.G.

Waldrum, Joseph to Marilda Jettun   20 July 1847
       Sol. 20 July 1847, A. H. Hanna, J.P.

Walker, Elijah to Mary E. Jones   24 Feb. 1851
       Sol. 25 Feb. 1851, Edmund Dillahunty, Judge

Walker, Isham to Larica Waldrum   2 Sept. 1843

Walker, John to Sarah S. Walker   23 Mar. 1839

Walker, John J. to Sarah W. Matthews   31 Dec. 1839
       Sol. 31 Dec. 1839, R. M. Galloway

Walker, Lorenzo D. to Martha J. Noles   20 Aug. 1844
       Sol. 21 Aug. 1844, John Mack, J.P.

Walker, Lysander to Elizabeth Kelly   2 Aug. 1844
       Sol. 5 Aug. 1844, E. Flocker, J.P.

Walker, Nathaniel W. to Arminta Holmes   18 Dec. 1850
       Sol. 18 Dec. 1850, Henry A. Miller, J.P.

Walker, Robert Tenham to Sarah J. Davis   4 July 1839
       Sol. 4 July 1839, H. H. Brown, E.M.E.C.

Walker, Thomas to Nancy J. Walters   1 Aug. 1848

Walker, Thomas C. to Eliza A. Gale   18 Oct. 1843
    Sol. 18 Oct. 1843, C. R. Osborne

Walker, Thomas G. to Mary E. Walker   2 Dec. 1850
    Sol. 3 Dec. 1850, Joseph Foster, J.P.

Walker, William D. to Harriet J. Moore   9 Dec. 1848
    Sol. 10 Dec. 1848, W. H. Baldridge, M.G.

Walker, Wyatt to Eliza Coffey   21 June 1850
    Sol. 25 June 1850, J. W. Westmoreland, J.P.

Wall, Beverly D. to Virginia A. Thurmond   15 July 1846

Wall, Thomas C. to Matilda Crowder   18 Dec. 1846

Wallace, John B. to Ann Jane Todd   22 July 1841

Wallis, Robert S. to Judith W. Bryant   4 Aug. 1851
    Sol. 7 Aug. 1851, Aroma Clark, J.P.

Walters, Bird to Eliza A. Cathey   11 Jan. 1841
    Sol. 12 Jan. 1841, W. H. Baldridge, M.G.

Walters, Joel to Elizabeth J. Gaskill   1 Feb. 1847
    Sol. 4 Feb. 1847, Ishmael Stevens, J.P.

Wantland, Abram to Nancy Goad   18 Dec. 1850
    Sol. 18 Dec. 1850, E. Hanks, M.G.

Wantland, Samuel W. to Eliza M. Craig   18 Dec. 1850
    Sol. 19 Dec. 1850, E. Hanks, M.G.

Ward, Hezekiah to Josephine E. Craig   22 July 1852
    Sol. 22 July 1852, M. W. Gray, M.G.

Ware, Edward H. to Nancy M. Rogers   12 Oct. 1840

Warren, George W. to Zilla Robinson   20 July 1847
    Sol. 21 July 1847, Ishmael Stevens, J.P.

Warren, John C. to Elizabeth F. Burney   7 Dec. 1848
    Sol. 9 Dec. 1848, R. A. Glenn, J.P.

Warren, Robert to Susan Nelms   3 Apr. 1849
    Sol. 5 Apr. 1849, W. H. Baldridge, M.G.

Warren, Thomas to Elvira E. Hendly   9 Apr. 1850
    Sol. 9 Apr. 1850, William Mack, M.G.

Warren, William C. to Margaret Hudspeth   23 Mar. 1838
    Sol. Britain Garner

Waterhouse, James T. to Almira E. Long   24 Feb. 1852
    Sol. 25 Feb. 1852, Edward C. Slater, M.G.

Watkins, Frederick H. to Penelope Williams   24 Aug. 1838
     Sol. 25 Aug. 1838, G. W. Mitchell, M.G.

Watkins, Frederick H. to Margaret A. Stephenson   12 June 1843
     Sol. 13 June 1843, James M. Arnell, Zion Pastor

Watkins, James M. to Lucy A. Scott   3 Oct. 1842
     Sol. 6 Oct. 1842, J. F. Campbell

Watson, George W. M. to Elizabeth H. Sheppard   16 Nov. 1848
     Sol. 16 Nov. 1848, John B. Hamilton, Methodist Minister

Watson, James L. P. to Sarah A. B. Toumbs   12 Mar. 1849
     Sol. 12 Mar. 1849, N. F. Modrall

Watson, Jesse E. to Lydia Ragsdale   16 Oct. 1843
     Sol. 16 Oct. 1843, Aaron Vestal, J.F.

Watson, Jonathon S. to Mary S. Andrews   29 Dec. 1842
     Sol. 29 Dec. 1842, J. G. Harris, J.P.

Watson, Samuel J. to Malissa Miller   18 Apr. 1838
     Sol. W. D. Williams, J.P.

Watt, Beverly D. to Caroline Mack   12 Nov. 1846

Watts, Benjamin F. to Nancy E. Robinson   4 May 1850
     Sol. 8 May 1850, J. T. Moss, M.G.

Wear, William D. to Nancy J. Kannon   14 Aug. 1850
     Sol. 14 Aug. 1850, W. H. Baldridge, M.G.

Weatherly, John to Mary Loftin   2 Feb. 1842
     Sol. 2 Feb. 1842, William Davis, M.G.

Weatherly, John to Lucretia Love   19 Dec. 1842
     Sol. 20 Dec. 1842, G. Cathey, J.F.

Weatherly, Samuel N. to Eliza Duncan   6 Aug. 1839

Weatherly, William to Mary Adkisson   27 Jan. 1846
     Sol. 28 Jan. 1846, Alfred Fleming, J.P.

Webb, Hiram to Mary M. Lotty (or Tolly)   20 Sept. 1847
     Sol. 21 Sept. 1847, John F. Hughes

Webster, F. G. to Margaret R. Crosby   7 June 1841
     Sol. 8 June 1841, Justinian Williams, M.G.

Webster, William J. to Mary Ann H. Booker   23 Oct. 1844
     Sol. 23 Oct. 1844, William Mack, M.G.

Weeks, Samuel to Rachel M. Austin   22 June 1840
     Sol. 22 June 1840, B. H. Hubbard

Welch, Francis H. to Martha Beasley   5 Dec. 1846
    Sol. F. F. Neeley

Welch, Robert W. to Mary Ann Nelson   30 Sept. 1839
    Sol. 1 Oct. 1839, Thomas F. Scott, V. D. M.

Wells, David to Lucinda Kennedy   14 Jan. 1846

Wells, James M. to Sarah A. Whaley   4 Feb. 1840
    Sol. 4 Feb. 1840, D. H. Hubbard, M.G., M.E. Church

Wells, Jesse to Martha A. Blackburn   15 Dec. 1838
    Sol. 18 Dec. 1838, W. D. Williams, J.P.

West, Thomas J. to Rebecca Wilson   7 May 1838
    Sol. 10 May 1838, Andrew Smith, M.G.

West, William to Elizabeth E. Johnston   20 Jan. 1840
    Sol. 22 Jan. 1840, G. W. Mitchell, M.G.

Westmoreland, John W. to Elizabeth D. Parke   10 Sept. 1839
    Sol. 12 Sept. 1839, Penony Gresham, J.P.

Westmoreland, Robert to Mary Moore   3 Jan. 1843
    Sol. 3 Jan. 1843, Hiram Anthony, J.P.

Weston, E. to Lucy Bolton   30 Oct. 1851
    Sol. 30 Oct. 1851, James M. White, J.P.

Wheatley, James C. to Lucretia Daimwood   2 Nov. 1838

Wheatley, Lewis R. to Martha Daimwood   28 Dec. 1840
    Sol. 29 Dec. 1840, Parke Street, J.P.

Wheeler, Benjamin F. to Mary W. Campbell   25 Nov. 1847
    Sol. 25 Nov. 1847, William Mack, M.G.

Wheeler, William H. to Alice A. Patton   27 Nov. 1852
    Sol. 29 Nov. 1852, W. H. Baldridge, M.G.

Wheeler, William W. to Mary J. Zollicoffer   27 Apr. 1846

Whitaker, J. L. to Sarah H. Foster   11 Dec. 1848
    Sol. 13 Dec. 1848, W. H. Baldridge, M.G.

Whitaker, Thomas J. to Mary A. L. S. Myrick   16 Aug. 1842
    Sol. 17 Aug. 1842, Thomas W. Randle, M.G.

Whitaker, William to Mary M. McCoy   31 Oct. 1838
    Sol. 31 Oct. 1838, E. Hanks, M.G.

Whitaker, William to Susan E. Patton   12 Jan. 1841
    Sol. 14 Jan. 1841, Joseph Brown, M.G.

Whitaker, William G. to Fernetha F. Dodson   19 Sept. 1849
    Sol. 20 Sept. 1849, M. D. Molloy, M.G.

White, Allen to Martha A. Daniel   25 Feb. 1845
     Sol. 27 Feb. 1845, William Mack, M.G.

White, Archelause M. to Harriet D. Bryant   6 Aug. 1841
     Sol. 12 Aug. 1841, Jonathon S. Hunt, J.P.

White, Cary B. to Elizabeth M. Turbeville   25 May 1840
     Sol. 26 May 1840, R. H. Hubbard, L.E.M.E.Church

White, Cary B. to Frances E. Sudberry   26 Feb. 1848
     Sol. 28 Feb. 1848, W. D. S. Saurie, M.G.

White, Cherry J. to Nancy M. Wilkes   30 Oct. 1850
     Sol. 30 Oct. 1850, A. T. Gray, J.P.

White, James P. to Martha M. Box   1 June 1847
     Sol. 2 June 1847, E. Gresham, J.P.

White, Luke S. to Nancy J. Sparkman   25 Dec. 1852
     Sol. 27 Dec. 1852, A. T. Gray, J.P.

White, Miles to Margaret S. W. Smith   11 Jan. 1850
     Sol. 11 Jan. 1850, B. H. Ragsdale

White, Reuben to Latitia S. Tyler   9 Jan. 1838
     Sol. 18 Jan. 1838, Alexander Dickson, T. Ela.

White, Robert to Katherine McCafferty   1 Feb. 1838

White, Samuel D. to Sarah E. Morris   13 Aug. 1850
     Sol. 14 Aug. 1850, J. T. Moss, M.G.

White, Shilo to Mary Ray   9 Feb. 1846

White, St. Ledger to Nancy Pickard   16 Mar. 1844

White, Thomas to Caroline A. Campbell   3 Feb. 1851
     Sol. 4 Feb. 1851, Wade Barnett, M.G., Christian Church

White, William to Margaret Carey   22 Feb. 1842
     Sol. 22 Feb. 1842, Alfred Fleming, J.P.

Whitfield, Henry W. to Susannah A. D. Oliphant   13 June 1850
     Sol. 13 June 1850, M. P. Erwin, J.P.

Whitfield, James G. to Sarah A. Foster   19 July 1838
     Sol. 19 July 1838, E. Hanks, M.G.

Whitfield, John W. to Catherine M. Dansbee   13 Apr. 1839
     Sol. 16 Apr. 1839, E. Hanks, M.G.

Whiteside, John F. to Mary J. Bingham   10 June 1839
     Sol. 11 June 1839, S. Whiteside, J.P.

Whiteside, Robert W. to Rachel A. Findly   30 Nov. 1840
     Sol. 1 Dec. 1840, Richard Anderson, J.P.

Whitfield, James E. to Mary L. Oliphant   3 Jan. 1845
     Sol. 3 Jan. 1845, E. Hanks, M.G.

Whitson, Samuel to Catherine Ledbetter   7 Feb. 1850
     Sol. 7 Feb. 1850, A. R. Dickson, Local Elder, M.E.C.

Whitted (or Whitten), James to Elizabeth Hawks   10 Mar. 1846
     Sol. 11 Mar. 1846, Henry A. Miller, J.P.

Whitted (or Whitten), John to Mary Johnson   15 Nov. 1849
     Sol. 15 Nov. 1849, James M. White, J.P.

Whitted (or Whitley or Whitten) Joseph P. to Mary J. Jackson 14 Mar. 1850
     Sol. 15 Mar. 1850, William R. Sharp, J.P.

Whitted (or Whitten), Levi C. to Elizabeth J. Evans 13 Dec. 1849
     Sol. 13 Dec. 1849, Joseph W. White J.P.

Whitthorne, W. C. to Matilda J. Campbell   4 July 1848
     Sol. 4 July 1848, Edmund Dillahunty

Whitworth, Melchioedock to Harriet Bond   11 Apr. 1844
     Sol. 11 Apr. 1844, I. N. Bills, J.I.

Wiggs, Henry W. to Margaret L. Lockhart   31 May 1838
     Sol. 31 May 1838, James Adkins, J.P.

Wiley, Ansel S. to Elizabeth J. Erwin   29 June 1840
     Sol. 15 July 1840, Alfred Fleming, J.P.

Wiley, James H. to Elizabeth Barnett   16 Sept. 1841
     Sol. 16 Sept. 1841, James W. Matthews, J.P.

Wiley, William to Evaline Frisby   18 Dec. 1848
     Sol. 21 Dec. 1848, F. A. Burke, J.P.

Wilks, James H. to Mary Macon   14 Aug. 1843
     Sol. 16 Aug. 1843, J. T. Moss

Wilkes, James H. to Mary Fielder   30 May 1848
     Sol. 31 May 1848, W. D. F. Saurie, M.G.

Wilkes, Richard to Elvira O. Moore   25 Oct. 1852

Wilkes, Washington L. to Jane C. Love   24 July 1844
     Sol. 25 July 1844, C. B. Harris, M.G.

Wilkes, William to Mary Amis   5 Jan. 1848
     Sol. 6 Jan. 1848, J. O. Church, M.G.

Wilks, William L. to Sarah E. Foster   9 June 1852
     Sol. 10 June 1852, E. Hanks, M.G.

Wilcoxon, Coleman W. to Mary A. Morrow   26 Mar. 1851
     Sol. 26 Mar. 1851, Joseph Brownlow, M.G.

Willcoxson, Daniel W. to Louisa E. Morrow   9 May 1848
     Sol. 11 June 1848, J. T. Moss, M.G.

Willcoxson, David to Nancy Bailey   27 June 1844
     Sol. 27 June 1844, J. T. Moss

Willcockson, John to Nancy Jane Ellis   25 Aug. 1838

Williams, Alvis to Sarah C. McMurry   3 Aug. 1846
     Sol. 4 Aug. 1846, B. R. Gant, M.G.

Williams, David G. to Fanny H. Cooper   2 Dec. 1851
     Sol. 4 Dec. 1851

Williams, Dewitt C. to Racena M. F. Jaggers   23 Sept. 1850
     Sol. 24 Sept. 1850

Williams, Edward to Lila A. McConnico   9 Oct. 1851
     Sol. 9 Oct. 1851, E. W. Benson, M.G.

Williams, Elijah D. to Nancy W. Alexander   28 Mar. 1844
     Sol. 28 Mar. 1844, Berryman Hamlett

Williams, Helman to Jane Coffey   20 Oct. 1840

Williams, John A. to Mary L. Hale   22 July 1848
     Sol. 23 July 1848, R. Sharp, J.P.

Williams, Marmaduke to Mary C. Chambers   13 Oct. 1838
     Sol. 13 Oct. 1838, Robert Foster, J.P.

Williams, Robert C. to Hattie A. Kercheval   28 Jan. 1852
     Sol. 29 Jan. 1852, William Mack, M.G.

Williams, Thomas to Lucinda Robison   28 Sept. 1841
     Sol. 30 Sept. 1841, G. W. Mitchell, M.G.

Williams, William to Nancy M. Lane   3 Oct. 1842

Williams, Will J. to Martha A. Gilmer   26 Mar. 1839
     Sol. 26 Mar. 1839, C. B. Porter

Williamson, Charles P. to Elizabeth L. Jackson   24 Nov. 1842
     Sol. 24 Nov. 1842, C. Cooke, J.P.

Williamson, William O. to Ann Brown   3 Oct. 1843
     Sol. 3 Oct. 1843, Joseph Sherman

Williford, Almaria H. to Nancy D. Harrington   20 Aug. 1838
     Sol. 21 Aug. 1838, Robert Hardin, M.G.

Willis, Charles W. to Mary Jane Brooks   7 Dec. 1843
     Sol. 7 Dec. 1843, J. E. Douglass

Wilis, James A. to Nancy C. Andrews   16 Oct. 1852
     Sol 17 Oct. 1852, J. E. McCord, M.G.

Willis, John S. to Martha Williams   22 Oct. 1838

Wilson, David F. to Leonora R. Wilson   6 Sept. 1842

Wilson, George W. to Elizabeth E. Jones   5 Jan. 1850
      Sol. 6 Jan. 1850, J. F. Holt, J.P.

Wilson, Henry A. to Elizabeth A. Williams   18 Nov. 1839
      Sol. 19 Nov. 1839, Samuel Wheatley, J.P.

Wilson, James M. to Martha M. Jackson   22 Jan. 1838
      Sol. 23 Jan. 1838, Samuel Wheatley, J.P.

Wilson, John C. to Mary Wright   29 June 1840
      Sol. 2 July 1840, Samuel Wheatley, J.P.

Wilson, John J. to Rebecca E. Fleming   4 Oct. 1851
      Sol. 6 Oct. 1851

Wilson, John M. to Susan E. Williams   17 Oct. 1844
      Sol. 17 Oct. 1844, G. W. Fly, J.P.

Wilson, Joseph N. to Cynthia Minor   30 Oct. 1848
      Sol. 6 Nov. 1848, R. A. Glenn, J.P.

Wilson, Junius A. to Maria J. Hales   19 Feb. 1865
      Sol. 19 Feb. 1865, R. W. Morris, E. M.E.C.

Wilson, Napier to Nancy Smith   31 Aug. 1843
      Sol. 31 Aug. 1843, R. H. Simmons, J.P.

Wilson, Robert D. to Mary J. Minor   6 Oct. 1848
      Sol. 7 Oct. 1848, R. A. Glenn, J.P.

Wilson, Samuel J. to Elizabeth K. Frierson   25 Oct. 1841
      Sol. 27 Oct. 1841, James M. Arnell, Pastor, Zion

Wilson, Thomas B. to Mary Brown   17 Oct. 1842

Wilson, William B. to Sarah E. McCarty   2 Nov. 1847
      Sol. 4 Nov. 1847, William Mack, M.G.

Wilson, William B. to Jsaru C. Hamilton   13 Aug. 1851
      Sol. 14 Aug. 1851, E. C. Slater, M.G.

Wilson, William H. to Eleanor L. Lusk   17 July 1839
      Sol. 18 July 1839, Richard Anderson

Winn, William M. to Mary S. Weakley   22 Oct. 1838
      Sol. 23 Oct. 1838, Wilie Ledbetter, E.M.E. Church

Wisner, James H. to Mary S. Harris   12 Sept. 1850
      Sol. 12 Sept. 1850, R. G. Irwin, M. G.

Witherspoon, John M. to Louisa J. Dowell   30 Sept. 1847
      Sol. 30 Sept. 1847, E. Hanks, M.G.

Witherspoon, Joshua T. to Malvina F. Dodson   16 Aug. 1841
     Sol. 18 Aug. 1841, W. H. Baldridge, M.G.

Wood, David to Cynthia E. Garrett   27 May 1847

Wood, James to Elizabeth Daniel   5 Mar. 1851
     Sol. 6 Mar. 1851, J. B. Hamilton, Methodist Minister

Wood, Joseph J. to Emily J. Salmon   19 Oct. 1847
     Sol. 20 Oct. 1847, James N. Edmiston

Wood, Norman D. to Mary P. Cooper   24 June 1841
     Sol. 24 June 1841, Joseph Sherman, M.G.

Wood, Samuel to Cisice Ragsdale   18 Apr. 1844

Wood, William A. to Frances E. Caldwell   23 Oct. 1844
     Sol. 24 Oct. 1844, Finch P. Scruggs, M.G.

Woods, John A. to Rachel C. McNeely   20 Dec. 1845
     Sol. J. C. Spinks, J.P.

Woods, Starke B. to Mary Fitzgerald   16 Dec. 1840
     Sol. 17 Dec. 1840, James W. Matthews, J.P.

Woodward, Chesley to Lavinia Renfro   16 Aug. 1842

Woodward, George W. to Sarah A. Renfro   7 Aug. 1838

Woody, Archibald to Elizabeth A. Beckum   10 Jan. 1839
     Sol. 10 Jan. 1839, E. Hanks, M.G.

Woody, William to Catherine Nelson   22 Oct. 1840
     Sol. 22 Oct. 1840, Ishmael Stevens, J.P.

Woolverton, William L. to Eliza J. V. Curtis   12 Nov. 1844
     Sol. 12 Nov. 1844, C. Cooke, J.P.

Worley, Stephen to Sophronia Dickey   16 Sept. 1844
     Sol. 17 Sept. 1844, E. R. Osborne, E.C.C.

Worley, Wiley to Margaret Strayhorn   19 Dec. 1838
     Sol. 20 Dec. 1838, G. W. Mitchell, M.G.

Worley, Wiley B. to Arminta E. Hunt   21 Sept. 1850
     Sol. 22 Sept. 1850, J. B. Hamilton, Methodist Elder

Wortham, Charles L. to Cornelia J. Williams   1 Oct. 1839
     Sol. 2 Oct. 1839, G. W. Mitchell, M.G.

Wortham, Edward L. to Emaline E. Spain   14 Sept. 1848
     Sol. 14 Sept. 1848, John F. Hughes

Wortham, James J. to Sarah H. Cross   26 Feb. 1848
     Sol. 26 Feb. 1848, L. W. Mitchell, M.G.

Wortham, Joseph D. to Saluda M. Sammond — 19 Sept. 1851
    Sol. 19 Sept. 1851, H. A. Miller, J.P.

Wortham, Robert S. to Martha J. Wortham — 14 Sept. 1838
    Sol. 19 Sept. 1838, Lewis G. Lanier, J.P.

Wortham, William G. D. to Charlotte M. Locke — 13 Feb. 1841
    Sol. 14 Feb. 1841, Joseph H. Wilkes, J.P.

Wray, John A. to Levina Hawkins — 17 Oct. 1849
    Sol. 18 Oct. 1849

Wrenn, Jesse S. to Mary E. Petty — 10 Dec. 1846
    Sol. 10 Dec. 1846, Ishmael Stevens, J.P.

Wrenn, Thomas to Martha A. Lyons — 5 Dec. 1842
    Sol. 13 Dec. 1842, Ishmael Stevens, J.P.

Wright, Daniel to Milly Sloan — 9 Aug. 1852
    Sol. 9 Aug. 1852, Joseph Foster, J.P.

Wright, James B. R. to Lucy C. Perry — 15 July 1846
    Sol. 17 July 1846, P. R. Gant, M.G.

Wright, John F. to Salina E. Meador — 15 June 1848
    Sol. 15 June 1848, A. H. Hanna, J.P.

Wright, John R. to Elizabeth C. Vaughn — 2 Apr. 1850
    Sol. 2 Apr. 1850, W. D. Werr, M.G.

Wright, Joseph A. to Mary S. Mitchell — 4 Feb. 1840
    Sol. 13 Feb. 1840, Andrew Smith, M.G.

Wright, Robert M. to Nancy J. Blackwood — 18 Dec. 1852
    Sol. 19 Dec. 1852, John T. Moss, M.G.

Wright, Robert N. to Nancy N. Smith — 16 Nov. 1846
    Sol. 16 Nov. 1846, John McKelvey, Methodist Minister

Wright, Thompson to Nancy Diamond — 18 Jan. 1843
    Sol. 19 Jan. 1843, Samuel Wheatley, J.P.

Wright, Washington to Harriet Lawrance — 18 Feb. 1852
    Sol. 19 Feb. 1852, A. T. Gray, J.P.

Wright, William B. to Sarah M. Law — 23 Oct. 1849
    Sol. 23 Oct. 1849, William Mack, M.G.

Wright, William J. to Louisa Moore — 4 July 1843
    Sol. 5 July 1843, D. Gresham, J.P.

Wyatt, John H. to Mary E. Brandon — 28 Mar. 1849

Y

Yancy, William to Jane Ray   8 Jan. 1842
    Sol. 8 Jan. 1842, Alfred Fleming, J.P.

Yancy, William J. to Margaret M. Kerry   24 Jan. 1842
    Sol. 27 Jan. 1842, Hugh Shaw, M.D.

Yate, Charles E. to Martha J. Cooper   9 Mar. 1843
    Sol. 10 Mar. 1843, E. Gresham, J.P.

Young, Amaziah to Mary E. Cherry   11 Aug. 1842
    Sol. 11 Aug. 1842, Taswell S. Alderson, J.P.

Young, Felix G. to Lurana J. Hill   20 Nov. 1843
    Sol. 21 Nov. 1843, Joseph Brown, M.G.

Young, George W. to Salina Blocker   2 Mar. 1843
    Sol. 2 Mar. 1843, Joseph Foster, J.P.

Young, John C. to Elizabeth Haley   20 Jan. 1851
    Sol. 20 Jan. 1851, Henry Harris, J.P.

Young, John M. to Susan R. Scribner   2 Oct. 1850
    Sol. 2 Oct. 1850, F. A. Burke, J.P.

Young, Joseph T. to Sophia E. Vestal   15 Dec. 1852

Young, Peter to Elizabeth Ray   31 July 1839
    Sol. 31 July 1839, Jonathon S. Hunt, J.P.

Young, William T. to Isabella M. Campbell   16 Feb. 1841
    Sol. 17 Feb. 1841, Joseph E. Walker, M.G.

Younger, William to Lucinda M. Dodson   25 Oct. 1852

York, James F. to Nancy Bolten   6 Nov. 1851
    Sol. 9 Nov. 1851, E. Hanks, M.G.

Z

Zellner, Arnold to Clarinda Johnson   27 July 1839
    Sol. 28 July 1839, William Davis, M.G.

Zellner, Arnold to Meeky M. Reaves   10 July 1843
    Sol. 12 July 1843, Adam J. Riggs, M.G.

Zellner, Henry to Martha J. Hughes   21 May 1839
    Sol. 21 May 1839, H. H. Brown, E.M.E.C.

NAME	DATE	BONDSMAN

1825

David R. Cockrell to Polly Due   5 Jan. 1825   Elisha Olgivie
   solemnized 6 Jan. 1825, John Matthews, J.P.

Joseph P. Crosswait to Mary Roberty Mack   14 Mar. 1825   J. P. Crosthwait
   her name also given on bond as Polly   John Mack

William Dikus to Sally Grinder   18 Feb. 1825   John Blackburn
                                                                    William Dikus

Thomas S. Logan to Jane Wortham   24 Aug. 1825

Ezekiah Waldrop to Sarah Knight   14 July 1825   Silas Wheat

1836

John H. Caldwell to Ruth Jones   15 Sept. 1836   John S. Caldwell

Josiah Cathey to Martha Ann Gunter   6 Aug. 1836   John C. Ware

William G. Cathey to Emily A. Brown   10 Aug. 1836   Nathan B. Akin

John W. Frierson to Lucy A. Mosly   14 Sept. 1836   James H. Frierson
                                                                    John J. Stephenson

Cambridge Green to Amy Holcomb   9 July 1836   James Rankin

William B. Hudson to Elizabeth B. Woolbright 30 June 1837   George Bradbury

Philip B. Johnson to Almira S. Black   14 Nov. 1836   Thomas Barbour

Astin Matthews to Milly Slaughter   5 Oct. 1836   Joel P. Hawkins

John N. Mozly to Egnis Galloway   14 Sept. 1836   Sion H. Hight

James McNeilly to Armin McDaniel   17 Sept. 1836   Miles McDaniel

John A. Murrell to Elizabeth Mangham   March 1829   Patton Churchwell

James J. Oliphant to Maria A. Maddux   15 Nov. 1837   Robert Reaves

Elijah H. Overstreet to Sarah D. Collins   16 March 1836   Lawrence Smith

Mac Donnall Small to Lemirah C. Bell   13 March 1836   Edward D. Moore

Joseph M. Sowell to Nancy J. Gordon   31 Oct. 1837
   Sol. 2 Nov. 1837, E. Hanks

Littleberry Turbyfill to Judy Hill   4 Oct. 1836   Charles Robason

Wiley B. Williams to Mary A. Harrington   27 Sept. 1836   Robert Carter

BONDS FOR 1838 - 1852

No bonds for the years 1844, 1845, 1846, 1849, 1850, 1851--missing.

Andrews, William B. to Nancy A. Turner   11 Oct. 1847 (see entry page 3)

Bailey, James to Elizabeth Craig   10 Oct. 1843   Alfred P. Buckner
   (see also license entry on page 6.)

Brandon, John L. to Izora Holt   17 March 1852   Benjamin F. Carter
   (see also entry on page 11.)

Brooks, Samuel to Jane Clendenin
   Sol, 22 July 1839 Ishmael Stevens, J.P. (see page 11.)

Cain, Samuel S. to Elizabeth Dillon   11 Oct. 1843   John P. Spindle
   (see also page 15.)

Causey, Zebulon to Lucy Wilson   22 Sept. 1847   James Tucker
   (her name also given as Nancy on bond. See also page 17.)

Childress, William P. to Mary Hare   12 Nov. 1847   James Garrett
   (see also page 19.)

Clemons, William to Joyce William   8 Jan. 1839
   (Sol. 9 Jan. 1839, E. Hanks, M.G.)

Cooper, George C. to Minerva Dial   2 Sept. 1847   Jonathan M. Fuller

Cooper, Charles L. to Tabitha Ostean   19 Aug. 1841   Zachariah Pogue

Crampton, James to Eleanor Towns   27 Dec. 1842   William N. Scott
   (see also entry page 24.)

Durham, Thomas to Nancy Mills   7 Feb. 1852   Daniel Durham
   (see Denham entry on page 26.)

Ereband, John W. to Martha Tenneson   20 Oct. 1847   Joseph Ham
   (see page 39.)

NAME	DATE	BONDSMAN
Guest, David to Martha Watson	2 Aug. 1852	Willford Due
(see also page 48)		
Guest, James L. to Emily J. Hill	18 Dec. 1839	
Gunnell, William to Dorothy A. Welch	26 Dec. 1842	Samuel H. Butler
(see also page 49)		
Hale, John to Sarah Williams	20 June 1840	
Sol. 20 June 1840, Samuel Wheatley, J.P.		
Hamner, Austin N. to Anna Eliza Anthony	26 Aug. 1847	T. G. Spindle
(see also p. 49) Her name also given as Armstrong.		
Harris, Daniel M. to Minerva White	28 July 1841	Blagrave T. Maxey
(see also page 51.)		
Hassell, John of Hickman County to Lavinia Polk	31 Mar. 1841	James Cooper of Hickman County
Hassell, William to Rebecca C. Partee	18 Nov. 1839	
Sol. 21 Nov. 1839, G. R. Hore, M. G.		
William Hassell was of Hickman County. See also page 53.		
Hassell, Zebulon to Sarah Graham	15 May 1843	Egin H. Spencer
(See also page 60.)		
Holcomb, Jason M. to Amanda Truelove	27 Nov. 1847	Thomas J. Holcomb
(See also page 56.)		
Isbell, James to Elizabeth A. Branch	4 Sept. 1840	
Sol. 8 Sept. 1840, Joseph Sherman		
Isom, George W. to Elizabeth Akin	8 Dec. 1840	
Sol. 9 Dec. 1840, Wilie Ledbetter, L.E.M,E.C.		
Jackson, Daniel to Sarah J. Kittrell	4 Jan. 1841	Evans Jones
Johnson, Hugh N. to Frances J. Tidwell	12 Nov. 1847	Jeremiah Capoots
(See also page 62.)		
King, James H. to Malissa Bell	25 Aug. 1847	Lee Pickard
(See also Ring entry on page 98.)		
Lancaster, William H. to Mary A. Hill	6 Jan. 1848	James W. V. Hughe
(See also Lamaster entry on page 67.)		
Landsberry, John S. to Sarah E. Lindsey	15 Nov. 1848	Charles Johnston
(See also Sandsberry entry on page 101.)		
Majors, Samuel to Matilda Byrum (see Magers entry on page 73.)		
Martin, Caswell C. to Elizabeth J. Johnson	27 Apr. 1852	John W. Gilmore
(See entry on page 73. On license her surname given as Smith.)		
Maxwell, Jesse W. E. (see entry on page 74.)		
(Attached to this bond was note postmarked Locust Grove, Tennessee, telling that he was teaching school and wished to post bond to marry Mrs. Ruth Hill)		
Moore, James P. to Mary A. Bunch	31 Jan. 1848	Robert J. Baugess
(see also page 82.)		
Murrey, William P. to Catherine E. Early	30 Nov. 1847	Austin Stanley
(see Maury entry on page 74.)		
McBride, James to Martha J. Jaggers	11 Jan. 1843	Jesse J. Bingham
(Bond gives her name as Martha J. Jaggers alias Martha J. Cunningham.)		
McNeelley, Erie to Sarah T. Gates	23 Aug. 1847	Moses M. Swim
(see also page 79 entry.)		
Neely, Samuel W. to Sarah Kerr	21 Dec. 1842	Thomas Journey
Park, John J. to Atthayer E. Oliver	17 Sept. 1839	
Sol. 18 Sept. 1839, E. Gresham, J.P.		
Partee, William B. to Sarah D. Todd	15 Sept. 1840	
(See entry page 93.)		
Payne, Isaac to Judith Mattox	28 July 1841	Thomas Payne
(See entry page 92.)		
Powell, Nathaniel to Susan C. Simmons	9 Oct. 1847	James Hutchcroft
(See Sowell entry on page 107. Name definitely Powell on bond.)		

NAME	DATE	BONDSMAN
nfro, Albert F. to Nancy R. Evans (See also page 96.)	23 Dec, 1847	Doctor B. Harrison
oss, Andrew F. to Irene W. Wortham (See also page 99) Sol. 26 March 1840.	23 March 1840	
ellers, Robert to Ann Good	29 June 1833	Arkey Y. Partee
nelby, Reece F. to Mary Ann Capoot (See Skelly entry on page 104.)	1 Feb. 1840	
nith, Clem to Nancy Tanner (See page 105.)	7 May 1839	
tewart, William A. to Mahala Powell (See also page 109.)	12 June 1852	Thomas Clendenin
nompson, John A. to Mary Ann Winn (See also page 113.)	7 Aug. 1852	R. B. Mayes
nurmon, Nathaniel to Mary Carter (See page 114)		
alker, James Simpson to Mariah Ann Nicholson	5 March 1818	Silas M. Caldwell
alker, Washington P. to Frances Taylor	26 Jan. 1852	Davis N. Coffey
eatherly, Samuel N. (see page 119) Sol. by James Smith, J.P.		
nite, William to Margaret Covey (See also page 121.)	21 Feb. 1842	Alexander Graves
lliamson, William A. to Ann Brown (See also page 123	3 Oct. 1843	Leonidas Walthall
ood, Daniel to Cynthia E. Garrett (See also page 125.)	27 May 1847	Thomas K. Young
ortham, William G. D. to Charlotte M. Cocke (See also page 126.)	13 Feb. 1841	Jacob Coffey
ight, Thompson to Nancy Daimwood	18 Jan. 1843	Samuel Gullett
ancy, William to Margaret Kerr (See also page 127.)	24 Jan. 1842	John W. Gilmer

DDITIONAL INFORMATION ON BOND AND NOT ON LICENSE

drews, William B. to Mary Hawks
    This entry is found on page 4 and her surname given as Hanks.
    Joseph A. Bruce was bondsman for Andrews.

derson, William to Nancy Wilks on page 2. His name William A. Alderson.

mpbell, John J. to Julia J. Mack on page 15. Their full names were:
    John Jackson Campbell to Julia Joanna Mack.

rney, John on page 35. Surname spelled Fearney on bond.

ierson, Samuel W. on page 41. Name on bond Samuel Wickliffe Frierson.

llespie, D. C. to R. M. E. Crews on page 44. Her name on bond given as
    Rosanna M. E. Crews.

een, John G. on page 47. Bond gives: John Burton Green to Sallie Naomi
    Walker.

een, W. E. B. on page 47. Bond: William E. B. Green.

Zocky M. Martin, page 71, name on bond: Zocky Maria Martin.

Alice Towler, page 85, name on bond: J. Alice Towler.

Noles, Tiny, page 86. On original license name: Tiry Noles.

Sherman, Daniel J. on page 103. On bond: Shannon, Daniel J.

Thomas, A. W. on page 112. On bond: Alfred Thomas.

Caldwell, Sarah Y., page 116. On bond: Sarah J. Caldwell.

Webb, Hiram to Mary M. Lotty, page 119. On bond: Mary M. Totty.

Whitaker, J. L., page 120. On bond: Josephus L. Whitaker.

INDEX TO BRIDES ON BONDS

INDEX

1

ADCOCK, Sally, 113
ADKERSON, Eliza, 115
ADKINS, Margaret J., 6
ADKISSON, Elizabeth, 17; Elizabeth D.,52;
    Henrietta, 44; Mary, 45; Mary, 119;
    Minerva M., 84; Ruth A., 53
AGNEW, Sarah E., 17
AKIN, Eliza, 15; Eliza T., 76; Elizabeth,
    110; Frances, 56; Manerva, 90:,
    Martha, 52; Mary C., 110; Sarah, 86;
    Susan O., 87
ALDERSON, Ann A., 29; Eliza, 52; Margaret,
    68; Martha A., 42; Mary, 80; Mary,
    88; Nancy, 33; Nancy C., 111;
    Sarah C., 2
ALDRED, Nancy A., 1
ALEXANDER, Caroline H., 102; Emily E.,15;
    Margaret B., 102; Margaret C., 109;
    Margaret J., 2; Mary A., 89; Matilda
    G., 101; Nancy W., 123;Sarah A.,87;
    Sarah E. L., 57
ALFORD, Minerva A., 47
ALLEN, Caroline, 79; Elizabeth K., 35;
    Martha H., 99; Mary J. C., 5
AMENT, Eliza, 35; L. B., 36, Malinda, 12
AMIS, Derinda A., 74; Frances N., 62;
    Martha J., 35; Mary, 122; Mary J., 91
    Nancy A., 85, Sarah D., 86
ANDERSON, Martha A., 106; Prudy, 108
ANDREWS, Mary S., 119; Nancy C., 123;
    Nancy W., 63; Permelia R., 4;
    Permelia R. O., 17
ANGLAND, Jane, 59
ANGLIN, Malinda, 25
ANTHONY, Ann Eliza, 49; Emily E., 13;
    Sarah D., 13
ARCHER, Mary J., 95
ARINGTON, Martha G., 104
ARMSTRONG, Agnes F., 84;Flora, 63·
ARNOLD, Martha Z., 11; Priscilla, 10;
    Ruth, 69; Sarah, 39; Sarah M., 6
ASHTON, Rachel, 116
ASHWORTH, Mahala, 107; M. J., 78;.
    Sarah A., 99
ATKERSON, Indiana S., 14; Mary M., 45
ATKINSON, Amanda P., 18; Samella, 64
AUSTIN, Rachel M., 119
AYDELOTTE, Edna B., 71; Rebecca A., 102
AYDELOTT, Rhoda, 115; Sarah J., 70
BACHELOR, Frances M., 101
BAILEY, Louisa, 1; Martha, 105; Nancy,123;
    Nancy C., 1; Nancy P., 90; Sarah, 88
BAILY, Elizabeth N., 91
BAIN, Amelia A., 103, Elizabeth C., 26;
    Hannah A., 23; Harriet E., 19

BAIRD (or BIRD), Mine J., 8
BAKER, Elizabeth H., 25; Mary, 14;
    Mary, 24; Permelia A., 70
BALDRIDGE, Isabella, 28; Jane E., 71;
    Margaret Y., 2; Mary A., 10:,
    Sarah E., 54.
BALEY, Derinda, 34; Eliza, 43
BALL, Margaret J., 56.
BANKS, Mary M., 10
BARBOUR, Elizabeth, 112
BARD, Mary J., 77
BARFIELD, Phebe E., 68
BARKER, Mary F., 116; Nancy, 80
    S. E., 11
BARNES, Charlotte A., 32; Cynthia, 30;
    Martha, 9, Mary E., 103; Sarah,1;
    Sarah, 1; Sarah, 91.
BARNETT, Caroline, 53; Elizabeth, 122;
    Mary, 6; Nancy J., 77.
BARNHEAD, Elizabeth, 40
BATES, Celia C., 114; Mahaly A., 51;
    Nancy E., 90
BATEY, Mary, 10
BATIN, Sarah, 56
BATY, Mildred, 112
BAUGUSS, Mary Jane, 79
BAZZELL, Permelia, 34
BEASLEY, Cynthia K., 83; Eliza A., 89;
    Martha, 120; Nancy, 7
BEATY, Nancy J., 6
BEAVER, Mary, 62
BECKUM, Elizabeth A., 125;Mary, 3;
    Mary G., 45
BELL, Malissa, 98; Tirzah E., 58
BENDERMAN, Sarah L., 107
BENNETT, Mary, 112
BERNAN, Rhoda, 46
BERRY, Mary M., 86
BIFFLE, Sarah, 102
BIGGERS, Elizabeth, 65
BILL, Margaret J., 47
BINGHAM, Frances J., 27; Mary A., 31;
    Mary J., 121; Mary M., 107;
    Myra E., 4; Sarah Jane, 64.
BISHOP, Grishen, 95
BLACK, Almelia F., 117; Maria A., 25;
    Mary A., 74; Parthena, 77
BLACKBURN, Frances J., 86; Frances O.,
    18; Martha A., 120; Matilda, 22;
    Sarah E., 71; Valera A., 76
BLACKMAN, Ann W., 40; Elizabeth C.,23;
    Laura, 34
BLACKWELL, Martha A., 15; Nancy C., 15
BLACKWOOD, Harriet E., 48; Nancy J.,
    126.

www.ingramcontent.com/pod-product-compliance
Lightning Source LLC
Chambersburg PA
CBHW021908020426
42334CB00013B/517